FUTURE OF SCRUM

YOUR GUIDE TO THE MOST POPULAR AGILE METHODOLOGY

FUTURE OF SCRUM

Your Guide to The Most Popular Agile Methodology

Agile Project Management Series

A Practical Guide to the future trend of Scrum Framework for Agile Managers, Scrum Masters, Product Owners and Agile Teams: Scrum Framework has been in existence for over two decades. Scrum is easy to grasp yet very hard to practice. Besides, it had its own challenges when trying to scale at enterprise level. Understanding how to make Scrum effective has been a challenge. No more! In this book, Future of Scrum, Jai Singhal (Coach Jay) and Anju Singhal give much needed insights to Scrum framework and fill in some of the gaps to understand the various aspects of agile methodology value and principles. You will gain deep insight to the framework, integration with other agile methodologies, processes and practices with strategies and tactics explained with easy to follow illustrations in the new paradigm. A MUST-HAVE reference because you need to excel in your pursuit of excellence.

Jai Singhal, MS, BE, SPC, PMI-ACP, PMP, CSP, CSM, CSPO
Anju Singhal, BE, PMP, CSM
Series Authors

Agiliants™
Act Smart. Be Agile.

Future of Scrum

Your guide to the most popular agile methodology

Agile Project Management Series

Printed in the United States of America
ISBN: 978-1-62829-019-6
ISBN-13: 978-1-62829-019-6
ISBN-10: 1628290196

www.Agiliants.com
Phone: +1 - (240) 654-5496
Fax: +1 - (301) 769-6253
Email: Info@Agiliants.com
Website: www.Agiliants.com

Dedication

This book is dedicated to our parents, teachers, coaches and mentors. Thank you all for being part of our lives and teaching us, to be better human beings, by sharing timeless wisdom and lessons.

Contents at a Glance

Contents at a Glance

Contents at a Glance

Contents

Contents

Contents

Contents

Contents

Contents

Contents

Contents

Figures

Figures

Figures

Figures

Future of Scrum

Figures

Figures

Acknowledgements

Authors' Acknowledgements

We are grateful to our teachers, coaches, mentors, and parents who continue to inspire us to learn, improve and grow every day of our lives. We have learned a lot in your company and continue to learn. Also, we are grateful to so many Agile thought leaders in introducing and continuing to inspire us on better ways to develop software and have a working environment that is fun. Agile is common sense; risk management just happens to be a part of it.

We are grateful to the publisher and many working partners who helped us bring this work to reality. This has been a long and strenuous journey. However, with Agile mindset, it has been rewarding, fulfilling, and satisfying to the core.

Publisher's Acknowledgements

Agiliants, Inc. would like to thank our partners and consumers who have contributed to this book. We would like to thank the authors for their diligence and constant effort in compiling the content in the book from timeless wisdom prevalent in various cultures around the world.

In advance, we would like to thank and encourage you to share your thoughts to help us improve. Please feel free to visit our site to learn from resources, provide feedback, and take a look at our online blog.

Contact Us

We would love to hear your feedback. Is there anything that you feel that has inspired you? Is there anything that helps you look past your current hurdle? Is there anything that you want to elaborate on? Is there anything you feel that should be included in this book? We would love to hear from you. Send an email to: FutureOfScrum@Agiliants.com

Acknowledgements

About the Authors

About Jai Singhal (Coach Jay)

Jai Singhal (Coach Jay) is an Agile Enterprise and Leadership Trainer and Coach. He provides training on Agile methodologies; especially Scrum, eXtreme Programming, Kanban and Agile-Lean. He also provides trainings on Leadership skills, Conflict management and Individual development skills. Coach Jay has trained hundreds of professions and students on Agile Project Management, Scrum, XP, Kanban, Lean-Agile, VersionOne, Rally, IBM-Rational tools including IBM-Rational Team Concert (RTC), BuildForge, RQM and RRC, OOA&D, and Management and Leadership skills.

Coach Jay has over 22 years of IT experience. He received Masters in Computer Science from Johns Hopkins University, MD, USA and Bachelor of Engineering (Electronics Engineering) from India. He is a certified PMI Agile Certified Practitioner (PMI-ACP)®, Project Management Professional (PMP)®, Certified SAFe Program Consultant (SPC), Certified Scrum Professional (CSP)®, Certified Scrum Master (CSM)®, Certified Scrum Product Owner (CSPO)®, and IBM-Rational Certified Specialist on Rational Unified Process (RUP) and OOAD since 2004. Coach Jay's started as Front-end Software Developer with Object Oriented Programming on OSF/Motif and C++ and transitioned to Internet Software Development technologies. He has been Lead Architect of Internet COE (1997), Development Manager (2000) and since then he has held many management and leadership positions and currently works as Vice President - IT. Transition to agile was a cool breeze as it was how he started with delivering functionality with complete features in short cycles. Agile immediately appealed to him and he took to agile practices naturally. As Lead Agile Leadership and Enterprise Trainer and Coach, he has coached many agile teams enterprise-wide. He enjoys inciting and inspiring collaboration and innovative ways of leading teams, Product Owners, Scrum Maters and Agile Coaches in their pursuit of excellence. He works closely with client PMO and Leadership teams to enable agile transition and help with seamless adoption.

In his spare time, Jai coaches his younger son's soccer team, regularly volunteers, lead regular open-door preaching, teaching and training programs like leadership skills and conflict management, and practices yoga at various yoga centers to empower individuals, organizations and communities.

About Anju Singhal

Anju Singhal is a Master Agile Trainer and Coach to help enterprises deliver great value in a humane way where teams outperform the expectations. Anju has trained hundreds of professionals in Technology and Tools since 1991. She is an internationally recognized expert in IT management and a highly sought after Senior IT executive, Agile and Scrum Trainer, Management Coach, Mentor, Advisor, and Author. In 1991, Anju started her career as Professional Trainer in Professional Services Organization of HCP-HP; a then HP subsidiary. She has over 22 years of IT experience mainly at Fortune 500 companies. She earned a Bachelor of Technology in Computer Science from MANIT, India. She has many technical certifications besides being a certified PMP® and CSM®.

Anju seeks to apply simple approaches to solving complex problems in simple innovative ways. She has found agile methodologies appealing due to the simplicity, ease and direct approach. While coaching collaboration, Customer focus and commitment has been her key areas of expertise. She has helped teams deliver valuable software and services quickly and continuously; to the customer as the highest priority.

In spare time, Anju actively volunteers and likes to spend quality time with her family.

About Agiliants, Inc.

Agiliants, Inc. is a thought-leader and innovator in IT project and program management trainings, coaching, and consulting services. Agiliants also provide complete solution including publications, class-room and work-group trainings, product development, mentoring, enterprise transformation, and valuable resources.

Agiliants attract clients due to three main values of personal, professional and social development combined with a unique combination of training, coaching and practices by:

1. Enhancing personal development with fun filled games, activities, and training programs
2. Enabling professional development with sharing timeless wisdom and building solid foundations
3. Empowering organizations, cultures, and social structures with brilliant initiatives based on time-tested principles and values.

These three simple aspects set us apart and have turned Agiliants into one of the fastest advancing agile management training and services organization.

Act Smart. Be Agile.™

Preface

As Scrum and Agile Trainers and Coaches, we have been seeking a comprehensive guide on Scrum Framework and other agile practices that fits nicely with it. While there are many great books, we were not able to find concise information with all areas covered and well-structured layout as a practical reference guide. Besides, the books were filled with text with few, scattered and hard-to-follow illustrations. A picture is worth a thousand words. Hence, we decided to write this book in the hope that you can learn and easily adapt to Scrum Framework and practice Scrum using this guide and reference.

What's Future of Scrum?

This guide covers in-detail the various aspects of Scrum – the most popular of agile methodologies. This information is currently scattered in over dozens of books with varying degree of experiences of the authors to various agile methodologies including Scrum. There has also been found differences in processes, practices, and the concepts identified by various authors and in some cases even by the same author. These texts have been thoroughly analyzed and simplified with suitable illustrations for better understanding. All these have been thoroughly investigated, researched and sorted to provide desired knowledge and common base as a useful yet complete guide. Hence, to make it easy, this book provides an excellent reference with knowledge gathered, structured and presented in a simpler fashion for reader's advantage. Studying all the books on Scrum Framework with scattered information could result in numerous hours spent. Thus, here all the important concepts have been well structured and streamlined for easy grasp. If you follow the text, it would allow you to grasp the critical aspects and prepare you well for the real world experience with Scrum. This guide hence provides a relevant reference as well to experienced Scrum practitioners.

Origin of this book

Originally we wrote this book in the form in which it is presented now. When the first book was published it was cut short to less than 200 pages without illustrations and without explanations for most of the original concepts and principles. In all our books, we provide insight from our and others practical experience on Agile projects and programs in the real world of the original techniques with tips and insightful strategies, tactics and facilitate those techniques, and their applications and practices enhanced by the knowledge and skills. Thus, the present effort is to offer as a manuscript of this well-structured and knowledge condensed in the book with full practical explanations in order to establish the concepts and principles more soundly and progressively.

Agile methodologies are genuine, natural, and adaptive, since they have evolved from proven concepts and principles over the time tested applications of values. Of all the agile methodologies, Scrum continues to be the most popular methodology for software development and other research projects, especially for the younger generations. It is becoming more and more interesting and appealing to seasoned IT professionals too. Seasoned and experienced IT professionals are driven to this book, so much so that they are utilizing the contained knowledge and able to relate the various instances of failures of waterfall and traditional project management practices to realize - what went wrong, where mistakes and assumptions were made, when it all started to fall apart, why the processes differ from the practices, and how it all led to project failure. Some of them said that it is great fortune to read this book containing crucial knowledge of IT project management and development practices. If we have any credit in this connection, it does not belong to us personally; rather it is due to our teachers, mentors, families, and colleagues.

Our only purpose is to present this book in order to enable the current practitioners and newcomers to delivery great valuable innovative products. We hope that the readers read, learn and grow professionally; finally to attain quality of life with worth and purpose deriving values and satisfaction. This purpose has been sought by IT professionals and management for decades yet was far from realization until now. Generally so called IT managers, advisers, scholars, philosophers and supervisors, without full knowledge of IT field and its ways, try to provide philosophical and imaginary concepts try to mislead the general populace. Such practices which are stringent and inflexible in their ways and prescriptive in nature continue to commit a great blunder. The result of such a blunder is that misguided readers feel bewildered when faced with IT management and guiding principles and will not be able to get the success or peace. Interpreting agile methodologies without any reference to the underlying values and principles is a great mistake. In order to take advantage of agile methodologies for one's individual advantage and use it as technical jargon to create self-directed methodologies without much experience and proven realizations would backfire and can result in just the opposite results. Avoid such mistakes. Try to understand the concepts as laid down by the methodologies, since these have evolved from proven and practical realizations. Such understanding of agile methodologies is really profitable and recommended to lead to fulfilling desired goal of quality work and success in developing innovative products and services.

Essential principles

Introduction focuses on origin of Scrum, the most popular agile methodology and its continuous adaptation for empirical processes. It identifies the change in perception of project success and changing criteria for development to help us see beyond the immediate. A new horizon seems to appear as we see software development process with a new perspective with customer focus.

Section I takes an enthusiast directly to the core values, principles and working of Scrum Framework. An overview with sufficient depth is provided for a clear understanding and foundation of Scrum Framework.

Section II focuses on Agile Manifesto and its principles at depth for a solid foundation. This is essential for understanding Scrum Framework and related core values and principles. This section continues to amaze a new comer to the workings of Scrum where many known challenges in traditional approach are easily overturned. Many insightful tips are provided for an Agile Practitioner to learn and grow while continue to revert back to this book as a constant companion and reference.

Section III discusses Scrum Backlogs - the heart of Scrum Framework. Product success is paramount for any project and this is directly related to how well the backlogs are groomed and kept aligned with the vision and market trend.

Section IV focuses on Project Management aspect. User Stories as Backlog items are discussed in detail. Estimation strategies to tie back the vision to schedule and cost constraints while delivering highest value product Sprint after Sprint. It provides a planning perspective with user stories, story points, velocity, and schedule estimation. User stories, Spikes, and story point concepts are from eXtreme Programming (XP).

Section V describes Scrum roles in detail. Individual chapter discusses each role, its characteristics, responsibilities and collaboration opportunities where various roles collaborate together to deliver valuable software to customer. The growth of each role, as experienced by real people on various projects, has been captured to show how to identify as one advances from one level to the next.

Section VI focuses on Scaling scrum for enterprises where large projects may have many teams working on product development and even at program and portfolio level the links are described.

Section VII describes various Scrum ceremonies. These ceremonies allow the artifacts and information radiators to allow changes to plan to adapt to optimal path.

Section VIII provides insights to an experienced Scrum Practitioner to go beyond current Scrum Framework. While Scrum Framework provides a set of core values, principles and practices, it still stays lightweight for the Team to define how the development is done. Many of XP and Lean practices can be adapted to as situation warrants. An experienced Agile Practitioner can see the insightful depth of Scrum Framework and can learn to adapt its practices. For this advanced level, we have provided further textbooks on ScrumBan, Kanban, Lean-Agile, and Agile Enterprise Evolution and Management.

Intended Audience

This book is intended for an expanded circle of readers ranging from someone new to Scrum who want to take the leap from traditional project management to Agile as well as seasoned Agile Practitioners have come to regard this as a practical reference to help them realign their understanding to learn, practice, and grow. Agile is all about common sense. Agile focuses on empirical processes and help transform command-and-control to the world of worth-and-purpose.

Tips on using this book

You can read any chapter in any order as each chapter discusses an independent topic. Introduction and Section-I is recommended if you are new to Scrum as they provide the essential concepts.

Introduction helps in understanding the domain agile influences. Further it helps identify the reasons why Agile continues to be so successful for empirical processes.

Section I, Overview, helps to understand Overview of Scrum Framework. Chapter 1 provides insights to why Scrum is so popular. Chapter 2 describes the foundational aspects to a new comer to Scrum and stakeholders who are not directly involved in Scrum methodology to understand the workings and their role. Chapter 4-7 address specific key areas of Scrum: Scrum Roles, Backlog, Ceremonies and Sprint.

Section II, Agile Principles, targets understanding of agile principles. Chapter 8 gives agile overview and describes the essence of Agile Manifesto and its principles. Chapters 9 through 12 discuss the essential aspects of agile values, principles and practices that form an essential part of empirical process control.

Section III, Scrum Backlogs – The Heart of Scrum, highlights various aspects of Scrum Backlogs – Heart of Scrum Framework. Scrum Backlogs are most essential aspect among all others that separate Scrum Framework from Traditional Iterative development methods like RUP. The product success is inherent in ensuring that these are well maintained and regularly groomed. Chapter 13 discusses various types of Backlogs. Chapter 14 describes Backlog Items in relation with the product vision and analysis. Chapter 15 discusses the different activities involved in Backlog grooming.

Section IV, Scrum Requirements and User Stories, focuses on in-depth understanding of requirements and user stories. Chapter 16 describes user stories; a concept adapted from eXtreme Programming. Chapter 17 delves deep into agile estimation strategies. Chapter 18, Team velocity, overcomes the common human factor in schedule planning aspects. Chapter 19 addresses Technical Debt – a monster in disguise. Chapter 20 describes various Information Radiators to make the progress visible.

Section V, Scrum Roles, covers three key Scrum Roles and their responsibilities. Chapter 21 describes the roles and responsibilities of Scrum Product Owner. Chapter 22 covers the roles and responsibilities of Scrum Master. Chapter 23 addresses the roles and responsibilities of the Development Team.

Section VI, Scaling Scrum, targets Scaling Scrum for enterprises. Chapter 24 goes deeper into the agile planning concepts. Chapter 25 starts to peel through the different layers of planning. Chapter 26 focuses on Product planning and strategies. Chapter 27 addresses Release planning where the product is realized at greater depth. Chapter 28 describes Sprint planning at greater depth. Chapter 29 focuses on tactical aspects covered during Daily planning.

Section VII, Scrum Ceremonies, focuses on Scrum Ceremonies. Chapter 30 covers insights and details to Planning Ceremonies. Chapter 31 provides essential aspects of Daily Scrum. Chapter 32 covers Scrum of Scrums where multiple teams collaborate. Chapter 33 focuses on essentials of Review Ceremonies. Chapter 34 covers Retrospectives; an essential aspect to inspect-and-adapt. Chapter 35 addresses the various reports at the strategic layer of agile planning onion.

Section VIII, What's next, provides some great insights even to a seasoned agile practitioner on advancing further as Scrum appears to feel like second nature. Chapter 36 discusses Story Mapping technique at length. Chapter 37 further explores the use of Story Map on a project. Chapter 38-40 discuss aspects of Scrum that make it very hard or easy to practice, common misconceptions about Scrum and how Scrum promotes agility. It is recommended that novice to Agile and Scrum should take to practice the intricacies of Scrum as identified in earlier chapters. This section needs realizations which are built on real-world experiences and as one gets to the very essence of Scrum and its intricate mechanism. It is also essential to have a strong foundation with required Scrum trainings and having a mentor, with rich Scrum experience, who can guide you and help you learn and grow as you get the same realizations and deeper understanding of Agile values and principles.

Conventions

We used various text connotations to highlight key area, aspects and references in the text. These are as follows:

- ❖ References are identified within square brackets [] with Author/Reference
- ❖ Abbreviations or other synonyms are in braces; if not explicitly stated.
- ❖ Bold and at times repetitions are used for emphasis of important terms or concepts
- ❖ Italics are used to share insights from external sources
- ❖ Repetition, though rare, is used to stress important concepts and on related topics

Introduction

"If you think you can do a thing or think you can't do a thing, you're right." - Henry Ford

Scrum Framework is built on the foundation of simple yet essential core values and principles. As a framework, Scrum provides a set of practices with rules, roles, artifacts, and process flow to deliver innovative valuable software quickly and frequently. Adapting to Scrum is easier when organization embrace complete framework on a pilot project and focus on embracing all the values and principles. The practices are simple, yet they require profound change of mindset. Failure of Scrum is normally a failure to adapt to Scrum mindset or its improper application.

Scrum is an agile methodology for empirical product development to develop great innovative products and services. Figure 1 shows a simple high-level view of Scrum Framework. All requirements are listed in Product Backlog. From Product backlog, a Sprint backlog is derived for features developed during Sprint and deliver at the end of Sprint as Incremental deliverable product. During the Sprint, Daily Scrums are conducted to proactively address any progress, roadblocks, and exceptions.

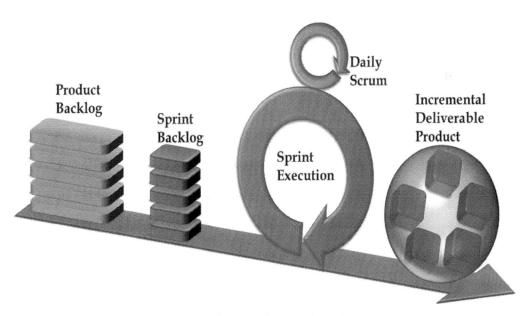

Figure 1 Scrum Overview

Origin of Scrum

The word 'Scrum' comes from "Scrummage" which is a variation of term "Scrimmage" in football or rugby. Scrummage means "the play that occurs between the teams from the instance the ball is snapped until moment it is declared dead." In software development, the term is meant to refer to the team members collaborating to deliver the incremental releasable product.

Scrum was first introduced in 1986 by Takeuchi, H. and I. Nonaka; known as Godfathers of Scrum Agile Process. They published the Scrum concept in a study "*The New New Product Development Game*" in Harvard Business Review in January-February 1986. They explained that historically small and cross functional teams have produced the best results at assembly line industries like Honda and Fuji-Xerox. This concept of high performance team was related to "Scrum" formation in football. Later in 1993, Jeff Sutherland introduced the Scrum process at Easel Corporation using the study as a basis for adopting their analogy for software development process. This process was later formalized worldwide by Ken Schwaber in his first published paper on Scrum at OOPSLA (Schwaber 1995). Then Ken Schwaber and Mike Beedle further popularized Scrum framework in 2001: Agile Project Management with Scrum. Later, again Jeff Sutherland and Ken Schwaber published Agile Project Management with Scrum in 2004, *ScrumGuide* in 2009, The *Official Scrum Guide* in 2011, and *Scrum Guide™* in July 2013.

Recent times have seen tremendous change due to Scrum as a widely growing practice for software development. This pertains to it being lightweight and unique approach to software development of complex projects. Scrum works on collaborative principle where the whole team gets together to deliver the product features. This is very different than the traditional waterfall model which can be compared to a *relay race* where one team finishes and passes on the baton to next team to work on the following phase in sequence.

Development domains

There are basically three domains that a software development projects can be in: Simple, Complex and Chaotic. Simple projects have deterministic process from start to end with no uncertainties. Complex projects have uncertainties in one or more of the followings: skills, domain, technology, processes, and needs. Complex projects are also commonly referred to employ one or more empirical processes due to the uncertainties involved. These projects require a need for managing risks arising due to uncertainties and constraints. A varying degree of feedback loop is needed to allow inspect-and-adapt to address uncertainties. Chaotic projects are filled with chaos – a lack of order. Chaos could be the result of unmanageable uncertainties or even be product of the environment itself.

Simple domain is characterized by the following factors:

1. Well-defined with all aspects known and available at the start of project
2. Skilled professionals are easy to find,
3. fairly easy to approach an agreement to requirements between the development team and customer, and
4. the solution is fairly certain as the project is not complex
5. The development process is well defined from start to end

Examples: Assembly line, production units, and simple jobs like bicycling

Complex domain is characterized by the following factors:

1. Technology or business domain is new and upcoming
2. Skilled professionals are not so easy to find
3. Unknown risks exist
4. Growing complexity hindering an easy approach to agreement to requirements and requires more dialog back and forth between the development team, and customer, and
5. the solution is not well defined

Examples: Software development in new domain, new technology, research project, or other aspects contributing to uncertainties.

Chaotic domain is characterized by the following factors:

1. Skilled professionals are almost impossible to find so whatever resource is available is used on the project,
2. Very hard to approach an agreement to requirements between the development team and customer, and
3. the solution is not even perceivable as the project is very complex and vision is not very clear
4. Chaotic culture and environment
5. Absence of guidelines, processes or framework

Scrum is able to influence the complex domain and is found most suitable and effective in delivering innovative products in complex domain. In fact, Scrum is common sense because it promotes to inspect-and-adapt to changes due to uncertainties and constraints.

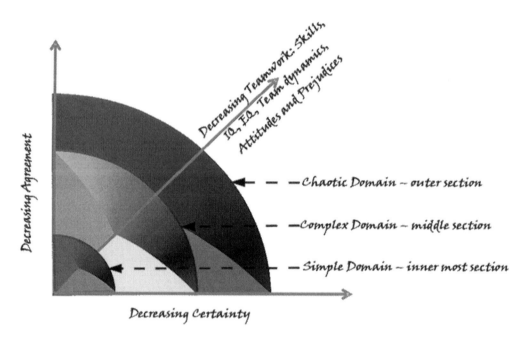

Figure 2: Simple-Complex-Chaotic Project Assessment Graph

Scrum Framework provides opportunity for products that are innovative, research based, thoughts provoking, creative, enticing, and defining new services. The SDLC (waterfall methodology) is applicable in simple scenarios where the complete set of product requirements are known upfront (in software development, to know everything to know at the start? who are you kidding, really!), non-changing during the development, a defined process with defined phases is identified with resources and skills already mature and available. This applies mostly to assembly line products where the different pieces are built, assembled, and "Voila! We have the product ready to market." This requires hardly any creative thinking as all pieces are well defined. However, with evolving market we need new methods and practices for complex projects. Yet Agile project management (APM) is within the domain between simple well-defined process and chaotic. Chaotic projects for product development are the other extreme where things are continuing to evolve and resulting in much waste and priorities keep changing over time. Such projects are out of reach as no process can be defined to contain chaos unless chaotic project can be deescalated to complex domain. History has proven that chaotic projects either dwindle away or come to the level of complex projects where they can be handled and managed.

Software development revolution

Software development had been in silos for decades. These silos came into existence from the distribution of software development into various phases like requirements analysis, design, development, testing and maintenance. This is the traditional waterfall model. This waterfall model evolved from the Deming cycle – PDCA – Plan-Do-Check-Act. In 1939, Walter Shewhart of Bell Labs originally developed the concept of Plan-Do-Check-Act (PDCA) cycle which was later popularized by W. Edwards Deming [Pyzdeck, 2003]. PDCA cycle enables integration of knowledge and practices for continuous improvement. The waterfall software development methodology had its struggle. Projects continued to fail as check and adapt aspects were hard to follow.

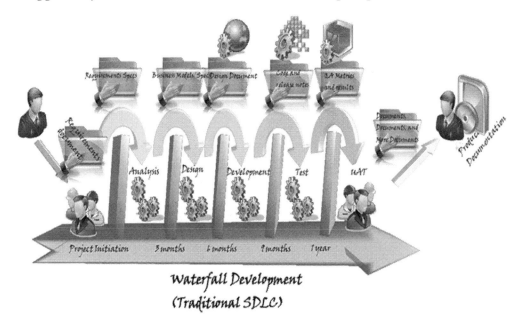

Figure 3 Waterfall Development

Then, came iterative development approach that divided software development process into multiple smaller iterative cycles. However, without the well-defined framework, iterative development suffered similar lags and management issues. Waterfall model is process and documentation driven as shown:

Then IBM-Rational introduced software development methodology based on iterative product development known as Rational Unified Process (RUP). RUP showed advantage over the waterfall development by providing processes, artifacts, and roles. Being heavyweight, RUP was hard to adopt and allow all processes, artifacts and roles to be streamlined. Not all project teams are built with the resources, people and demands as it identified. Hence, it was adapted at varying flavor. RUP provided specific ways to do things. It added flexibility. However, it still acknowledged transition different phases of SDLC. One of its contributions is providing a common language.

In essence, iterative development works as smaller waterfall cycles. It does have advantage over waterfall model as it helps with shorter delivery cycles, risk management, performance optimization, and resource utilization. The progression of phases is identical except that the complete cycle has been split into smaller iterations. Iterations allow getting early delivery of products and receive quick feedbacks. These appear very close to the approach taken in Scrum and XP – agile methodologies.

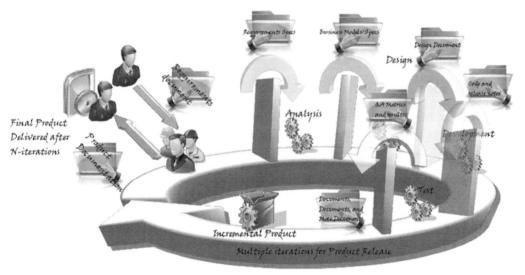

Iterative Development (RUP)

Figure 4: Iterative Development

What sets Scrum apart is the value driven aspect. In Scrum, the highest value features are delivered as part of the incremental product. Then in each sprint, the highest value features are delivered. Iterative development and waterfall methodologies do not promote focus on value-driven delivery. Mostly the easiest feature is delivered early. Unlike waterfall or iterative development methods, in Scrum, another aspect is scrimmage where the development team works hand-in-hand to deliver incremental product. All phases appear to be executing simultaneously. These coupled with agile practices built atop core values and principles provide a collaborative environment to inspect and adapt with ease.

Requirement gathering

Waterfall methodology expects all the requirements be defined upfront. Any change to the requirements is then tracked through Change Management process. The change management discourages agility and customer collaboration. Iterative development seeks to address all requirements as a piecemeal without making any differentiation. Agile requirements gathering encourages prioritizing and then focusing on refining and detailing requirements with the highest value first.

To understand the differences and individual concepts, we setup activities during our training and coaching sessions. One such activity is done with 5-6 participants. There are 4-5 members who are identified as customers. Each customer is provided a deck of cards with different numbers of unsorted cards in each deck. Each customer keeps a deck of cards faced down. One person acts as listener to record the readings of values. The remaining team records the timings. Time duration is recorded to identify:

1. Duration it takes to record the first deck of cards
2. Duration it takes to record all the cards.

Waterfall scenario: Each customer flips a card at the same time and tells the value. All customers are saying the values at the same time. It appears that soon everyone starts raising voice so as to be heard and even shouting. The one who loudest is heard – time duration is really long for recording as too much distraction occurs without a strategy and one with most power prevails. When first deck is done, the duration is recorded and when all decks are done, the second reading is taken.

Iterative scenario: Everyone flips one card at a time as round-robin polling is done for reading and only one card value is recorded each time and processed. The cards are read until all the decks are recorded.

Agile scenario: Cards are read similar to that of iterative. However, order is value-driven where highest value deck is covered first. Person with highest value deck flips a card at a time and the value is recorded. Once the deck is done, the next highest value deck is recorded and so on.

At the end, the data is analyzed and compared. First reading shows that Waterfall process scenario takes a long time to complete the first deck and second reading is very close to the first reading when all the decks are recorded. Notably, this scenario is very close to being chaotic. Iterative process shows similar relationship in the two readings though much better than that of Waterfall. The first reading finishes earlier. While with similar pattern where first set of cards, takes a long duration and complete duration is close enough to the first reading. Agile methodology exercise timings show that the first reading to be very small; just as that of iterative scenario where the first deck of cards could take longer and then, all the cards are done in the same time.

Below are results from one of the sessions:

Agile game: Requirements Reading durations>	First deck recording	All decks recorded
Waterfall	213 seconds	343 seconds
Iterative	154 seconds	181 seconds
Agile	27 seconds	173 seconds

Then, participants are asked to analyze if the same run occurs in half the time it took to run the waterfall scenario. The following are the observations:

- ❖ Waterfall is unable to complete any set or a few set and identifies project failure
- ❖ Iterative process takes a long time to complete first deck though it is faster than that of waterfall scenario and would fail to complete the full set
- ❖ Agile scenario shows that the highest value decks are recorded early and provide maximum benefit while may still fall short of completing all decks of cards

Agile ways

All customers collaborate through Product Owner. Product Owner is the internal representative of customers and end-users. Figure 5 shows a Product Owner who collaborates with customers, end-users and business stakeholders in gathering and managing requirements using Product Backlog. This backlog is organized and refined over time and continuously detailed and expanded upon. Product Owner owns the Product Backlog. Different grooming activities are identified using legend and explained later in detail.

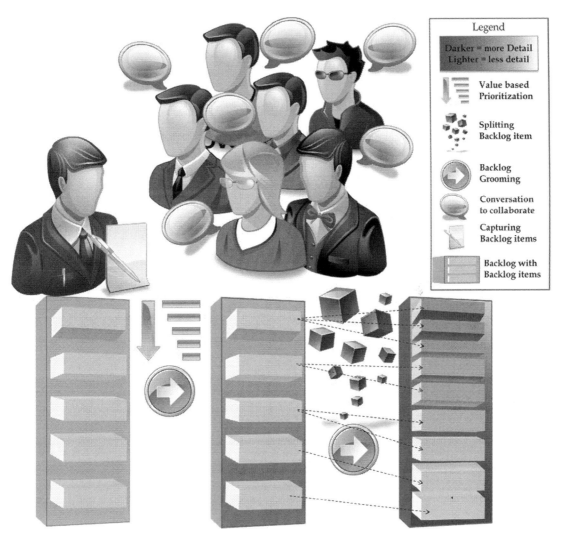

Figure 5: Backlog Grooming

Product Owner performs the following activities; not necessarily in the listed order:

❖ Gather data: Story-writing workshops, Reviews and Market analysis sessions
❖ Effort cost and schedule estimation with management, leads/architect and tester and innovation games to re-prioritize based on value
❖ Generate insights: Brainstorm to find options and alternatives
❖ Backlog Grooming sessions using various strategies like MoSCoW and Kano analysis to perform value-based prioritization
❖ Decide what to do: Planning session where the team commits to develop features
❖ Backlog reshuffled and prep for planning session

Backlog grooming – an activity where requirements are managed - is recommended to occur at twice the frequency than the sprint length. For two week long sprint, weekly backlog grooming is recommended. For a month long sprint, bi-weekly backlog grooming sessions are recommended. It is performed frequently when something new is known. The session does not stop from Product Owner communicating any higher priority item as it has been identified for the backlog. If a stakeholder approaches Product Owner to add a new high priority item, Product Owner can communicate to other stakeholders as he moves the item to higher priority. The customers would then follow-up with the one who asked for the new features and close the loop at the customer level it is to occur. Product Owner reviews all the changes since last backlog grooming session in the next session to provide an opportunity to further collaborate and optimize ROI.

All requirements whether they are changes, defects, enhancements and even risks are listed in one place – the Product Backlog. This allows only one source for all of the product requirements. These requirements are referred to as Product Backlog Items (PBI's).

Product Development

Waterfall methodology expects all the development to be completed before testing and release. Any change to a developed feature is then tracked through Change Management process. Besides discouraging agility and customer collaboration, change control process delays product development and hence, its release to customer. Iterative development seeks to address all requirements as piecemeal without making any differentiation. Agile requirements gathering encourages prioritizing and then focusing on completing requirements with highest value first.

To understand the differences and individual concepts, we setup activities during our training and team coaching activities. One such activity is done with 5-6 participants. There are 4-5 members who are identified as customers. There are equal number of deck of cards with different number of cards and values in each deck. Each customer keeps a deck of cards faced down. One person acts as listener to record the readings. The listener multiplies the values of all cards in the deck each time a value is identified and lists the total value. In order to keep it feasible, each scenario is given 3 minutes to run. In this case, the number of decks completed and the processed value is recorded for:

1. Duration it takes to process the first deck of cards and total value of the deck
2. Number of decks processed and total sum of all values for completed decks.

Waterfall: Every customer flips one card at the same time and tells the value. All customers are saying at the same time. It seem that soon everyone starts shouting and the one who shouts the most is heard – time duration is really long as too much distraction without prioritization and power prevails. When first deck is done, the duration is recorded and when all decks are done, the second reading is taken.

Iterative: Each deck contains different numbers of cards. The customer with smallest number of cards in the deck goes first. The number of cards represents that easiest features are done early and often; as evident in iterative development. The customer flips one card at a time as the total value is processed for the deck. Then the next customer with smallest number reads the card value at a time and so on.

Agile: Reading is done similar to that of iterative. However, the order is value-driven where highest value deck is processed first. Person with highest value deck flips a card at a time and the value is recorded. Then the next highest value deck is recorded and so on.

At the end, the data is analyzed and compared. In Waterfall process scenario, First reading would shows that it takes a long time to process the first deck. The second reading is very close to that of the first reading. In tough time constraints, as in this case, it is possible that no value is realized for investment. Notably again, this scenario is very close to being chaotic. Multiplying the values is hard when so many people are breathing down your neck. Many participants shared that they had experienced similar behavior when they do projects in waterfall methodology, where management and customers are always demanding and distracting them. In such an environment, it is easy to lose focus. Iterative process shows that the first reading finishes much earlier but may not be of highest value; while all the decks are read within the time duration.

Agile methodology exercise shows the first reading to be of highest value as is the focus; as its distinct advantage. Thus, agile outperforms others in value. Then, participants are asked to analyze if the same run occurs in half the time it took to run the waterfall scenario. The following are the observations:

❖ Waterfall scenario is unable to complete any deck which identifies project failure; in this case. At times, it does complete a few decks but mostly those are of low value overall. This is how its execution is experienced in complex domain as well.

❖ Iterative process scenario shows the maximum number of decks processed and the value is not the highest

❖ Agile scenario results show that the highest value decks are recorded early and provide maximum benefit. It still falls short of completing all decks of cards and could be less than the number of decks covered in iterative scenario.

The deck of cards contained the following values:

Deck 1: 100, 40, 20, 13, 8, 5, 3, 2, 1 (Multiplication value: 249,600,000)
Deck 2: 40, 20, 13, 8, 5, 3, 2, 1 (Multiplication value: 2,496,000)
Deck 3: 20, 13, 8, 5, 3, 2, and 1 (Multiplication value: 62,400)
Deck 4: 1, 2, 3 (Multiplication value: 6)

Below are results from one of the sessions:

Agile game: Development Readings:	First deck readings durations, value >	Second readings durations, value >
Waterfall	Time expired, zero value as no deck is processed completely	Time expired, zero value as no deck is processed completely
Iterative	16 seconds, value = 6	Number of decks = 4 Value = 2,558,406
Agile	107 seconds, value = 249,600,000	Number of decks = 3, Value=252,158,400

Agile methodology provides maximum benefit even with less coverage of overall requirements as it focuses on delivering the highest value first. This signifies that ROI is optimized in Agile methodology due to value prioritization.

Another variation of above game is done where the values are not identified in iterative and the decks contain same number of cards. This scenario is not the behavior seen in iterative development so let's call it unsorted-scenario. In this case, the value of first deck and overall value to be the largest ones is a matter of luck in unsorted-scenario while it is guaranteed in the case of agile scenario. This assurance of highest value is what sets agile apart from waterfall and iterative development methods. Besides this, many other interesting games and team activities are in our book: *Agile games*™.

Waterfall product development analogy

We have seen many examples of traditional (Waterfall) projects analogies as shown using swing metaphor in Figure 6.

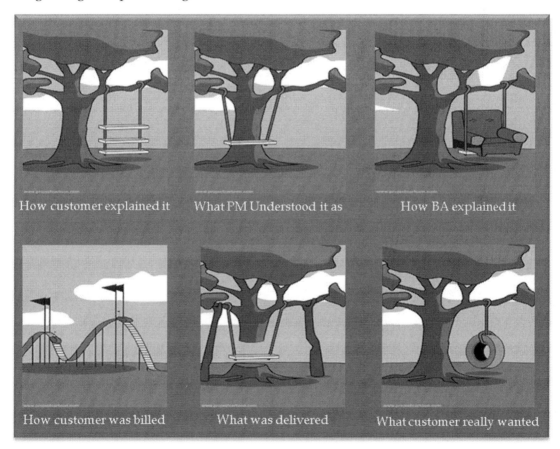

Figure 6: Waterfall analogy

This cartoon is among many yet it shows how a complex project can lose its track. The plan is to be followed to the letter. However, there is no consideration of competitive advantage of the customer. There are many factors that would need customer's input like:

> Changing market trend
> Customer not able to visualize in case of new product development and gets perspective when he sees first prototype or deliverable
> Communication is close ended with contract negotiations and frozen requirements
> Customer not able to visualize the product under development to provide feedback and thus, to inspect and adapt appropriately
> Customer may have new changes to the initial product requirement, however, is constrained by the contract negotiations
> Project team is unable to clear ambiguities and gain insights to business domain
> Business analysts could be mapping the business needs with development efforts while nothing to validate their conclusions against

Agile addresses these in clear perspectives for customer's competitive advantage and the team is able to deliver incremental product early and often with constant customer interactions for feedback yet allowing changes to be accepted even late in the process. This can be visualized as shown in Figure 7 using metaphor of a swing; to reflect agile development project.

This pictorial series identifies an important aspect of Agile Project Management (APM). APM provides many advantages to both the customer and the development team. This is basis of the guiding principles and Agile manifesto as developed in February 2001 by 17 software developers who gathered at Snowbird, Utah resort to discuss lightweight development methods now known as agile software development.

This metaphor, in Figure 7, highlights the aspect that even though there are differences in various perspectives, these differences are brought in open where the customer and the project team can collaborate to understand the differences. Various risks are identified early on and addressed as early as possible. Customer provides a prioritized Backlog which may still have a many more features than the customer could afford. The affordability and backlog could be out of sync. The project team would take one aspect based on early understanding. However, being agile in nature, various risks can become evident.

Figure 7: Agile analogy

In this metaphor, there is a risk of rope breaking or even the tree branch breaking. Besides, the ground under the tree may pose other risks. The project team works with customer to address these where requirements are updated and flexibly a new solution emerges to meet and address all these risks timely to deliver a viable and valuable product. Such risks need to be recognized early and addressed. This is depicted in another metaphor for Agile development where risks are identified which are either addressed to optimize ROI or project encourages fast-fail; a concept discussed later.

An Agile Project approach

Agile project teams work in a much different way than the traditional waterfall teams that work in different silos based on their functional domains. Agile teams are structured so as to:

1. Work as one team; where no walls or partitions exist; and open communication is encouraged
2. Work in short sprints; where they deliver an incremental releasable product to the users
3. Deliver something in each sprint; where the product is a complete functional unit including documentation
4. Focus on business priorities; so the most important and valued features are delivered sooner

Inspect and adapt; the product based on users' feedback and valuable insights as well as optimize the development process.

Project governance

With the expansion of APM taking over software development industry, a common discussion prevails on comparing project governance from waterfall versus iterative versus agile project management approaches. Executives are interested in mainly two aspects for project governance; viz. investment and risk.

Governance pertains to making decisions in uncertain environment with varying market conditions, demands and needs of customers, and so forth. Executives hence seek to assess ROI, associated risks, and probability of success on early payback on the investment. We will discuss the calculations in detail later. Currently, the comparison with transition from waterfall to iterative to agile is essential to grasp. An essential aspect is the fact that for research based exploration projects, risks are not identified by specifying requirements upfront. Risks are reduced by exploring, analyzing the problem domain, investigating, creating simulations, prototypes or research and development efforts.

Waterfall approach assumes that when all the requirements are defined, the risk is reduced. Besides, it sets the criteria for return on investment (ROI). However, reality is that the value is recognized at delivery of product to the customer and not at the time of requirement definition. Unless we have a production line project where the problem domain and solution domain are both known which allows clearly defined requirements and plan on developing the product as if in an assembly-line, waterfall model fails to manage risks and investments; and thus, in turn fails to manage returns on investments. Hence, for an exploratory project, with higher level of uncertainty and complexity, waterfall methodology experiences an inherent shortcoming as not everything is known at every phase.

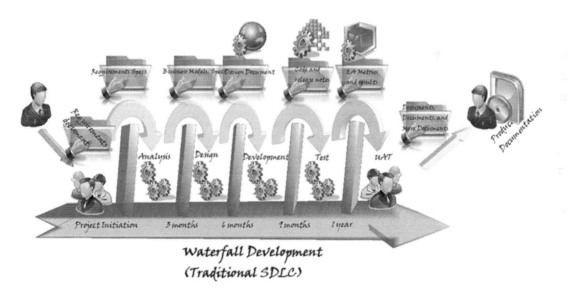

Figure 8: Waterfall Development (Traditional SDLC)

While an iterative approach breaks this into smaller cycles, however, it does not bring inspection and adaptation; due to the limitations and restrictions imposed by the processes. Iterative development faces the drawback and gets overburdened by the artifacts, processes and roles involved. The transitions from one phase to next phase goes through a phase-gate progression where decision of go/no-go are made as the project continues to progress further.

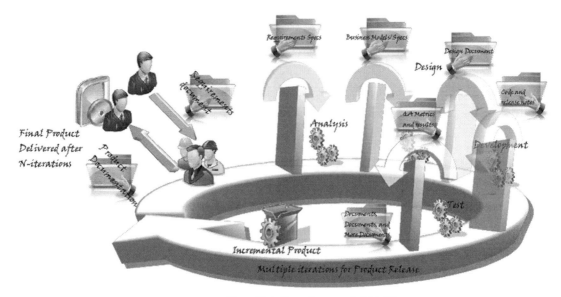

Figure 9: Iterative Development

Agile methodology provides the phase-gate progression where the governance and operational modes executes separately in parallel. Executive perspective is a series of linear phases while operational mode is a series of iterative planning followed by delivery. With delivery a constant approach to review the product and the process of product development provides the essential feedback loop to be able to inspect and adapt to optimize the value driven while managing and maintaining the quality of the product.

Performance management

Agile brings a new perspective to performance management. Traditional project management measures performance by strict adherence to the Iron triangle: scope, budget and schedule. APM measures team performance using value-driven triangle called "Agile Triangle," that consists of value, quality, and constraints.

Often Traditional Project management and Governance body do not take value into consideration. They are focused on scope to be met within time and cost constraints. Value has been ignored as if it'd be self-managed once time, resources and cost constraints are managed. For traditional project managers, the assumption is that delivering on scope, schedule and cost equates to delivering value. This is hardly true if practices are not promoting the value factor. APM addresses this by bringing in Value and Quality as major factors while time, scope, resources, technology, and other limitations as constraints.

Change, adaptation, and flexibility are the trademarks of agile projects. While conforming to plan is the trademark of traditional projects. APM streamlines the performance management to meet the set goals as per development and practices.

In traditional project management, Iron triangle is followed consisting of scope, schedule, and time. Mostly scope is primary driving factor due to false assumption of knowing the scope early. Thus, cost and schedule vary to meet the scope; while plan was devised to lock all three down early on and even refactored periodically.

The second – Agile Iron triangle evolved during early agile development where schedule was fixed as end date of delivery (timebox) while scope was allowed to vary and time was a fixed constraint. This approach still had plans define success by identifying schedule and tasks and was not adaptive to the nature of complex projects. This brings us to the Agile triangle [HIGHSMITH, 2009]. The factors of Agile Triangle are: Value (to the customer), Quality (attain to deliver value to customer), and constraints (scope, schedule, and cost). The primary factor in APM is value and constraints need to be adjusted as project progresses to maximize value. Schedule (timebox) may still be a constraint, yet scope and cost are managed to deliver highest value. Hence, adjusting constraints to meet value with intrinsic quality helps organization meet the customer needs.

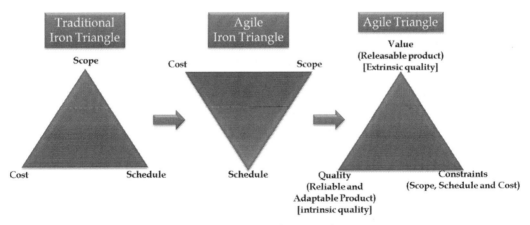

Figure 10: Agile Triangle

In an Agile Triangle, where dimensions are individually discussed, as transitioned occurred from Iron triangle to Agile Iron triangle, as goals are:

1   *Value goal*: Develop a releasable product of highest value early
2   *Quality goal:* Develop a reliable and adaptable product
3   *Constraints goal*: Attain highest value and intrinsic quality goals within acceptable constraints of scope, schedule and Cost.

Agile triangle recognizes the fact that the value of a product is recognized at the point of sale or release to the customer instead of the scope defined at the point of inception.

For agile values, the measurements systems that support these values need to evolve to support and measure the success. The success factors are seriously impacted as we set the bar for value delivery. Sometimes project goals are set low just to meet the success factor and then at times a project is driven more like a production unit with stable yet outdated technology to meet the demand. These projects can very well be driven in waterfall methodology. The difference is set when a project is in complex domain with uncertainty where cultural factors are imposed and it is hard to find the skilled and experienced personnel would force a project to be more suitable to accept agile methodology to be successful. This is due to the value driven product delivery while maintaining high quality and managing the constraints. Further toppled with the compliance and regulatory demands, it may appear that agile methodology is not suitable. That is not the case. When there are compliance and demands, say extensive testing requirement, it is easier to still follow agile methodology. However, it provides delivery of product, in releases or even at different levels of roadmap, when extensive testing has been performed. A project recently done had two sprints lag in a release to meet the extensive compliance without development teams stopping to do the testing. This was achieved using different intermediate deployment stages where the code was delivered with extensive testing performed with automated test suites before they completed the phase-gate transition to the next level.

Risk Management

Risk management is managed differently in Waterfall and Agile methodologies. Waterfall projects tend to plan for risks (constraints and uncertainties) early on. The monitoring and risk management plan is tracked during the project progresses. Most of these risks are dealt with in reactive manner due to the traditional approach towards risk management.

Waterfall projects seek to reduce risks during the initial planning phase and then seek to address upcoming risks during the development process. This is discussed in detail later as well. Agile project seeks to manage risks by increasing the probability of opportunities and decreasing the probability of threats to the project. The uncertainties, thus, need to be managed and a risk management plan is identified. [Adapted from Laufer, 1996]

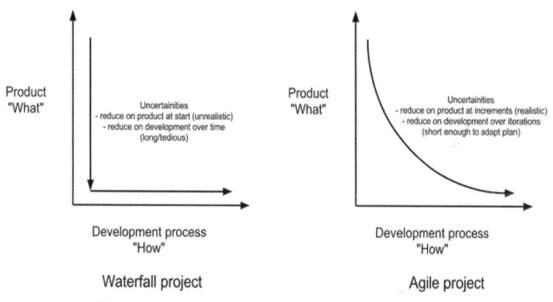

Figure 11: Risk management: Waterfall vs. Agile [Laufer, 1996]

The common risk management issues encountered are:

1. Failing to describe risks due to the process
2. Improper time the risks are focused on
3. Weak risk management which could cause project failures if not project suspension
4. Wrong time to address risk management

Agile project address the risk management as progressive cycle as shown below:

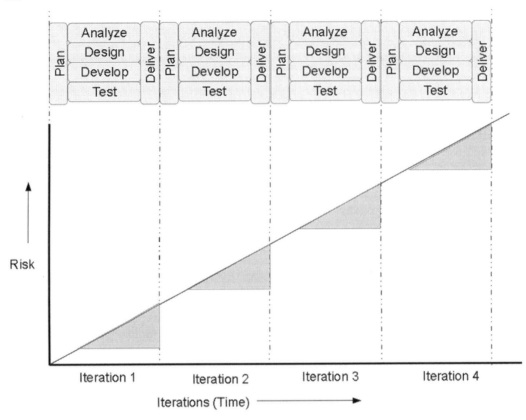

Figure 12: Risk managed as rolling wave planning

Compare this with Waterfall model where the risk continues to accumulate in each phase and discovered in the test or UAT is costly.

Waterfall project continues to accumulate risks all the way till testing phase and sometimes when the project is hampered due to quality issues, the risks are not fully discovered even when the product is deployed. Hence, risks continue to creep in and it could be over a year before serious risks and quality issues related to early phases are visible. By this time, it is too costly to address the issues. The application team continues to struggle in trying to manage risks all the way during the maintenance.

It is interesting to observe that risks are hidden and not visible for a long duration in waterfall methodology based projects.

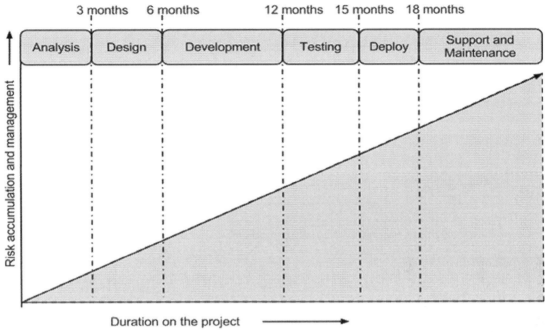

Risk management on a project with Waterfall methodology

Figure 13: Risk Management on a waterfall project

While iterative development provides an advantage over Waterfall project risks are not visible until the end of iteration. In iterative development, iteration is still traditionally 3 months to 6 months long. This is too long a period to be blind sighted. The quality issues and risks are not apparent until the application is in testing phase and the delays result in further compromising the quality. Thus, the response cannot be sufficiently prepared to manage the risks. Hence, iterative development process addresses the risk management as progressive cycle as shown below:

The risks are not visible on iterative project for months and can cause serious delays. Agile projects address these in short sprints. Hence, sometimes the fanatical approach to manage risks is prevalent as a saying: You don't need risk management on agile projects; Agile Project Management is risk management!

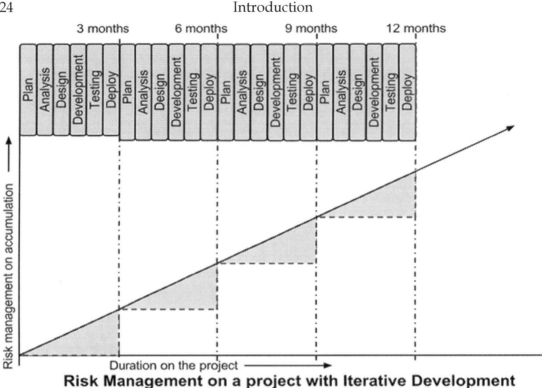

Figure 14: Risk management on an iterative development

Value Comparison analysis

While many differences are discussed, the most profound and important is to assess the success from various aspects: time to deliver, ROI, and customer satisfaction. Even when a product is developed using the best of methodologies, if it fails to meet these three factors, it would be considered unsuccessful.

This is further revealed from our review of three similar software development projects using different methodologies; namely Waterfall, Iterative and Scrum. The project started as waterfall project and resulted in delivering the product in twice the time period than originally anticipated while still having quality issues, budget overruns, negative ROI, and poor customer satisfaction. Another similar project using iterative development did fair in customer satisfaction, however, it still had 33% drop in ROI and was delivered one month late. Third project started with Scrum Framework adaptation where we helped the teams to understand the workings and got it started with customer and team collaboration. The project completed in the time anticipated, exceeding the ROI by 50% (200 to 300) and customer satisfaction was amazing as the complete team was praised. Constantly delivering incremental product every Sprint allowed customers to access software early. Early access further promoted quick feedback for improvements, change of direction, and market analysis to improve project alignment to changing needs. This agility is needed in today's dynamic environment.

Project	Estimated	Actual	ROI	Satisfaction
Waterfall	3 months	6 months	< 100%	Poor
Iterative	3 months	4 months	150%	Fair
Agile	3 months	3 months	300%	Excellent

Figure 15: Comparison analysis of waterfall, iterative and agile methodologies

Summary

This section explores the origin of Scrum as an agile methodology. We compared agile methodology with Waterfall and Iterative development methods. Influence in complex domain is discussed at length. This is undertaken to show that agile methodologies have an identified domain of impact. A lot more and in-depth analysis is provided in another reference: In our book - "Coaching Agile Enterprises and Leadership Teams" we detailed scaling of Agile framework at enterprise level with many strategies and techniques. Scaling pertains to the simple and complex domains where coaching and enablement of Agile methodologies is discussed from project to enterprise level.

We utilize various Agile games™ and activities, as discussed in this chapter, to train teams to learn the core values and principles. Many more such games are presented in our book: *Agile games™*. It is fun for the teams to play and learn and ROI from these games is amazing as we ourselves have seen from start where teams were able to achieve great results from the get-go!

Figure 16: Agile Games™

In the next chapter, we describe, why Scrum continues to be the most popular among Agile methodologies.

Section I
Overview

Chapter 1 Why Scrum?

"Be a yardstick of quality. Some people aren't used to an environment where excellence is expected." - Steve Jobs

Why does Scrum continue to be so popular?

Scrum is an Agile Framework for software development for complex projects. It has gained a lot of success and popularity in software industry in last two decades. It is one of the lightweight Agile methodologies. Scrum is very easy to learn. Scrum is very hard to practice; as its core values and principles hold the key for successful execution. Scrum allows you to adopt the processes and practices within its framework. It helps in managing complexity of empirical process where the project can utilize the key processes for further improvements.

Comparison with other Agile methodologies

VersionOne survey for 2010 reveals the top Agile methodologies. Scrum and Scrum hybrids contributed to [58+17(Scrum/XP)+3(ScrumBan)] 78% of market!

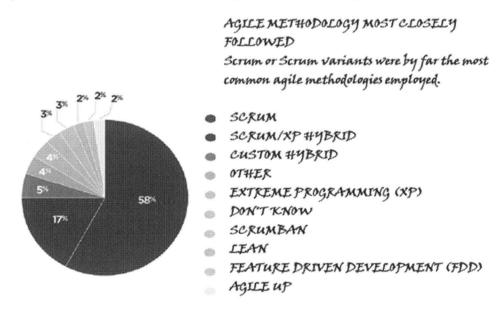

Figure 1-1: VersionOne 2010 Survey - Agile methodologies most closely followed

There are many agile methodologies and more continue to evolve and practiced. These methodologies comply with Agile manifesto, Agile guiding principles, and Agile Declaration of Interdependence [DOI 2005]. The common ones are Scrum (1995), Extreme Programming (XP) (1996), Lean, Crystal Clear, Adaptive Software Development, Feature Driven Development (FDD), and Dynamic Systems Development Method (DSDM) (1995).

VersionOne 2011 survey results still show increasing trend in Figure 1-2. Scrum or Scrum variants continue to make up more than two-thirds (Scrum 52%, Scrum/XP hybrid 14% and ScrumBan 3%) of the methodologies being used, while Kanban has entered the scene this year as a meager player. The only category that saw growth this year was Custom Hybrids (9% up from 5%).

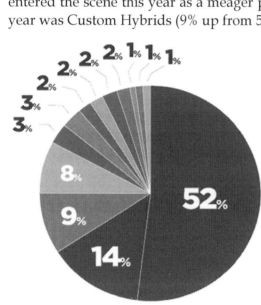

Scrum or Scrum variants continue to make up more than two-thirds of the methodologies being used, while Kanban has entered the scene this year as a meager player. The only category that saw growth this year was Custom Hybrids (9% up from 5%).
- Scrum 52%
- Scrum/XP Hybrid 14%
- Custom Hybrid 9%
- Don't Know 8%
- Kanban 3%
- Scrumban 3%
- Feature-Driven Development 2%
- Extreme Programming XP 2%
- Lean 2%
- Other 2%
- Agile Unified Process (AgileUP) 1%
- Agile Modeling 1%
- Dynamic Systems Development Method 1%

Figure 1-2: VersionOne 2011 Survey - Agile methodologies most closely followed

Lean-Agile and Kanban methodologies promote practices on managing work-in-progress through process and Kanban board, which is too ingrained at development level. Kanban still holds more promise as it is based on Lean principles. Lean principles focus on eliminating waste and are universally applicable in all domains.

Domain of direct impact

The popularity of Scrum can be due to the Framework provided with a unique set of ingredients. The direct impact is identified for development focus efforts. This is easy to grasp and understand. This becomes a good starting point where it is encouraged in organization. While implementing Scrum, teams learn and discover the intricacies and difficulties. In most cases, team is able to overcome those. Figure 1-3 shows how the direct impact is focused on Sprint level.

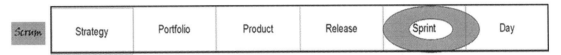

Figure 1-3: Direct impact domain of Scrum

Yet Scrum as practiced today can easily allow other practices to add on. Adding a Release level delivery around Sprints makes the next level. Scrum makes a subtle and profound change through the reviews and retrospectives where product and process improvements are made on constant basis.

We find a lot of text where Scrum Practitioners become defensive[i] when Scrum is compared to other methodologists. The direct impact is actually a major advantage. Two other Agile methodologies seem to be on the two sides of Scrum: Kanban and XP. Kanban (aka Lean-Agile) methodology is based on Lean principles. Yet it does not appeal for easy adoption. The processes and practices are not easy to grasp and a lot of variety exists in practice. XP is the other extreme with a lot of identified practices like TDD, Pair-programming, Continuous Integration, etc. These are common in mature teams. Seasoned development resources seem to take onto XP due to the frantic approach to quality. Scrum provides a balance in an imbalance world. As below diagram shows how easy a team can expand the impact of Scrum to apply from a Sprint to Release level.

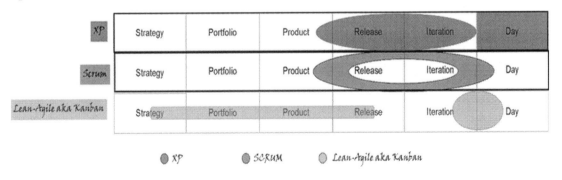

Figure 1-4: Direct impact domain of top three Agile methodologies

Scrum of Scrums provide structure for larger teams as well. Scrum just continues to grow. Yet allows teams to use what works best to get the highest value product features delivered time and again.

Initial expansion of Scrum was first observed shortly after Agile manifesto was compiled in 2001. Scrum was already propagating values identified in the manifesto. Now it is common to see Scrum to have Sprints from 1 week to 30 day long period. Two week Sprints are most common. Sprint length pertains to sustainable pace of delivering completed product features.

Domain of influence or indirect impact

Though Scrum has a limited direct impact but its influence ripples up to the enterprise level. The practices are accommodated specific to situation. Scrum framework provides much structure to allow enablement of Agile values and principles at Enterprise level.

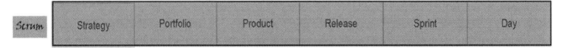

Scrum	Strategy	Portfolio	Product	Release	Sprint	Day

Figure 1-5: Domain of Influence of Scrum Framework

From the initial inception of Scrum, the influence is observed throughout the organization level. The Strategy and Portfolio seem to grasp on with customer focus and value driven delivery.

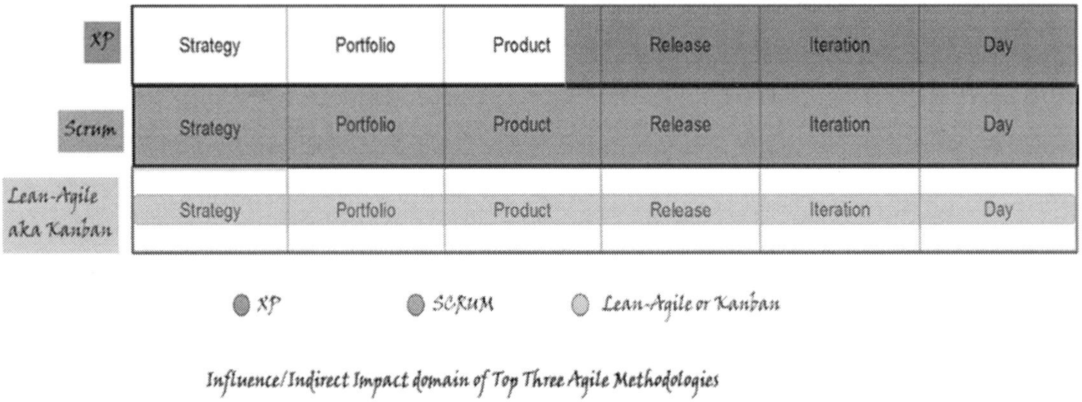

	Strategy	Portfolio	Product	Release	Iteration	Day
XP	Strategy	Portfolio	Product	Release	Iteration	Day
Scrum	Strategy	Portfolio	Product	Release	Iteration	Day
Lean-Agile aka Kanban	Strategy	Portfolio	Product	Release	Iteration	Day

● XP   ● SCRUM   ○ Lean-Agile or Kanban

Influence/Indirect Impact domain of Top Three Agile Methodologies

Figure 1-6: Domains of Influence of top three Agile methodologies

Defined framework

As a Scrum practitioner for years, we have been amazed at the flexibility and influence of Scrum Framework time and again. Scrum framework provides a unique structure with a set of roles, ceremonies, and artifacts that truly promote value-driven development. It allows teams to grow based on their own experiences. It allows the transition time while letting teams adopt various practices to make the best decisions. Instead of being prescriptive, it allows the framework that teams can use for development. This is its best feature. Hence, over the years, Scrum has grown to include various practices from other methodologies and teams transition to hybrid methodologies like Scrum/XP, ScrumBan, and so forth.

Summary

In this chapter we discussed the reasons behind popularity of Scrum. We have analyzed the direct impact promoting early inception of Scrum. Scrum framework is unique as it is not too heavy or too light-weight but just the right balance. The framework would be elaborated in subsequent chapters.

In the next chapter, we will provide Scrum overview covering the framework aspects.

---

i *Scrum® in Action: Agile Software Project Management and Development by Andrew Pham* – Introduction section and Chapter 1 – seek to correct information about Scrum in its support, while Alan Shalloway and his team discuss some of Scrum shortcomings in *Lean-Agile Software Development Achieving Enterprise Agility* (p. 84–92).

Chapter 2 Foundation

"Of all that is good, sublimity is supreme. Succeeding is the coming together of all that is beautiful. Furtherance is the agreement of all that is just. Perseverance is the foundation of all actions." - Lao Tzu

Introduction

This chapter provides an overview of Scrum foundation pillars, core values, principles, concepts and practices. Scrum framework consists of a set of roles, ceremonies, and artifacts. All these elements are bound together by Scrum rules. Each element in Scrum contributes to specific purpose and is an essential integrated part of the whole. Each of these aspects is then explored in subsequent chapters to help you grasp the essential values and principles. Besides, Agile values and principles are explained to build deeper understanding.

Scrum values

Scrum values are: **Commitment, Focus, Openness, Respect and Courage.**

Commitment: Scrum seeks individuals to be able to make commitment. Team commits to Sprint goal. Scrum provides and promotes people to be able to meet the commitment. Hence, Scrum identifies and differentiates the committed team from the extended team. Everyone on the committed team is committed to project success. Everyone in the extended team is involved and is a stakeholder.

Focus: Focus is on the goal identified as product vision and the aligned Sprint goal. All efforts are made towards working and delivering the committed goals. Hence, during the Sprint, team focuses on development of features and functionality. Further, framework provides ways to protect the team from external as well as internal unwanted interruptions.

Openness: Everything needs to be transparent about the project at all times. Team members are encouraged to openly ask questions and share any concerns that can impact the project. Various ceremonies especially Daily Scrums seek to provide this openness to allow for inspection and adaptation.

Respect: Everyone act in respectful manner with every other member. This allows the teams to grow and allow sharing of ideas, experiences, and their background. Scrum seeks to promote respect where every individual feels ability to contribute and thrive. Everyone is committed to product success. Thus, respect is an integral part.

Courage: To be able to provide complete transparency on an ongoing basis requires one to be courageous. Courage is needed to be able to make commitments in each Sprint. Courage is needed in owning tasks during planning. Courage is needed to share and provide team ownership for committed goals, sharing of ideas, raising early concerns, and team collaboration efforts. Everyone is responsible for product success and hence courage is essential and in-turn everyone gives and expects respect. *Courage is the first of human qualities because it is the quality which guarantees the others. - Aristotle*

Three pillars of Scrum

Complex projects recognize that not everything is known at the start of the project. There are unknowns. This requires constant generation of feedback loops to be able to build valuable product efficiently and effectively. Uncertainty, constraints and variations are encountered during empirical development process. These pose constant challenge to leadership and management teams. In order to seek quick and frequent feedbacks, to align the direction, Scrum values promote to uphold the three pillars of Scrum viz. *Transparency, Inspection, and Adaptation* [SCHWABER, 2001] and is collectively referred to as *"empirical process control."*

Transparency brings forth the current status in clear vision for the team and stakeholders; to be able to inspect and adapt for better efficiency, value and quality can be explored. Transparency means that both process and product development be visible and identifiable, without any speck of deception. For example, when a feature is identified as "done," everyone should be clear on what 'done' means. The definition of "done" must be clearly identified during the planning ceremony.

Inspection addresses the various aspects of process and product frequently and consistently. Inspection identifies ability to analyze, where the individual(s) must be skilled to assess the product and process.

Adaptation addresses the ability to adjust when new information is available. Adaptation demands immediate adjustments to eliminate further deviation. Inspection and adaptation is achieved by the ceremonies performed at specific time during the Sprint. Ability to adapt is an essential aspect of team agility and dynamics.

The uncertainties are uncovered using root-cause analysis techniques like W5H: Who, What, When, Where, and How. Empirical process control [SCHWABER, 2001] enables these to be known through the feedback loops at varying levels in different stages of Scrum. Feedback precedes adaptation; to be able to optimize the next course of action. This is very much like a road trip to a new destination. You do some planning and start your journey. Frequently checking your progress with the route map, using empirical process control (Transparency, Inspection and adaptation), to assess where you are on your way. In case of any deviation, adapt by planning to get on the most suitable route to reach the destination unless you travelled in opposite direction or know no other shorter way. Generally returning back to the start is not the most suitable decision. Bean counters know this; so, they don't look at sunk cost.

Figure 2-1: Scrum Skeleton

In Scrum Skeleton, as depicted above in Figure 2-1, the development cycle is kept small where the development is kept visible so that it can be inspected and adapted to optimal results. The components of Scrum skeleton are described as:

- Lower horizontal loop represents the *Sprint* (a term for *'iteration'* in XP or iterative development methodology like RUP) where development activities occurs repeatedly in short duration cycle
- The input to sprint is the list of requirements, referred to as Sprint Backlog
- The output of sprint is an incremental deliverable product; of value to end-user
- The upper circle represents the daily inspection during the sprint, in which the team meets to inspect each other's activities and make appropriate adaptations
- The cycle repeats until the project meets its vision or is no longer funded

Some roots of practices promoted in Scrum

"In all planning you make a list and you set priorities." - Alan Lakein

Agile methodologies patterns and techniques are discussed in detail in our book: *Solving Problems – The Agile Way*. These patterns show that Scrum Framework is built on proven principles and concepts that have stood the test of time and has provided an easier way to manage empirical processes.

Backlog

*Charles Schwab hired a time management consultant for US$25,000 in 1936 to help him best manage this precious commodity – **time**! He realized that time is an irreplaceable resource, an asset which cannot be recovered once spent. The consultant's advice was to start the day with a "To Do Task list" and then prioritize the vital few after sorting them from trivial many. Attain to these vital few instead of addressing all tasks as they appear. Besides, start with a task list with highest priority tasks based on their value and importance in descending order from top to bottom. Then, take up the topmost task which is of highest value. Then the next one and so on go down the list. Revise the list everyday by adding new task item in respective priority, removing the completed tasks off the list and updating the priorities of tasks based on their importance at the time. Time is money. Spend it wisely. [SINGHAL, PoH, 2013]*

Backlog is a list of items that are of value to the customer. Customer, here, refers to any entity that can derive value from the product like end-user, dealer, retailer, vendor, etc. The backlog is sorted with highest value items on the top and lower priorities below; in that order.

Sprint

Product Backlog contains many items that could take months to develop. Sprint is a specified amount of time duration, ranging from a week to 30 days in length, in which identified and committed to backlog items, constitute Sprint backlog, are developed and delivered. At the end of the Sprint, an incremental product is delivered that can be used by the customer. Commonly 2 weeks timeboxed sprints are widely used currently. However, sprint 0 and hardening sprints are commonly kept 1 week each as a common practice.

Timebox

Timebox is a time management technique to manage scope and organize work effort to complete the scope while working at a sustainable pace. A Timebox has a definite start and end time period.

Scrum ceremonies are timebox activities. Timebox means that each session is like a container of specific time. It must finish within the timebox. This helps the members to focus on the agenda and strive to seek resolution within the timebox. The timeboxed activity is adjourned when time expires. This is like a container of time where the team continues to fill in various contents and at the end either the agenda is achieved or the container fills up. The advantage of containing within time helps from dragging the issue and meeting timelessly without any direction or focus.

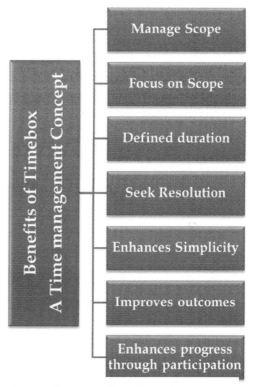

Sprints and various ceremonies in Scrum are timeboxed. Sprints are normally from 1 week to 30 days

Figure 2-2: Benefits of Timebox

timebox. All Sprints in a project are generally the same duration. The team strives to select backlog items for Sprint. These backlog items constitute Sprint backlog. The development team commits to deliver Sprint backlog items for the Sprint. Sprint utilizes iterative and incremental development.

Scrum ceremonies have a specific agenda. Scrum ceremonies identify specific goals and target that need to be achieved during the session. The members focus on meeting these needs during the identified timebox.

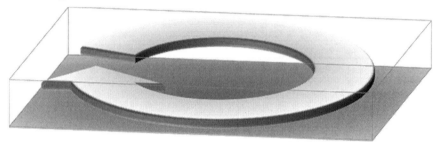

Figure 2-3: Sprint is a timebox

Timebox is an important aspect for the ceremonies. Timebox is not just a specific duration of time as a formality. Rather the duration of time to introduce a sense of time pressure in reaching a decision and restrict the ceremony to overrun time and decision indefinitely, providing a time constraint helps the members to focus on the agenda at hand and seek to reach the solution with identified focus, commitment, scope and level of granularity for the session. Hence, the effect of time seems to propagate the unanimous message to keep the focus on agenda and achieve the result. Further with progressive elaboration and rolling wave planning, it allows the team to take the result from the ceremony as sufficient to proceed further.

Figure 2-4: Timebox enforces focus and commitment

Sprints are further protected as no requirement changes are entertained within the Sprint. Customer can make updates to the Product Backlog but not to the committed items in the Sprint. This safeguards the development where the team can focus on committed functionality to deliver incremental valuable product at the end of Sprint. The scope creep is managed while customer can still continue to update the requirements without affecting the development progress. This aspect is further elaborated in the next chapter: Scrum Overview.

Last Responsive Moment

Last responsive moment (LRM) is another one of effective time management strategy Scrum has embraced from Lean principles. Scrum teams delay commitment and execution until the last responsive moment. Mary Poppendieck and Tom Poppendieck [Poppendieck, 2003] identified this term initially when experiencing a reverse effect of not making prompt decision when the moment is right. Last responsive moment is a reverse of gold plating mindset. It follows the principle of: "Strike while iron is hot." It is always economical, time saving and simplest to take decision at last responsible moment.

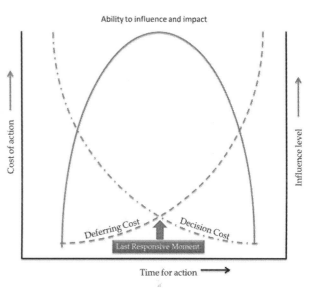

Figure 2-5: Highest impact of decision at Last Responsive Moment

Identifying last responsive moment is a constant challenge. We have seen two strategies that work in helping made decisions at the Last Response Moment (LRM). First approach is based on insight that planning is hard looking forward and can lead to gold plating and possibly cause rework. Hence, the approach is to see immediate impact due to upcoming work that could lead to differing cost to exceed if dependent decision is not taken. Second approach is similar to the strategy used in aerospace engineering. Engineers inspect and evaluate the impact of wing damage to an aircraft and additional impact due to the next flight. If a wing has 2 inch long crack but, say, 10 inches is the threshold. Then the decision is not to fix it immediately. An analysis of flight duration, weather and other aspects are considered and then the flight may be allowed. When the aircraft reaches the next airport, the crack is inspected. When it approaches closer to the threshold, it is fixed. Similarly, if the upcoming work is not impacting the area of impact while a delivery timeline approaches soon, it is better to defer decision and track it on the backlog. Then prioritizing it for next Sprint allows better alternative.

For this reason, Scum practices have expanded to rolling wave planning and progressive elaboration to allow the details to be defined as the product backlog is groomed continuously. At Sprint planning, the backlog should have sufficient level of details, for the team, to be able to make commitment.

When the uncertainty is high and indefinite, as is normally in the early stage of planning, delaying commitment and decisions enhances the accuracy. Further during Sprint planning, if the team feels that the details are not well-defined, the team can delay decision and continues to collaborate with the customer. This improves the effectiveness, discourages ambiguous workload, eliminates or at the least reduces rework, and enhances accuracy of dependent decisions. This further enhances agility and improves performance.

Decisions made early in the project where uncertainties are high is risky; as is prevalent in traditional software development. Scrum overcomes this as it includes planning to change as part of its plan. Not making a decision is itself a decision and hence, when the opportunity comes knocking, the team makes the decision and not let go of the "last possible moment." These are illustrated in Figure 2-5 where ability to influence is highest at Last Responsive Moment and where most is known and can be impacted.

Just-in-Time (JIT)

Just-in-Time (JIT) is another time management technique where work is undertaken just when they are needed. This optimizes time utilization and avoids wastes like waiting. This is further extended and applied to progressive elaboration and rolling wave planning.

We learned it as part of software development process that decisions have to be taken just in time when the information is known and clear. Believing that at least the architecture needs to be well-defined upfront has fired back where the discoveries in later phases have revealed that any guess or predicted architecture decisions had to be revisited and changed. Then on a couple of projects, utilizing Just-in-time technique, we keep the simple approach of building architecture and design only when warranted by the features in development. This expedited the process, kept the updates to a minimum, allowed early and quick adaption and provided flexible design. It is better to take decisions Jut-in-time to keep the process lightweight and effective for optimal performance. If we fail to make decision in time by waiting out longer, results in decisions being made for us as we lose control and technical debt starts to set in as well.

Progressive elaboration

Agile methodologies utilize progressive elaboration technique for backlog grooming. Backlog grooming is the estimation and planning aspect where each item in the backlog is visited top-down i.e. from highest priority item to next priority and so on. As each item is visited, it is elaborated to the desired level of details for the progressive stage. Agile methodologies support different progressive levels in product development. These levels are identified in agile onion and are closely related to rolling wave planning. Progressive elaboration applies to plans, estimates, risk assessments, requirements definitions, architectural designs, acceptance criteria and test scenarios.

The details pertain to each sprint level. For release level, the details in the estimation and planning pertain to the waves contained in the release. For Wave level, the estimation and planning pertain to the sprints contained in the wave. For Sprint level, the estimation and planning are detailed so that they can be covered by activities taken up for development during the Sprint. The plan so developed at each the beginning of each level is known as *rolling lookahead plan* as it outlines the expectations to be met and committed to during the timebox.

Rolling wave planning

Agile utilizes this aspect in Product Backlog technique. This aspect of making the prioritized list, with top-down processing, allows the highest priority items to be visited more frequently than the lower priority items. This enforces focus on highest value items to get more elaborated and detailed over time. Scrum encourages the Product Backlog to be groomed constantly to get details for the development to be effective. The

Figure 2-6: Agile Onion

planning does not assume all details upfront, rather includes constant inspect-and-adapt at each planning stage. The various levels of planning is shown in Figure 4-3 and further elaborated in agile planning onion [Mike Cohn 2005]. This is covered in detail in Chapter 25: Planning layers.

Scrum keeps an adaptive approach to be able to flexibly change its course to the optimum path at any time. Keeping this simple, lightweight and only addressing current known factors while recognizing the unknowns safeguard from going overboard. This brings agility to the development process for quick response time when there is a change in course of actions desired.

Information Radiator

Graphs and charts visible to make the progress easy to convey with ease. Information refrigerators are opposite where the information is kept hidden in secured sites, restricted locations or emails.

Collaboration

Collaboration is a negotiation style that promotes mutual interest of all parties involved where they working together for mutual interests. This negotiation style focuses on interests instead of positions. All parties join hands to help seek collective goal. Collaboration is the way the team scrums together toward a common goal.

Tacit knowledge

Tacit knowledge is the implied business domain knowledge that occurs when working closely with customers and end-user. Tacit knowledge is easier to build when customer is collocated with the Development Team and works together on daily basis.

Osmotic Communication

Osmotic communication is also known as cocktail party effect. Team members can experience osmotic communication by picking up other conversations by sitting in the same room. Communication occurs by just being in the vicinity. This occurs where other folks are discussing as if in unconscious eavesdropping. Osmotic communication is promoted heavily in agile software development. The Product Owner, the Scrum

Master and the Development Team – all are encouraged to be collocated in same area to promote osmotic communication.

Osmotic communications help in promoting team collaboration:

1. To gain tacit knowledge about business domain
2. To become self-organized, self-disciplined and autonomous
3. Information sharing occurs automatically in an informal setting
4. Team collaboration picks up
5. Common perception and understanding builds around the solution domain as more brainstorming sessions get triggered due to osmotic communication
6. To keep the team communication focused, committed and open
7. Informal setting where information flows in the background for easy pickup

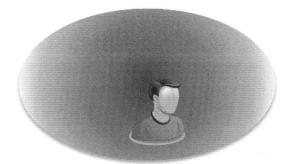

Figure 2-7 Osmotic region of influence of an individual

Closer a conversation occurs; easier it is to pick it up. It appears like an invisible zone around a person that fades with distance. This is depicted in Figure 2-7 and 2-8.

Figure 2-8 No osmotic communication

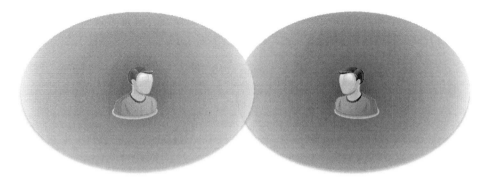

Figure 2-9 Little osmotic communication

When a person is conversing, another person can pick up. For example, when a designer and developer were discussing on UI layer, a tester sitting in the vicinity can quickly become aware of the changes. This promotes team collaboration. The tester, in possession of additional information, can quickly inform them of required acceptance criteria to ensure complete coverage. This is shown in Figures 2-9 through 2-11.

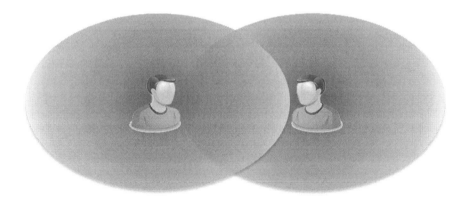

Figure 2-10 Effective osmotic communication

When two team members are conversing, all the people in the vicinity become aware. This allows others to associate the topic with their individual domain. Two developers working together on a module could be conversing while analysts, designers and testers in the same room can stay aware. Such team environment fosters collaboration.

Figure 2-11 Osmotic communication

Collocation

Residing at the same location – same floor and building are implied. Collocation promotes osmotic communication and enables effective modes of communication. The ability to just be at same location allows expedites a group to build ties and become an entity with aligned objectives.

Teamwork

A group of motivated individuals working closely on a common goal with aligned visions. Everyone brings their abilities to best achieve the goal. Team performs as a well-oiled engine where each team member feel themselves part of a single entity. Hence, TEAM is also expressed as an entity where Together Each Achieves More.

Summary

This chapter describes Scrum values and the three pillars of Scrum. These enable Scrum framework to stay lightweight and focus on delivering value in empirical process.

Next chapter discusses the overview of Scrum where we discover more insights on how empirical control process helps in complex project domain.

Chapter 3 Overview

"You will never do anything in this world without courage. It is the greatest quality of the mind next to honor." - Aristotle

Introduction

This chapter provides an overview of Scrum and its practices. Scrum framework consists of a set of roles, ceremonies, and artifacts. All these elements are bound together by Scrum rules. Each element in Scrum contributes to specific purpose and is an essential integrated part of the whole. Each of these is then explored in subsequent chapters to help you grasp the essential concepts and principles. We shall later discuss agile values and principles to gain deeper understanding.

This chapter would help you understand the original Scrum framework. A serious evolution of framework has occurred in Scrum since 2001. Scrum framework has since extended from Sprint to Release and even to Project/Product level. User stories and story points from XP have not been adopted and considered an integral part of Scrum. We shall cover those aspects in detail in later chapters to help you grasp the concepts, framework working and underlying principles.

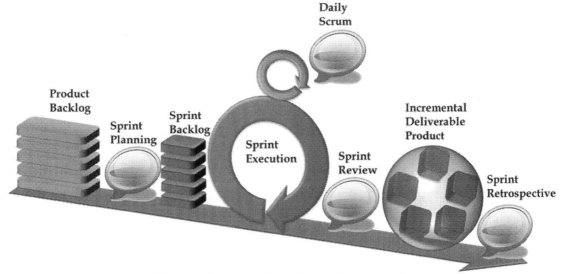

Figure 3-1: Scrum Overview with ceremonies

Scrum Framework Overview

Scrum framework provides a structure for software development to deliver incremental release of product with highest value delivered in every Sprint. It is not a prescriptive process. It is not a discipline though it requires a disciplined approach. Scrum rules are essential to tie the roles, ceremonies, and artifacts into the whole as a framework for software development.

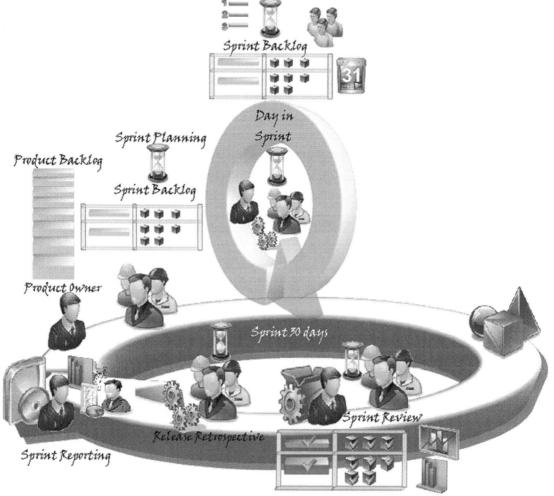

Figure 3-2: Scrum Framework Overview

The overview elaborates on Scrum Skeleton discussed earlier in the previous chapter. Scrum maintains one artifact – Product Backlog as single source of all product features and requirements. Sprint is a defined duration where some of the items from the Product Backlog are taken to create a Sprint Backlog. The Sprint backlog is worked on to develop and deliver an incremental product at the end of the Sprint. The cycle continues until all the items in the Product Backlog are implemented or any other agreed upon criteria has been met through collaboration.

Scrum Ingredients

Scrum ingredients are sets of: 3 roles, 4 ceremonies, 5 artifacts and a development period (known as Sprint):

- Scrum Roles
  - Product Owner
  - Scrum Master
  - The Team
- Scrum Ceremonies
  - Sprint Planning meeting
  - Daily Scrum
  - Sprint Review
  - Sprint Retrospective
- Scrum Artifacts
  - Product Backlog
  - Sprint Backlog
  - Product Increment
  - Sprint Reports
  - Product Backlog Burndown Report
- Sprint

There are two additional ceremonies that are getting included in recent practice of Scrum: Scrum of Scrums and Backlog Grooming. These are more prevalent on large projects.

Scrum Roles

There are two types of project members in Scrum as derived from an analogy: pigs and chickens. **Pigs** are ones who are totally committed and accountable for the product success. **Chickens** are ones who are involved, consult on the project, and are kept informed of the progress. These two types of roles are referenced in Figure 3-3.

The joke identifies that the Pig being able to provide a sacrificial offering, for which the Pig must die in order to provide bacon versus the Chicken which provides non-sacrificial offering of eggs.

Sometimes, this joke is presented as a riddle:

Question: *In Bacon-and-egg breakfast, what is the difference between the Chicken and the Pig?*

Answer: *The Chicken is **involved**, but the Pig is **committed**!*

For Scrum project, Scrum Master, Product Owner, and Team are considered committed to the project while other stakeholders including customers, management and leadership teams are considered involved in the project. Committed members are referred to as Core Scrum Team. Involved stakeholders are referred to as 'Extended team.' If a project fails or lags, the neck of committed members is on the line while involved members are affected but not that severely. The distinction between committed versus involved is made to incite motivation, development, accountability, and eliminate floundering.

Figure 3-3: Chicken and Pig story

Product Owner

Primary responsibility of Product Owner is to ensure that a common vision is pursued, establish priorities to the user needs so that highest valued features are delivered early, and optimize Return on investment (ROI). Product Owner represents the interests of stakeholders including users, purchasers, and customers of the project deliverable, be it a product or a service. The Product Owner accrues funding for the project, manages requirements, Return-on-Investment (ROI) objectives, and release plans. Product Owner uses Product Backlog to ensure most valuable functionality gets implemented first.

Product Owner keeps the Product Backlog prioritized based on value. The development team helps develop and deliver the product features to Product Owner in a Sprint. A Sprint is the iterative development duration of fixed time. Earlier text referred to this as duration of 30 days as originally introduced. The Development Team works with Product Owner and commits to deliver a set of features in a Sprint. This set of features forms what is known as Sprint Backlog and is specific to the Sprint.

Scrum Master

 Scrum Master is responsible for the Scrum process. Scrum Master educates on Scrum principles, values, concepts, and practices to everyone involved on the project; including the team and the Product Owner. Scrum Master helps organization adapt to Scrum practices. As the Development Team matures and inspects the development process, Scrum Master facilitates *Process tailoring* to deliver expected benefits in compliance with Scrum principles and values.

Scrum Master is responsible to seeing that Scrum rules are upheld during each Sprint. Master assists the Product Owner with Product Backlog. Scrum Master is mentor and teacher for the Team. Scrum Master acts as a Servant-Leader for the Team. Scrum As the servant leader, Scrum Master provides necessary resources to the team, protects the team from external influences and interruptions, and removes roadblocks so that the team can focus on Sprint goals. Scrum Master is accountable for Scrum framework processes and to ensure that Scrum rules are followed on the project. An agile coach or Scrum coach can take up the role of Scrum Master on a project.

The Development Team

The Development Team is responsible for developing the product during the Scrum process, an incremental development process. The team is self-organizing, empowered, adaptive, and cross-functional. Team is sized as 7 ± 2 members ideally. Note: team of 7 ± 2 developers translates to a team size of 5 to 9 developers.

Figure 3-4: The Development Team

People assigned to these roles are committed to the project. The distinction is made to instill momentum, productivity, accountability, and end floundering.

The Team develops the features during the Sprint while continuing to inspect and adapt daily. At the end of the Sprint, the Team delivers the releasable product features to the Product Owner. The Product Owner accepts features meeting agreed upon criteria. The Team inspects and adapts to improve the development process for next Sprint. In next Sprint, again the team collaborates with the Product Owner to work on product features development.

Scrum Ceremonies

Practices of Scrum are specific to the three pillars of implementation of empirical process control: transparency, inspection and adaptation.

Transparency/Visibility means that both process and product development be visible and identifiable, without any spec of deception. For example, when someone identifies that a feature is "done" it should be clear as to what "done" means. **Inspection** addresses the various aspects of process and product frequently and consistently. Inspection identifies the role of Inspector, where the individual(s) **must be skilled to** *assess the product and/or process under inspection. Adaptation* addresses the adjustments in the various visible aspects if inspection reveals that the results are unacceptable; be it the aspects of the process or the resulting product. Adaptation demands immediate adjustments to eliminate further deviation.

There are four major Scrum ceremonies: Sprint planning, Daily Scrum, Sprint review and Sprint retrospective. These are performed at identified time in a Sprint, as shown in Figure 3-5.

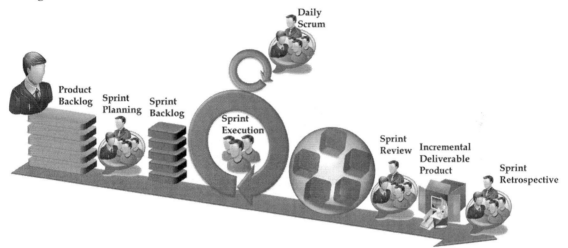

Figure 3-5: Sprint Ceremonies in Scrum

The three pillars are guided by five different practices in Scrum of which last two provide visibility aspect while later three provide opportunity to inspect and opportunity to adapt. These ceremonies that promote visibility are:

Sprint planning ceremony

Sprint planning ceremony is the first event in a Sprint. The Team meets with the Product Owner and reviews the Product Backlog and commits to a set of backlog items to deliver for the Sprint. Sprint planning ceremony is attended by Product Owner, Scrum Master and the Team.

Sprint planning ceremony is a timebox. For two week Sprint, it is normally a 4 hour timebox and consists of two sessions. In the first half, the Product Owner describes various items in the backlog. The team inquires to understand each item. Then, the team commits to the set of items for the Sprint. In the later half, team collaborates and identifies the tasks that need to be performed to complete each backlog item.

Figure 3-6: Sprint Planning ceremony

Daily Scrums

Daily Scrums are 15 minutes timebox sessions focused on bringing the current short term tasks status sharing so later team can focus on adapting. These are short ceremonies where 3 questions are answered by every team member. Attendees are the Team, the Scrum Master and the Product Owner. Only team members speak in this meeting, extended team members are only spectators.

Every team member answers three questions:

1. What have you done since the Last Daily Scrum on this project?
2. What do you plan to do before the next Daily Scrum on this project?
3. Is there any impediment or roadblock in your way on this project?

Figure 3-7: Daily Scrum

Sprint Review

Sprint Review ceremonies are conducted on the last day of Sprint. The Team conducts a demo of product features completed during the sprint. The individual features are covered in demo. After demo, the features are accepted and included as part of the incremental product.

As part of inspection, product improvement and updates based on stakeholders' feedback are collected. These inputs are then used to groom the Product Backlog and prepare for the next Sprint.

Sprint Review ceremony is attended by the committed and extended teams. These include Scrum Master, Product Owner, the Team, and the essential Stakeholders.

Figure 3-8: Sprint Review ceremony

Sprint Retrospectives

Sprint Retrospective is normally conducted after Sprint Review. Sprint Retrospective is geared towards improving the development process. This ceremony is attended by The Team, Scrum Master, and the Product Owner. Product Owner used to be optional for this ceremony. Sprint Retrospective is facilitated by Scrum Master.

Sprint Retrospective is an essential part where the development process is inspected to improve upon. The Development Team seeks to improve the development process where focus is on: people, processes and resources. It is customary to share appreciations and kudos near the end of this ceremony.

Figure 3-9: Sprint Retrospective

Scrum of Scrums

Currently, Scrum of Scrums ceremonies were introduced for large team sizes or multiple teams working at project or program level. These apply to larger teams where development representatives from each Scrum team meet regularly to collaborate with other teams. These ceremonies occur once or twice a week to focus on project progress. This is a short ceremony; similar to Daily Scrum as focus is on providing transparency.

Each Scrum core team representative answers the following four questions:

1. What has your team done since we last met?
2. What will your team do before we meet again?
3. Is there anything slowing your team down or any roadblock is in its way?
4. Are you about to put anything in other team's/teams' way?

Figure 3-10: Scrum of Scrums

Scrum Artifacts

Backlog

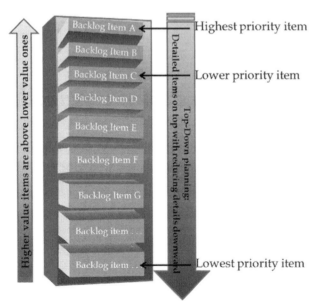

Backlog is a prioritized list of items based on value driven approach. In the beginning, there were two main types of backlogs in Scrum: Product Backlog and Sprint Backlog. An item in Backlog is known as Backlog Item (BI). As shown in Figure 3-11. In time, additional backlogs are identified with scaling of Scrum; based on evolution of rolling wave planning where various layers were added like Risk, Release and wave. These are discussed at length in Chapter 16: Scrum Backlogs.

Figure 3-11: Backlog with Backlog items

Product Backlog

Product backlog is a dynamic and prioritized stack of an evolving set of product requirements for the system or product being developed on the project(s). Individual product functionality is referred to as *Product Backlog item*. The most valued feature to the customer is at the top of the stack with decreasing order in value. Product Owner is accountable and responsible for maintaining this Product Backlog for the contents, prioritization, and availability. Product Owner updates the Product Backlog, not the team. Team only provides cost, complexity, risk, and time input factors for the Product Backlog items for Product Owner to manage the Product Backlog. Product Backlog is never complete and evolves as the product is built with each Sprint. Product Backlog constantly changes as "done" Product Backlog items are removed, new Product Backlog items are added, current ones updated, re-prioritized and managed to maximize customer value. Product Owner prepares the Product Backlog with sorted list of backlog items with highest valued at the top. Product Backlog items at the top of the Product Backlog are appropriately detailed. Product Backlog should be **D**etailed appropriately, **E**mergent, **E**stimated, and **P**rioritized (DEEP) [Roman Pichler and Mike Cohn, 2010].

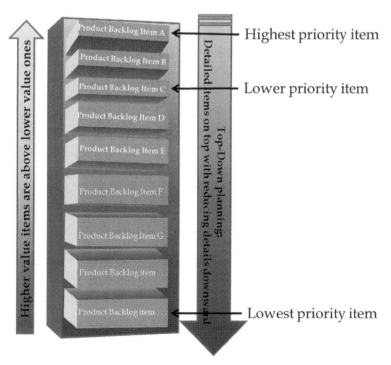

Figure 3-12: Product Backlog with PBIs

Sprint Backlog

Sprint Backlog is a prioritized stack of backlog items and related *tasks* committed to by the team to develop the incremental product for the Sprint. Team owns the Sprint Backlog. Hence, the Team can make any changes and updates to the Sprint Backlog, not the Product Owner or Scrum Master. At the end of Sprint, during Sprint Review ceremony, team reviews and conducts demo of the fully functional incremental product to the Product Owner and the stakeholders. Backlog Items on Sprint Backlog are referred to as *Sprint Backlog Item (SBI)*.

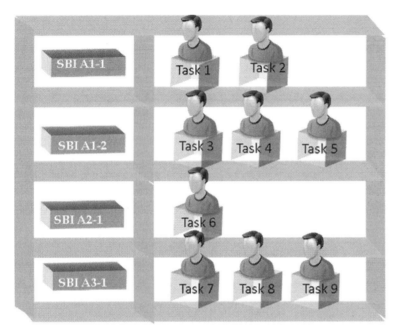

Figure 3-13: Sprint Backlog with SBIs and Tasks

Backlog item (BI)

Backlog item is a product feature, function, defect, risk or service of value desired to meet an end-user need. Backlog items are initially created as part of Product Backlog. In Product Backlog, they are known as *Product Backlog items (PBI)*. When a backlog item is assigned to Sprint, it is known as *Sprint Backlog Item (SBI)*. At the end of Sprint, when the backlog item is identified as 'done' it becomes part of Incremental product. When a backlog item is not considered 'done' in Sprint Review, it is added back to Product Backlog.

Sprint Reports

At the end of the Sprint, the Product Owner and the Scrum Master are responsible for four reports:

1   The Product Backlog at the start of the previous Sprint
2   The Product Backlog at the start of the new Sprint
3   The Changes report that details all of the differences between the Product Backlogs in the first two reports
4   The Product Backlog Burndown chart: Burndown chart shows the amount of work remaining across time.

Incremental Product

After a Sprint, the Team reviews the completed features with Product Owner and stakeholders. The completed features are marked 'done' and become part of the incremental product. This incremental product must be a releasable product which would fulfill the end user needs and provide the highest value. The change report identifies the features added to this incremental product during the Sprint. Over a number of Sprints, Incremental product grows as it collectively represents all the backlog items *'done'* in all the Sprints.

Sprint

Sprint used to be a 30 days timebox. Sprint is now a timebox of two weeks to 30 days timebox. All Sprints are kept the same length. During Sprint, the Development Team works on building the product features. Sprint allows sustainable pace with an incremental product delivery at the end of the Sprint. At the start of Sprint, during Sprint planning ceremony, the Team commits to deliver a set of features known as Sprint Backlog. The team then collaborates to develop the product features. Daily Scrums are held at the same place, same time for the team to inspect and adapt development efforts. The Team reports estimate of completed effort every day to reflect on Sprint Burndown chart. Product Owner is available during the Sprint to get any clarification. The Team stays focused on Sprint Backlog during the Sprint. On the last day of Sprint, the Team reviews the completed features with the Product Owner and the stakeholders. During Sprint Review, 'done' items are marked and become part of the Incremental product. Backlog items not 'done' are added back to the Product Backlog. The Team and Product Owner gather feedback from the stakeholders. The new or enhanced features are then included in the Product Backlog. After the Sprint Review ceremony, Sprint Retrospective is held. The Team reflects back on the development process during the Sprint and seeks to improve it. Product Owner and

Scrum Master prepare the Sprint reports. Product Owner prepares the Product Backlog for the next Sprint.

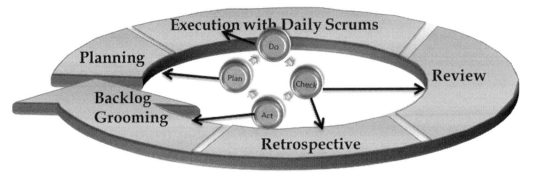

Figure 3-14: Sprint in Scrum

Summary

In this chapter, we described Scrum overview with coverage on various roles, ceremonies, artifacts and the sequence of events as provided by Scrum framework. These elements are discussed with greater depth in subsequent chapters. Since 2001, additional practices and artifacts have been included in Scrum. These will be covered in the subsequent chapters at length too.

Chapter 4 Roles

"Innovation distinguishes between a leader and a follower." - Steve Jobs

Introduction

Scrum Framework warrants three different entity roles to enable the delivery of valuable product. These three roles are: Scrum Master, Product Owner and the development team as shown in Figure 4-1. The Scrum Master understands the core values, principles and practices of Scrum Framework and is responsible for implementing Scrum Framework. The Product Owner is the internal representative of the customer and decides what would be built and in what order. The development team is the delivery team which decides how the features would be built and provides estimate insights required for the effort. These three roles form the core team. All other stakeholders form the extended team and are discussed later.

Scrum Master	Product Owner	The Team
• Responsible for Scrum process • Servant-Leader • Situational Leadership style • Acts as: Teacher, Mentor, Coach, Facilitator, conflict navigator, problem solver, and more. • Helps Product Owner understand the Technical jargon • Helps the Team understand the business langue	• Acts as Product Champion • Owns Product Backlog • Defines product features, functions, and approves Release and Sprint Backlogs • Can change features in Product Backlog • Owns the vision • Manages the stakeholders • Decides what to build and in what order	• Empowered team • Small sized: 7±2 • Collocated: caves and commons workspace • All skills to deliver the product features • Makes all decisions for the team and product development effort • Owns Sprint Backlog • Works together to build the product • Self-organizing • Self-managing • Self-motivated

Figure 4-1: Scrum Roles: Core Team

Scrum Master

Scrum Master (SM) is the Process Champion. The Scrum Master upholds Scrum Framework and helps train, coach, mentor and implement Scrum Framework for the project. Scrum Master is key person to help with Scrum Framework adaption and guides the core team and extended team members. In essence, the Scrum Master manages principles. The principles manage process.

Scrum Master performs as servant leader where the responsibilities include removing impediments, safeguarding team from external influence (foxes), and supporting and providing the necessary support and environment to focus on delivering value. Scrum Master seeks to provide

Scrum Master acts as Change Agent and utilizes various facilitator role and activities to help the Product Owner and the development team with various practices. In addition, Scrum master facilitates changes to improve the development process. Scrum Master acts as facilitator at various Scrum ceremonies and helps foster the environment for the Product Owner and the development team to make decisions and commitments.

Chapter 22 provides additional details on the Scrum Master role.

Product Owner

Product Owner (PO) is the Product Champion. Product Owner creates product vision, maintains ROI analysis, performs regular market analysis, user and market needs, and provides them to the development team.

The Product Owner collaborates with the Scrum Master and the Development Team, and vice-versa. The Product Owner participates in all Scrum ceremonies and normally facilitates the Review ceremonies.

The Product Owner is representative of customer, end-users and other stakeholders like marketing team and sales team. All requirements, defects, enhancements and changes come through the Product Owner. The Product Owner is solely responsible for what is to be built; when it is built; and in what order. The Product Owner ensures this through Product Backlog and team collaboration.

The Product Owner owns, manages, updates and prioritizes the Product Backlog. The Product Owner provides details about Product Backlog items (PBIs) to the team, Collaborates with the team to provide support and answers or gets all their questions answered. Product Owner collects estimates from team and uses it to carry out Product Backlog grooming sessions and activities like innovation games.

Until 2009, there was a misconception that the Product Owner is involved member (chicken) and not a committed member (pig). However, in time it was realized that the Product Owner is a committed member (pig). For instance, if a product fails even though the Scrum Master ensured that Scrum Framework was embraced to the very last principle and the team developed and delivered all features and functionality on or before time but the Product Owner failed to do the market analysis and led to product failure. Who would be responsible for project failure in this case? We hope you got the point.

Chapter 21 provides additional details on the Product Owner role.

The Development Team

The Development Team is the Product Delivery champion and is known as "Delivery team" or "The Team." Scrum defines the Development Team as autonomous, self-organizing, self-managing, and self-motivated. The Development Team is autonomous; which signifies that the Team has all required skills viz. analysis, design, development, test, deployment, and operations, to deliver the product from concept to reality. The Development team size is five to nine (7 $\pm$ 2) team members. The Team collaborates internally and utilizes techniques like consensus building approaches (CBA), Planning poker, and development practices.

The Team collaborates with Scrum Master and Product Owner. The Team is instrumental in executing the empirical process control aspects viz. Transparency, Inspection and Adaptation. The Development Team participates in all Scrum ceremonies.

The Team is accountable for delivery of incremental deployable product and its features and not individual members. The Team collaborates with the Product Owner to understand the product features and functionality. The Team commits to the Sprint goal in Sprint Planning ceremony. The Team members demo the product features during Review ceremonies. The Team provides effort estimates to the Product Owner and commits to deliver the prioritized list in Sprint Backlog. The Team owns Sprint Backlog and tracks Sprint progress through information radiators. The Scrum Master facilitates, mentors, and supports to help the Team gain insights. The Team collaborates in retrospectives to inspect and tune its development process.

Chapter 23 provides additional details on the Development Team roles and responsibilities.

Extended Team (Stakeholders)

Stakeholders who are not member of the Core team are part of extended team. These members interface with Product Owner as a single point of contact to request product features and improvements. Extended team members are invited to Sprint Review sessions.

For Scrum project, Scrum Master, Product Owner, and The Development Team are considered [Pigs] committed to the project; while other stakeholders including customers, vendors, support organizations and management are considered [Chickens]; as they are involved in the project. Committed members are referred to as Core Scrum Team. Involved stakeholders are referred to as 'Extended team.' Hence, all management responsibilities in a Scrum project are divided among the three roles.

Problem Domain vs. Solution Domain

As discussed earlier in Scrum overview, Scrum identifies two sets of teams: Scrum Core Team and Extended team. All roles are further segregated in two domains: Problem Domain and Solution domain.

Problem domain is commonly referred to as Business Domain. In Problem domain, product needs arises for the product. The customer, end-user, marketing team, sales team and members related to business domain are part of the Problem Domain. They collaborate with the Product Owner for various needs. Besides, they provide support, insights and answers related to the Problem Domain to the Core Team. Product Owner is the internal representative for Problem Domain. Product Owner performs initial business domain analysis and develops product vision, project charter and Product Vision box.

Solution domain is commonly referred to as Development domain. Solution Domain is where the solution is developed. Solution Domain Team is referred to as Development Leadership Team or Delivery Leadership Team. Scrum Master acts as the internal representative of Solution Domain.

The Development Team collaborates with the Scrum Master and the Product Owner to get insights and can directly communicate with the two domains to develop and deliver the incremental product at the end of Sprint. In Figure 4-2, the two domains with the two representatives are identified where the top semi-circle represents the Solution domain and the bottom semi-circle represents the Problem or Business domain. The Development Team can directly communicate with members of these two domains. Face to face communication is preferred. The information in-flow and escalation occurs through internal representatives to ensure team stays focus but is not a limiting factor. Team members can directly collaborate with members in the two domains. This encourages tacit knowledge to spread quickly and allows the two domains to understand various terms prevalent in the other domain. Scrum Master helps spread, facilitate, and support sharing of the domain knowledge.

Figure 4-2: Scrum Core Team and Extended Team

Summary

This chapter describes three Scrum roles: Product Owner, Scrum Master and the Development Team. These are described in length from Chapters 21-23. These three roles form the Core Team and are committed to the product success. All other stakeholders are part of Extended Team. The Extended Teams are further split in two domains: Problem domain or Business domain and Solution domain or Delivery domain.

In the next chapter, we shall discuss the various artifacts that empirical process control. These are normally in the form of big charts, graphs, and bulleted lists. Most of these artifacts are commonly referred to as "Information Radiators" and are posted in visible areas and Team room.

Chapter 5 Artifacts

"Finally, strategy must have continuity. It can't be constantly reinvented." - Michael Porter

Introduction

This chapter discusses various Scrum Artifacts that help deliver valuable software often and frequently to the customer. The focus is on the highest priority; which is to deliver valuable software to customer. The artifacts are utilized as part of the empirical process control viz. Transparency, Inspection and Adaptation.

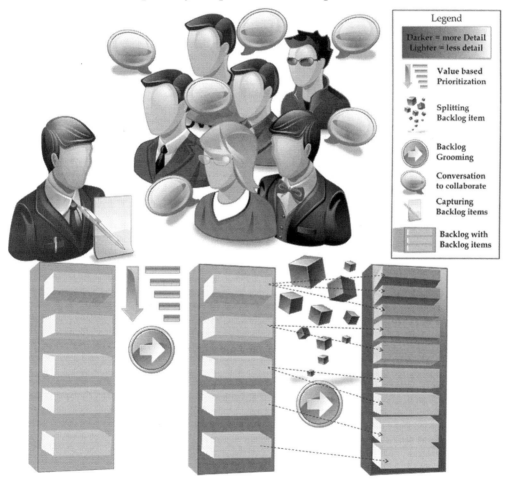

Figure 5-1: Product Backlog

Product Backlog

Product backlog is a dynamic and prioritized collection of an evolving set of product requirements for the system or product being developed. This is discussed in detail in Chapter 13.

Sprint Backlog

Sprint Backlog is developed from the Product Backlog during Sprint Planning ceremony. The Product Owner describes different PBIs and the team selects and commits to a set of PBIs. The team then analyzes each PBI and identifies the list of tasks that would need to be performed to deliver each PBI. Then each task is owned.

Figure 5-2: Developing Sprint Backlog from Product Backlog

Change Report

Product Owner and Scrum Master are together accountable for generating Reports at the end of each Sprint. Change report is one of the reports generated. Change report is the listing of backlog items that have been delivered in the Sprint and the list of new or updated backlog items. These are the difference of the Product Backlog from the beginning of the Sprint to that at the end of the Sprint. Change report is determined after the review ceremony.

Burndown Reports

Burndown report shows the rate at which the backlog items are delivered. It shows the reduction in estimates of the Backlog over time.

Product Burndown Graph

At the end of each Sprint, the total effort estimate reduces for a Product Backlog. A simple example is displayed where in first Sprint, 70 units were estimated and 84 units were achieved and so on.

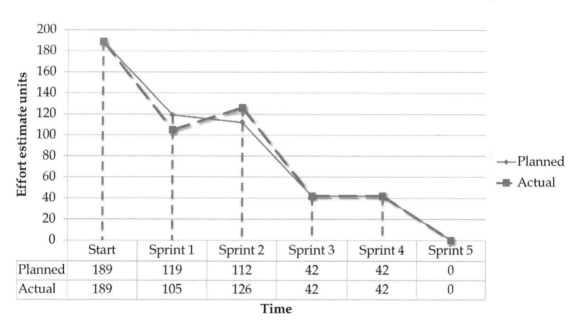

	Start	Sprint 1	Sprint 2	Sprint 3	Sprint 4	Sprint 5
Planned	189	119	112	42	42	0
Actual	189	105	126	42	42	0

Figure 5-3: Product Burndown Report

Sprint Burndown Graph

Sprint Burndown graph tracks the amount of effort completed each day. In the past when there were no Agile tools, the Scrum Master normally used to track the hours of work completed based on the reported completed hours by the Development Team. Currently, many agile tools like VersionOne, Rally, and Rational Team Concert can capture these values based on reported hours of effort completed for each day. Below Figure 5-4 shows an estimated vs. actual hours of work completed for a 14 day Sprint.

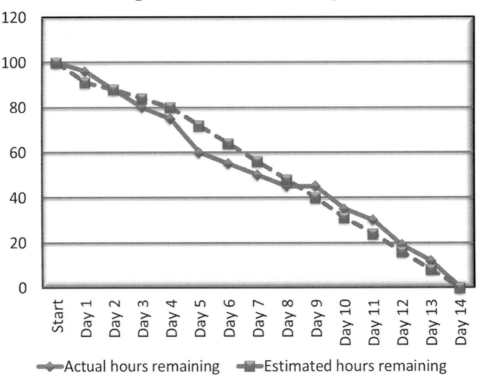

Figure 5-4: Sprint Burndown Graph

Summary

This chapter describes Scrum artifacts used to tracking the progress during the Sprint. These artifacts provide needed insight to progress and help the Team inspect-and-adapt accordingly.

Scrum Framework is lightweight and these graphs are very easy to manually prepare as shown here. The graph is easy to analyze, track, inspect and adapt.

We shall discuss various types of Scrum ceremonies in the next chapter.

Chapter 6 Ceremonies

"We are what we repeatedly do. Excellence, then, is not an act, but a habit." - Aristotle

Introduction

Together, the Sprint Planning ceremony, the Daily Scrum, the Sprint Review, and the Sprint Retrospective constitute the empirical inspection and adaptation practices of Scrum. These are the four major ceremonies conducted during a Sprint. The Scrum Master manages, enforces, and coaches Scrum rules and principles. . Scrum Master manages the principles. The principles manage the process and the Team. Scrum values and principles are introduced through these ceremonies and collaborative sessions. Hence, Scrum Master facilitates these ceremonies and ensures the values and principles are practiced.

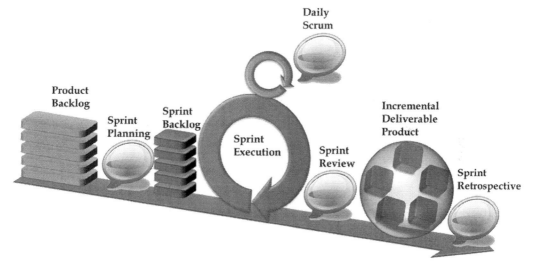

Figure 6-1: Scrum Ceremonies in Sprint

Sprint Planning

For a 30 day Sprint, the Sprint planning ceremony is timeboxed to 8 hours. The Sprint planning ceremony has two sessions of 4 hours each: During the first session, the Product Owner presents the value prioritized Product Backlog to the Team. The Product Owner discusses the Product Backlog items (PBIs) in detail with the Team.

The acceptance criteria are clearly defined for each PBI. This is known as definition of 'done' where meeting the criteria helps the team asses when the development for a PBI is done. When the Team understands enough, the Team selects and commits to the Product Backlog items that it feels can be delivered in the Sprint. During the second session, the Team plans out the Sprint Backlog with tasks. The Team visits each Product Backlog item and identifies the tasks it needs to perform to complete the PBI. These tasks are placed in the Sprint Backlog against PBI. The Team may add, update, or delete the tasks in the Sprint Backlog during the Sprint.

Important rules of conducting the planning ceremony are:

- The Sprint planning ceremony is attended by the Scrum Master, the Product Owner and the Development Team
- Scrum Master facilitates the Sprint planning ceremony. In absence of Scrum Master, another Scrum Master, Scrum Coach or Agile Coach can facilitate the ceremony. Scrum Master must coordinate to ensure a facilitator is assigned.
- The Product Owner provides the prioritized Product Backlog and help the team understand the Product Backlog items
- The Development Team seeks to create a Sprint Backlog with Backlog items and required tasks to complete the Backlog items.
- No chickens (other stakeholders) are allowed unless provisioned by the Product Owner. Other team members acting as SMEs and required support personnel are allowed.
- The Product Owner provides the updated and prioritized Product Backlog prior to the meeting
- In absence of the Product Owner, the Scrum Master prepares an adequate Product Backlog and stands in for the Product Owner
- The Team selects the Product Backlog items from the top (highest priority) to identify the items it can commit to. The Team determines what it will attempt to achieve during the Sprint.
- The Product Owner decides what items constitute the backlog for the Sprint.
- The team can offer suggestions and recommendations though for the Product Owner's consideration. Team calendar, velocity and other radiators are used for this analysis.
- Further analysis on Product Backlog items (PBIs) can be done during the Sprint.

- Product Owner is responsible to address any inquiries the Team has for understanding PBIs.
- During the second half, the Team breaks down each PBI into the various tasks needed to perform to achieve the PBI. The Product Owner must be present to provide answers to the Team. However, the discussion on analysis can continue during the Sprint, if both the parties agree as the ceremony is timeboxed.
- The Team manages the Sprint Backlog. The Team organizes Sprint plan to deliver the PBIs during the Sprint. Hence, the Team is responsible for deriving tasks needed to deliver each PBI. The Team collaborates with other stakeholders in case of inquiries or when it needs support.
- A set of rules apply to the Sprint and are thus, addressed in that section
- Every PBI in Sprint Backlog must have acceptance criteria defined (as to what 'done' means") to estimate effort and know when PBI is complete. The definition of 'done' should be defined and core team (the Product Owner, the Scrum Master, and the Development Team) agree as to what "done" means. During the Sprint, any changes to this definition must be agreed upon by the Product Owner and the Development Team.

Figure 6-2: Sprint planning ceremony

At the start of the second session of the Sprint Planning meeting, the Sprint has started. The Outcome of the Sprint planning ceremony is the Sprint Backlog. The Sprint Backlog is owned by the team and the Team is responsible for making any changes to it. Product Owner can continue to make changes to the Product Backlog but cannot make any updates to the Sprint Backlog during the Sprint.

Daily Scrum

Daily Scrum is a 15 minute timebox ceremony that occurs at the same place and the same time every day of the Sprint. In XP, Daily Scrum is also known as Daily Stand-up ceremony though it does not imply that everyone must stand during this meeting, though encouraged. Rather it is to identify the time sensitivity and focus. Daily Scrum occurs every day where the Team gathers where every member of the team answers three questions:

1. What have you done since the Last Daily Scrum on this project?
2. What do you plan to do before the next Daily Scrum on this project?
3. Is there any impediment in your way on this project?

Figure 6-3: Daily Scrum

Team members take turn to answer these questions and share the status with the team. This provides daily *visibility* to the team for *inspection and adaptation* opportunity in a later session during the day. Purpose is to synchronize the work of all Team members, schedule any required ceremonies, and remove any impediments team is encountering. Scrum Master is responsible to ensure these ceremonies happen, the rules of Scrum are followed, and any impediments identified are addressed for resolution. As per the rules of Scrum, following aspects are important and the Scrum Master is responsible to enforce these rules:

- The Daily Scrum is conducted at the same time and same place every day
- Everyone needs to be punctual to Daily Scrum Ceremony
- Daily Scrum ceremonies are timeboxed to 15 minutes duration
- Participants are the Core Team members: the Scrum Master, the Product Owner, and The Team. Extended Team members may attend as observers and are not allowed to speak during the ceremony.
- Scrum Master facilitates the ceremony. In absence of Scrum Master, another Scrum Master, Scrum Coach or Agile Coach can facilitate the ceremony. Scrum Master must coordinate to ensure a facilitator is present with the agenda.
- Only the three questions [as stated above] are answered by the team members
- Only one conversation continues where a team member answers the three questions
- No one other than the team members can speak in these ceremonies. Only one team member talks at a time and answers the three questions.
- Anyone can request specifics on any item of interest for parking lot and plan for a follow-up ceremony to discuss them with the Team or team member.
- No lengthy solutions to any identified impediments are discussed during the ceremony. These are recorded as parking lot item. Parking lot items are tackled in a follow-up session by the Team, Scrum Master and the Product Owner.
- Participation is normally decided by the team for extended team members which includes stakeholders
- If a team member cannot attend, he or she must provide the status beforehand or provide a proxy with the status
- The Scrum Master can limit the attendance of participants other than the team and the Product Owner.

- For team members not following the rules, the Scrum Master can remove them from the Team if unable to get compliance

Though these rules are followed, a mature Scrum Master uses soft-skills and leadership skills to make these ceremonies interesting. Outcome of Daily Scrum ceremony is current status and list of any impediments the Team has. Thus, any follow-up session can be held to address those and achieve the short-term deliverables. As evident, extended team members are not allowed to speak and are only observers. So they cannot provide instructions and direction to the team on how to complete the work.

Sprint Review

For a 30 day Sprint, the review ceremony is 4 hour timebox. Sprint Review ceremony occurs at the end of a Sprint. Review ceremony consists of two parts: First part where the Team presents the developed product and functionality during the Sprint. Then during the second session, stakeholders provide their feedback on the product demo and deliverables. Purpose is to encourage customer collaboration and gather product feedback for the Team and the Product Owner, as well. This enhances understanding of the product and planning for next Sprint.

The rules pertaining to Sprint Review ceremony are:

- Sprint review ceremony is attended by the Core Team viz. the Scrum Master, the Team and the Product Owner, and essential stakeholders.
- Only PBI(s) that are "done" based on the acceptance criteria established during the Planning ceremony are addressed. Any PBI not done is not addressed during the ceremony.
- Any work item not part of Sprint Backlog can be presented. This is to discourage gold plating
- PBI completed during the Sprint is presented (demoed) on a production or production like workstations closest to the production configuration
- Completed PBIs are presented by the team though it is a growing practice for the Product Owner to present the completed functionality to the stakeholders
- During the second half, the Product Backlog is updated with "done" PBIs noted, additional PBIs identified for consideration based on stakeholders' feedback and input

- The Product Backlog updates and prioritization is the responsibility of the Product Owner
- Product Owner facilitates Sprint Review ceremony and in the absence of Product Owner, it can be covered by the Scrum Master. Product Owner is responsible for ensuring the coordination to ensure a facilitator is available with agenda for the ceremony.
- In first half of the ceremony, the Team demos the product deliverables
- In second half, backlog items are accepted and reviews received

Figure 6-4: Sprint Review Ceremony

The outcome of Sprint Review ceremony is the accepted PBIs during the Sprint; additional PBI(s) for Product Owner to include in the Product Backlog; feedback to team on be able to optimize on managing the quality; and constraints and risks aspects for the product. The Product Owner takes input from the Review ceremony to update and reprioritize the Product Backlog. The Product Owner can seek anyone's help and advice to manage the Product Backlog.

Sprint Retrospective

For 30 day Sprint, the retrospective ceremony is timeboxed to 3 hours. This ceremony occurs as the last event for a Sprint; normally after the Sprint review and prior to the next Sprint Planning ceremony. Scrum Master holds this ceremony with the Team to inspect and review, within the Scrum process Framework, the development process to make it more effective and enjoyable for the upcoming Sprint.

The rules pertaining to Sprint Retrospective ceremony are:

- Sprint Retrospective ceremony is attended by the Scrum Master, the Product Owner and the Development Team.
- Scrum Master facilitates the Sprint planning ceremony. In absence of Scrum Master, another Scrum Master, Scrum Coach or Agile Coach can facilitate the ceremony. Scrum Master must coordinate to ensure a facilitator is present with the agenda.
- Attendees are the Core Team members: the Scrum Master, the Product Owner, and The Team.
- The Product Owner's participation is optional. No chickens are allowed.
- Sprint retrospective ceremonies do not have a specific format of questions but must address the following two at the minimum:
  - What went well during the Sprint?
  - What could be improved in the upcoming Sprint?

Additional questions that should be addressed are:

- What did not go well during the Sprint?
- What process improvements from past Sprint(s) are still applicable?
- Any new ideas that can be tried to improve current process?
- Any appreciations for the team and others for the last Sprint?

These additional questions provide further retrospection as part of continuous improvement goals.

Figure 6-5: Sprint Retrospective

As per the references from Ken Schwaber, Sprint Retrospective and the first half of Sprint Planning ceremony are not included in the Sprint timebox. A common fear of this mindset is that what is not included is left out. Rather safer approach is to realize that those two activities do not contribute to development but are essential for success.

Backlog Grooming (New*)

Product Owner gathers inputs from Sprint Review, feedback from stakeholders, and any impact due to external factors including cultural factors, compliance, and market conditions. Backlog grooming ceremony is not identified in the initial references of Scrum. However, it has been found critical for the project success. Backlog grooming is conducted at two levels:

- Product Owner working with involved stakeholders (Chickens) including users, purchases, and customers to develop, normalize, and prioritize the Product Backlog items representing functionality
- Product Owner working with the Team and the Scrum Master; to identify the cost, complexity, time, and risk factors for the Product Backlog items

Figure 6-6: Backlog Grooming Overview

Backlog grooming ceremony has different focus at product and Sprint levels. During the Sprint, the Product Owner gets inputs from the Development Team on Backlog items pertaining to technology and user experience. These are also groomed to ensure complete coverage. The backlog grooming ceremony raises many essential unknowns, constraints and risks that should be resolved to ensure DEEP backlog for Sprint planning.

Figure 6-7: Product Backlog must be DEEP

The rules pertaining to Backlog Grooming ceremony are:

- Backlog grooming ceremony is attended by the Product Owner, the Scrum Master, the Development Team and essential stakeholders.

- Product Owner identifies the agenda where activities and exercises are planned focus on the specific goal of Product Backlog grooming
- For Business domain, business stakeholders are active members while solution domain members can attend as observers; and vice versa.
- PBIs in the backlog are discussed top-down from highest priority and is refined, detailed, split and prioritized accordingly
- The Product Backlog updates and prioritization is the responsibility of the Product Owner
- Product Owner facilitates Backlog grooming ceremonies and seek to prepare a Product Backlog that is Detailed appropriately, Emergent, Estimated, and Prioritized (DEEP) [Roman Pichler and Mike Cohn, 2010]
- In the absence of Product Owner, it can be covered by the Scrum Master. Product Owner is responsible for ensuring the coordination to ensure a facilitator is available with agenda for the ceremony.

Backlog grooming is discussed in detail in Chapter 15: Backlog grooming.

Scrum of Scrums

Many organizations use "Scrum of Scrums" to allow Scrum to scale to the enterprise level. Scrum of Scrums gets the projects development teams to collaborate. Basic principle is to have team representatives, mostly technical leads, get together to collaborate and share visibility to their projects areas and identify and dependencies. This is utilized for a project where large team is split into individual teams based on functional domains and then technical representatives gather periodically (not necessarily daily). Team representatives plan to meet weekly or more frequently based on agreed terms and need of inspection.

The agenda is in two parts: first 15 minute timebox and second session as follow-up discussion on parking lot items.

During the first session, 15 minute timebox, each member (technical representative from each team) addresses the following four questions:

1. What has your team done on this project since we last met?
2. What will your team do on this project before we meet again?
3. Is there anything slowing your team down or any roadblock in its way?

4. Are you about to put anything in other team's/teams' way on this project?

Figure 6-8: Scrum of Scrums ceremony

During the Second part, the participants collaborate and discuss any outstanding issues on the teams' backlogs. Common flaw is: "Failing to see the forest for the trees" expression as each team is focused on their project areas and may fail to see enterprise, product, or intermediate level impact.

Scrum of Scrums ceremony is most effective when following aspects are sought:

1. Status progress across teams
2. Requirements that span across multiple teams
3. Development dependencies of work between teams
4. Technical knowledge dependencies between teams
5. Common development modules sharing and development by multiple teams
6. Development updates dependencies of one team on another
7. Multiple teams sharing code or working in same integration project for continuous integration and continuous delivery
8. Common libraries, tools and interfaces used by multiple teams
9. Knowledge dependencies among teams
10. Architecture and support dependencies of one team on another

It is essential that the objectives, perspectives, and goals of all the teams represented in Scrum of Scrums are aligned. In absence of the driving factors and shared vision, the ceremony encounters ambiguities, challenges and could fail to be effective.

As per the rules of Scrum, following aspects are important and the Scrum Master is responsible to enforce these rules:

- The Scrum of Scrums is conducted at the same time and same place every day
- Everyone needs to be punctual to Scrum of Scrums Ceremony; as they are kept short and quick
- Scrum of Scrums ceremonies are timeboxed to 15 minutes duration
- Attendees are the Core Team members: Scrum Master(s), and individual Development Team leads or representatives.
- Scrum Coach or one of the Scrum Masters facilitates the Scrum of Scrums ceremony. In absence of Scrum Master, another Scrum Master, Scrum Coach or Agile Coach can facilitate the ceremony. Scrum Master must coordinate to ensure a facilitator is present with the agenda.
- Only the four questions [as stated above] are answered by the team members
- Only one conversation continues where a team member answers the questions
- No one other than the team members can speak in these ceremonies. Only one team member talks at a time and answers the questions.
- Anyone can note specifics on any item of interest and plan for a follow-up ceremony to discuss them with the Team or team member. However, extended team members are not allowed to provide instructions and direction to the team on how to complete the work.
- No lengthy solutions to any identified impediments are discussed during the ceremony. These are recorded as parking lot item. Parking lot items are tackled in a follow-up session by the Team, Scrum Master and the Product Owner.
- Participation is normally decided by the team for extended team members which includes stakeholders
- If a team member cannot attend, he or she must provide the status beforehand or provide a proxy with the status

- The Scrum master can limit the attendance of participants other than the team. For team members not following the rules, the Scrum Master can remove them from the Team

Summary

This chapter describes various Scrum ceremonies. Scrum Framework provides these set of ceremonies to allow value delivery of incremental deployable product every Sprint. Each ceremony serves a specific purpose and feeds into the process to inspect-and-adapt to optimize the value delivery.

Chapter 7 Sprint

"By failing to prepare, you are preparing to fail." - Benjamin Franklin

Introduction

A Sprint is a timebox used for development process. In every Sprint, the Development Team collaborates to deliver incremental product from the Sprint Backlog. Traditionally original Sprints were 30 days long, though they could be as short as one week in duration. Two weeks Sprints are becoming a norm but it's not prescriptive.

Scrum Rules for Sprint

The rules pertaining to Sprint are:

- The Team can continue to organize work and tactics like identify additional tasks, update or remove tasks in the Sprint Backlog during the Sprint
- The Product Owner should be available during the Sprint for the Team to get clarification for any PBI on the Sprint Backlog
- The Product Owner cannot make any changes to the Sprint Backlog. However, the Product Owner can continue to make changes to the Product Backlog
- If the Team feels that it cannot complete some PBIs in Sprint Backlog, it can consult with the Product Owner. If Sprint Backlog seems to have lost its value, the Scrum Master can abnormally terminate the Sprint.
- If the Team feels that it can complete additional PBIs in the Sprint, it can consult with the Product Owner to identify additional high priority PBI(s) to tackle in the Sprint.
- If the Product Owner has a high priority PBI for the team which is not part of the Sprint, it can raise it to the Team. The Scrum Master identifies that either the Product Owner hold off the time until the next planning ceremony else the Sprint is cancelled and a Planning ceremony for new Sprint is conducted to incorporate the priority item.
- No one outside the team provides direction, instructions or organization to the Team during the Sprint. The Team can seek outside help, support and advice as needed.

The Team is a self-managing, self-disciplined, self-motivated, and contained unit responsible for delivering the Sprint Backlog during the Sprint.

Sprint Overview

Scrum project is split into various development timeboxes called *Sprints (aka Iteration)*. In initial references, Sprint is identified as 30 day long timebox. While in practice, a Sprint could be from one week to a month long. Two week long Sprints are becoming a norm. Sprint timebox is kept constant for the duration of the project. Exceptions to this rule are: initial or zero iteration and hardening iteration. The timebox is determined based on value delivery aspect and sustainable pace. All product development work is done in Sprints. The output of Sprint is a fully releasable incremental product.

In the beginning of Sprint, *Sprint planning* ceremony occurs. Pre-requisite for Sprint Planning ceremony is a prioritized Product Backlog with stack of product functionality in descending order of value - sorted top-down. During the Sprint planning meeting, Product Owner and team works together to plan for the Sprint based on delivering an incremental product; with maximum value. During Sprint Planning session one, Team enquires from Product Owner to understand Product Backlog items and identify it can deliver for the Sprint. During the second session, team identifies the tasks for the Sprint. Second session marks the start of Sprint (timebox period). Team can continue to add/update/enhance tasks in the Sprint Backlog throughout the Sprint. Not all tasks are required to be defined in the Sprint Planning ceremony. Besides, not all tasks are expected to be completed for the Sprint to meet the commitment for the Sprint. At the end of the Sprint, any leftover tasks for completed functionality are removed from the Sprint Backlog.

At the end of Sprint, *Sprint Review ceremony* is conducted where product is reviewed and demo occurs. This marks the end of the Sprint. Product Owner accepts the product backlog item based on acceptance criteria set during the planning ceremony. Then, the team meets for *Sprint Retrospective ceremony* where process is inspected and tuned.

Every day, Sprint Daily Scrum/Stand-up ceremony occurs at same place and time for empirical process control. The Team uses Daily Scrums as opportunity to inspect-and-adapt its tactics on daily basis and various development practices are used to provide further inspection-and-adaptation at smaller time intervals. When something new is learned or an issue is encountered, the team doesn't wait for Daily Scrum. Rather the team members collaborate to discuss and seek resolution as early as possible.

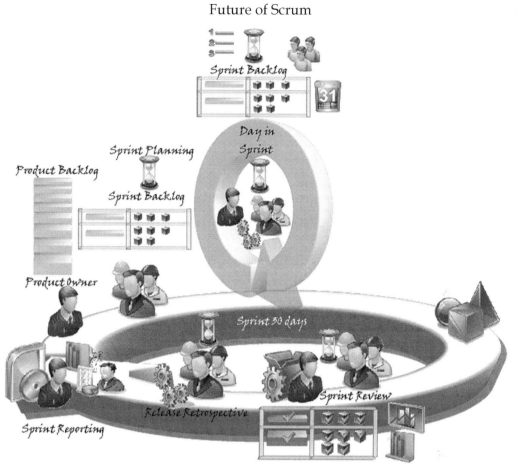

Original Scrum in Practice

Figure 7-1: Original Sprint Overview

At the end of the Sprint, a Sprint review ceremony is held where Scrum Master facilitates the Team, Product Owner, and the stakeholders (optional) to inspect the Sprint deliverable - the incremental product functionalities and thus, adapt by gathering feedback from stakeholders. This ceremony marks the end of the Sprint. Next a Sprint Retrospective is held with the Team where Scrum Master encourages the team to inspect the process and adapt to improve for the upcoming Sprint.

Most books focus on keeping the decade old Scrum methodology as propagated by Jeff Sutherland and Ken Schwaber. With current industry practice the concept has been expanded further at release level otherwise the Sprints would go on indefinitely without a defined releasable product definition. This is done to identify the concept of a deliverable functionality at the end of each Sprint.

The release aspect is an important one and hence, it has been included as it is essential to identify the delivery capacity (velocity) of the team in a Sprint. This forms an essential component to the planning aspect to manage the constraints (cost, scope, and schedule).

Another essential aspect is Product Backlog grooming. These are discussed later in detail.

Activities during the Sprint

Activities during the Sprint are as follow:

- Starts off by Sprint Planning
- A Day in Sprint
  - Daily Scrum
  - Scrum of Scrums (1 or 2 times a week)
  - Team activities for the Sprint
  - Update Sprint Burndown chart at COB
- Exceptional event: Sprint cancellation
- Last day of Sprint:
  - Sprint Review
  - Sprint Retrospective
  - Sprint Closure
- Optional ceremony: Backlog grooming (Mid-Sprint and End of Sprint timebox)

Sprint starts off during Sprint Planning

For a 30 day Sprint, the Sprint planning ceremony is timeboxed to 8 hours. The Sprint planning ceremony has two sessions of 4 hours each: During the first session, the Product Owner presents the value prioritized Product Backlog to the Team. The Team enquires from the Product Owner to understand the Product Backlog items. The "done" criteria is clearly defined here whether it means. When the Team understands enough, the Team selects and commits for the Product Backlog items that it feels it can deliver in the Sprint as functionality or a fully shippable incremental product. During the second session, the Team plan out the Sprint as the Team is self-organizing. The Team visits each Product Backlog item and identifies the tasks it needs to meet the functionality. These tasks are placed in the Sprint Backlog. The Team may add, update, or delete the tasks in the Sprint Backlog during the Sprint. Team owns the Sprint Backlog, while the Product Owner owns the Product Backlog.

At the start of the second session of the Sprint Planning meeting, the Sprint has started. The Outcome of the Sprint planning ceremony is the Sprint Backlog. The Sprint Backlog is owned by the team and the Team is responsible for making any changes to it. Product Owner can continue to make changes to the Product Backlog but cannot make any updates to the Sprint Backlog during the Sprint.

Sprint planning meeting provide outstanding questions and parking lot items for the Product Owner to investigate further. These contain essential inputs to Product backlog grooming ceremony.

A Day in Sprint

A typical day in a Sprint normally starts off with Daily Scrum where team members share their achievements during the past day, plan of action for next day and any impediments in their way. Daily Scrum provides the visibility for team to further have follow-up discussions and escalations of action items so team can focus on achieving the desired result. Team members then work throughout the day in completing the tasks on Sprint Backlog. At the end of the day, team reports the estimate of completed effort. This when collected over a period provides Sprint Burndown chart.

Daily Scrum

In XP, this ceremony is known as Daily Stand-up ceremony; though it does not imply that everyone must stand during this meeting, though encouraged. We normally have team members gather around the Team board or display from projector of our Sprint Dashboard and team members gather around in semi-circle for Daily Scrums. Daily Scrum is time sensitivity and focus ceremony. It occurs every day where the Team gathers for 15 minute timebox, where every member of the team answers three questions:

- What have you done since the Last Daily Scrum ceremony on this project?
- What do you plan to do before the next Daily Scrum ceremony on this project?
- Is there any impediment in your way on this project?

Team members take turn to answer these questions and share the status with the team. This provides daily *visibility* to the team for *inspection and adaptation* opportunity in a later session during the day. Purpose is to synchronize the work of all Team members, schedule any required meetings, and remove any impediments team is encountering. Scrum Master is responsible to ensure these ceremonies happen, the rules of Scrum are followed, and any impediments identified are removed. Scrum of Scrums

Team activities for the Sprint

During the day, team members collaborate to deliver the backlog items. The development effort allows the team to use the most effective development process. Scrum teams can effectively use the optimal process based on the skills and collaborative efforts. Development is open to use any of the practices like pair-programming, continuous integration, Test Driven Development (TTD), etc. Scrum Master protects the Team from external interruptions including Product Owner. Product Owner is collocated and is available for the team for any clarification. Scrum Master acts as servant leader, coach, mentor, conflict navigator, facilitator and any other role needed to serve the Team and Product Owner. Scrum Master is responsible for Scrum process and acts as teacher when the core team members deviate from Scrum rules.

Sprint Backlog stays constant during the Sprint. Any new backlog item need to wait until next Sprint planning ceremony to be included for development.

Update Sprint Burndown chart at COB

At the end of a Sprint day, team members reflect the completed effort for the day. This is then tracked on the Sprint Burndown chart. Task board is updated to reflect the work-in-progress and completed tasks.

Exceptional event: Sprint cancellation

A Sprint can be cancelled before the Sprint duration. Only the Product Owner is authorized to cancel a Sprint. There are mainly two main reasons when a Sprint is cancelled, besides external factors:

1. Product Owner decides that current Sprint Backlog is not of desired value as:
    a. Product Owner may have new set of PBIs that are of higher value
    b. Product Owner feel that current Sprint does not deliver the desired result
    c. Current Sprint backlog items have changed due to external factors

2. The Team identifies to the Product Owner their inability to deliver the Sprint Backlog with reasons, insights and possible alternatives that may include:
    a. Team encounters fast failure due to risky items
    b. Team faces an impasse
    c. The Team finds that the Sprint Backlog was incorrectly estimated and need to re-estimate the backlog items
    d. The Team identifies dependency on another Backlog item not in Sprint
    e. The team discovers major unknowns and risks during Sprint

When a Sprint is cancelled, Sprint Review is immediately held followed by Sprint Retrospective and Sprint Closure.

Last day of Sprint

On the last day of Sprint, two Scrum ceremonies are held to seek updates and improvements to the product and development process.

Sprint Review

This has been discussed at length in earlier section. Goal is to move 'done' backlog items to incremental product and to move not 'done' items back to the Product Backlog. Further feedback is received from the stakeholders for product improvement.

The feedback received during Sprint review is critical and provides essential inputs for the Product Backlog grooming ceremonies.

Sprint Retrospective

The Core Team meets during Sprint Retrospective ceremony to optimize the development process. Sprint retrospective has been discussed at length in Chapter 34.

Sprint Closure

As part of Sprint closure, Scrum Master and Product Owner are responsible for preparing the four Sprint Reports:

1   The Product Backlog at the start of the previous Sprint
2   The Product Backlog at the start of the new Sprint
3   The Changes report that details all of the differences between the Product Backlogs in the first two reports
4   The Product Backlog Burndown chart: a Burndown chart that shows the amount of work remaining across time.

Summary

This chapter describes a typical Sprint in Scrum. The description has been kept as close to the common configuration with perception of the most common and established practices.

Until now, we have been focusing on Scrum Framework overview and highlighting the various Scrum rules, core values, principles and practices. In the next chapter, we shall explore Agile manifesto and its twelve principles. These form the essential foundation that led to further scaling of Scrum Framework.

Section II
Agile Principles

Chapter 8 Agile Overview

"The whole is more than the sum of its parts." - Aristotle

Introduction

In February 2001, seventeen lightweight methodologists met in Snowbird, Utah. The purpose of the meeting was to discuss and discover the shared values and principles. These methodologies had discovered the timeless values based on collaboration, consensus building approach (CBA), customer focus, and self-organizing teams delivering values.

We are uncovering better ways of developing software by doing it and helping others do it. Through this work we have come to value:

Individuals and interactions over *processes and tools*
Working software over *comprehensive documentatio*
Customer collaboration over *contract negotiation*
Responding to change over *following a plan*

That is, while there is value in the items on the right, we value the items on the left more.

Kent Beck	James Grenning	Robert C. Martin
Mike Beedle	Jim Highsmith	Steve Mellor
Arie van Bennekum	Andrew Hunt	Ken Schwaber
Alistair Cockburn	Ron Jeffries	Jeff Sutherland
Ward Cunningham	Jon Kern	Dave Thomas
Martin Fowler	Brian Marick	

© 2001, the above authors this declaration may be freely copied in any form, but only in its entirety through this notice.

Figure 8-1 Agile Manifesto

With the recent struggles where traditional project management approach continues to fail in complex domain, they experienced that lightweight methodologies are advantageous and effective. Agile manifesto evolved during this gathering where better ways of development software was shared. Its twelve principles are established as the foundation that a lightweight methodology needs to support to be agile.

Individuals and interactions over processes and tools

Agile teams value "individuals and interaction" over "processes and tools" because great people build great products, not great tools; and collaboration and communication help more than defined heavy laid down processes. For optimal results, having great individuals who are collaborating while utilizing well defined lightweight processes and great tools provide ideal environment. Agile teams are built around motivated individuals instead of extensive tools and processes. Agile team members contain mix of skills where the complete team together is able to deliver the incremental product. Such a team includes designers, developers, testers, and other skilled professionals who are needed to complete the incremental in every Sprint. The hallmark of agile team is not just the skills of individual team-member. Rather hallmark is collaboration of the team members performing together and able to step in to help each other. The team delivers while grows with collective knowledge in mutual domains as well. This results in evolution of cross-functional team. Agile methodologies even go as far as to collocate the customer with the Team. The customer collaborates daily with the team. Customer works with the Team to understand business perspective while gaining technical insight for value optimization. "Strength lies in unity!" truly holds here. Agile teams are self-managing, self-motivated, self-organizing, and autonomous while protected from management interference. Such empowered teams take direction from management. Team members collaborate to make the necessary decisions to deliver the Sprint goal. While processes and tools can help and add value, such processes and tools are utilized by the team to meet their goal. However, individuals working together can review and optimize the processes and utilization of tools to value driven delivery aspects. It is not the tools that drive individual interaction, rather tools and processes are utilized by the team to provide the necessary support for value delivery.

Working software over comprehensive documentation

Agile teams value "working software" over "comprehensive documentation." Delivering an incremental product where users provide frequent feedback on value and desired valuable features. This provides opportunities to improved ROI for the product. While documentation is important to provide maintenance and support, it is not the main deliverable on its own. Hence, agile teams seek to provide necessary documentation, documentation that adds value like online help, support documentation, installation and release notes. Agile teams discourage waste and creating outdated documentation or efforts that lead to such waste. The Standish Group chaos report findings that more than 64% of software functionality is rarely or never used speaks to the waste. Traditional teams generate huge amount of product specifications document that fill pages after pages and are never even read by the users or customers. Agile teams value delivery of product more than high-cost and high-maintenance materials like extensive documentation, simulations, and models of actual product. A requirement document verifies a successful collection of a set of requirements. Releasable working software gives a working tangible product of value to customer. Further it enhances early feedback - a critical success factor.

Customer collaboration over contract negotiation

Agile team values "customer collaboration" over "contract negotiation" as it brings both parties together against the same goal. They work regularly with open communication to build the product as highest priority. This avoids the two parties of sitting across the negotiation table and play hard-ball on trying get the best for themselves and not the product. Contracts are essential to agree on the terms for the customer and vendor. Contracts promoting fixed price, fixed schedule, fixed scope perspectives seem to drive a complex project to death march far too often. The customer holding the vendor responsible to deliver as per contract while failing to provide the necessary information leads to finger pointing and finally to lose-lose. Further the development teams overworking 80 hours a week while burning their night lamps to deliver the product to customer at all cost cause burnouts. The turnover increases as team members leave to find stable environment. Enterprises are realizing the flux due to high turnovers and are striving to provide stable environments. Recently a lot of changes are emerging in contracts and negotiations. "Money for nothing, change for free" is a contract which includes clauses to encourage customer collaboration. Cost responsibility sharing as discussed by Mary and Tom Poppendieck is one such example which based on Toyota's practice as discussed "Cost targeted contracts." When vendor and customers act as rivals, project failure is ensured. Hard negotiations cause customer to get as many features at least cost, optimal quality, and shortest schedule; while the goals are still uncertain. For our son, we got a

"Cooperative game" which quickly exemplifies on the advantages where team members collaborate to save 8 whales from oil spills and other impediments.

Responding to change over following a plan

Agile teams value "responding to change" over "following a plan" as the focus is on delivering highest valued features. Most valued set of features are delivered to the customers as soon as possible. The priority is customer satisfaction. If there is a need to incorporate a change which would result in high value, agile teams make every effort to incorporate the change even late in the process. Iterative development to provide incremental product enables this approach. Agile teams focus on progressive refinement over rolling wave planning throughout the project instead of upfront plans. Extensive upfront plans render useless when not everything is well determined and known in the beginning. Users cannot know every detail of every feature in the beginning. Agile teams focus on what (product features) based on value for customers' competitive advantage and satisfaction.

Agile teams do not ignore plan, as is a common myth. Agile teams plan iteratively using top down planning which is referred to it as "Rolling wave planning." Agile teams plan Just in Time (JIT) when the details are more known and uncertainties are to be addressed in the upcoming sprint for the highest value PBI. Simplicity in planning and design is essential to value delivery and to avoid waste. Simplicity enhances agility – ability to quickly adapt to changes.

As a metaphor, consider a road trip. When you start the journey, planning is done where you have a route planned. During the drive, the close items are visible in greater details and allow us to adjust our route with further impact to corresponding approximations. Starting at say point A to get to point B (destination) and realizing on the way, say point C, that we have lost our way, the best alternative is to find the path from point C to point B – as responding to change implies; and not going back to point A to start the journey again – as following a plan would suggest. Road map and initial planning is crucial. An agile planning incorporates the ability to adapt to changes in the plan. Hence, to change the plan when need arises is part of the plan.

Agile projects still could fail which mostly caused by the wrong people or wrong initiatives; rather than the failure of practices. Agile methodologies improve performance. Yet agile is not a silver bullet; even though, Agile Manifesto holds true on most aspects.

Agile is not defined by a set of practices and techniques. Agile is not prescriptive. Agile helps deliver complex products through an adaptive environment that supports change. Every Sprint, creative, innovative, adaptive, self-organizing, and self-disciplined development team delivers an incremental releasable product where speed, mobility, and quality lead to success.

Principles behind the Agile Manifesto

Principles behind the Agile Manifesto
We follow these principles:
1. Our highest priority is to satisfy the customer through early and continuous delivery of valuable software.
2. Welcome changing requirements, even late in development. Agile processes harness change for the customer's competitive advantage.
3. Deliver working software frequently, from a couple of weeks to a couple of months, with a preference to the shorter timescale.
4. Business people and developers must work together daily throughout the project.
5. Build projects around motivated individuals. Give them the environment and support they need, and trust them to get the job done.
6. The most efficient and effective method of conveying information to and within a development team is face-to-face conversation.
7. Working software is the primary measure of progress.
8. Agile processes promote sustainable development. The sponsors, developers, and users should be able to maintain a constant pace indefinitely.
9. Continuous attention to technical excellence and good design enhances agility.
10. Simplicity--the art of maximizing the amount of work not done--is essential.
11. The best architectures, requirements, and designs emerge from self-organizing teams.
12. At regular intervals, the team reflects on how to become more effective, then tunes and adjusts its behavior accordingly.

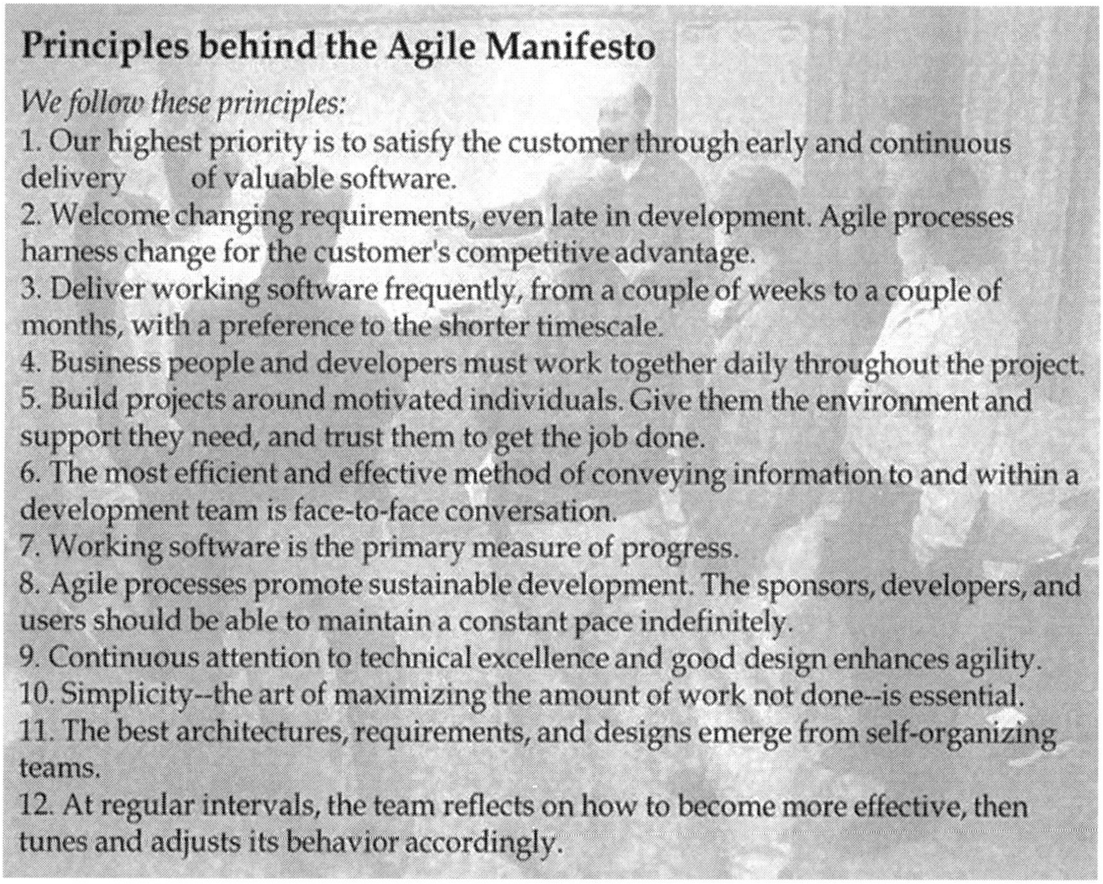

Figure 8-2: Guiding Principles of Agile Manifesto

Agile manifesto has twelve guiding principles for software development that extend core values for Agile methodologies.

We follow these principles:

1. Our **highest priority** is to **satisfy** the customer *through* **early** and **continuous** *delivery* of **valuable software**.

2. Welcome changing requirements, *even late in development*. Agile processes harness *change* for the **customer's competitive advantage**.

3. Deliver working software **frequently**, *from a couple of weeks to a couple of months*, with a *preference* to the **shorter timescale**.

4. **Business people and developers** must work together **daily** *throughout the project*.

5. **Build** projects *around* **motivated individuals**. **Give** them the *environment* and **support** they *need*, and **trust** them to *get the job done*.

6. The **most** *efficient and effective* method of *conveying* **information** to and within a development team is **face-to-face** conversation.

7. Working software is the **primary measure** of progress.

8. Agile **processes** promote **sustainable development**. The sponsors, developers, and users should be able to **maintain** a **constant pace indefinitely**.

9. Continuous *attention* to technical excellence and good design enhances agility.

10. **Simplicity**--the art of *maximizing* the *amount* of **work not done**--is **essential**.

11. The best architectures, requirements, and designs emerge from self-organizing teams.

12. At **regular intervals**, the team **reflects** on *how to become* more **effective**, then **tunes** and **adjusts** its *behavior accordingly*.

The important aspects in each principle are in bold and italics to help **memorize** for better understanding. We shall elaborate each principle to greater depth. In real world, if there appear to be multiple valid options then the option supporting agile manifesto and the principles of agile development prevails. Agile manifesto and principles are directed towards software developers not the project leads or project managers.

Principle 1: Our highest priority is to satisfy the customer through early and continuous delivery of valuable software

This ties closely to the agile values as focus is on providing value driven incremental product to users for rapid and frequent feedback. Continuous delivery is met using sustainable pace and iterative development. Providing valued feature with just enough documentation allows optimal ROI for project success. Agile gives maximum benefit to the users' needs. Though the principle is directed towards developers, it is applicable to Agile Project Management (APM).

Agile teams achieve this by developing product features in the order identified by the customer. The customer is responsible for prioritizing the features. This order is expected to be in declining order of value to the users. Team further helps in estimating the effort for the features. Then, the team develops these features to be delivered in incremental product releases instead of just performing individual tasks.

Standish group study reported that 64% of the features are never used while 20% features are often/always used. Thus, agile teams focus on delivering value first and early to the users. This provides an opportunity to customers to avoid waste and optimize ROI.

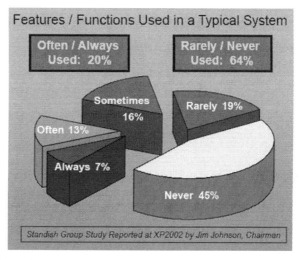

Figure 8-3: Features/Functions used in a Typical System

Besides, there is Pareto's rule: 80 percent of the value comes from 20 percent of the work. This is 80/20 Rule. [SHALLOWAY et al, 2009]

Principle 2: Welcome changing requirements, even late in development. Agile processes harness change for the customer's competitive advantage

Iterative development with frequent incremental product delivered to users help the users gain competitive advantage. This principle focuses on allowing changes for customer's competitive advantage, not just for customer satisfaction as is commonly interpreted. ROI is optimized for both the team's and customer's benefit. Early customer feedback; product with highly valued features; and early delivery of maximum value are just the effects which turn this into win-win for both parties.

Agile teams seek customer's competitive advantage to allow change even late in development. The team continues to develop a product in Sprint. These sprints are constant duration of time (aka timebox) which works to provide sustainable pace for the team and for customer advantage provide a duration where customer's valued features can be planned and implemented. On an average, an idea of feature to the feature delivery can be realized in 1.5 sprint duration. For two week long sprint, if the customer has a high valued idea feature to implement, on an average they would have to just wait half the sprint duration to the planning session of next sprint when it can be planned for delivery at the end of sprint.

Principle 3: Deliver working software frequently, from a couple of weeks to a couple of months, with a preference to the shorter timescale

An agile team works in short sprint which ranges from two weeks to up to two months. The focus is on shorter timescales (aka iterations in XP or Sprints in Scrum). The timebox implies that they halt development even if the work is not complete. Working on sprint allows the team to gain sustainable pace. While with longer durations, traditional waterfall teams would experience slack in work and heavy work crunch near the release date. This would cause working weekends, heavy escaped defects, everyone scrambling to get the work done with gaps all over and finally, resulting in pointing fingers and dissatisfied customers. Agile teams use timeboxed sprints to allow a sustainable pace where they continue to deliver releasable product to the customers at the end of sprint. This promotes gathering feedback from the stakeholders for product improvement. While some feels that incremental product delivery misses the "Wow!" moment, most welcome the elimination of "Uh-Oh!" moment. Frequent working software delivery tend to handle risk and allow product improvement early and often for project success.

Principle 4: Business people and developers must work together daily throughout the project

APM promotes agile teams to collaborate with business experts. The sprints allow identifying business stakeholders to prioritize features where highest priority items are delivered to maximize value delivery to customer. The customer may have idea on how the system should work, yet they may not be able to visualize this concept until they see something concrete. During product development, agile teams work with customer to understand any gaps in the needs. At the end of sprint, agile teams deliver a releasable product to customer. Business people get the opportunity to provide rapid early feedback during review, demo sessions and based on their expectations from using the product from sprints. Daily standups provide teams to inspect and adapt on daily basis. Sprint reviews and retrospectives provide sprint level feedbacks. Finally, the release reviews and retrospectives provide the release level feedback and inspections to the business. Customer collaboration is such an essential aspect that it is part of Agile manifesto and principles. Collaboration is gaining popularity in agile contracts as most favorable negotiation style [SINGHAL, SP, 2013].

Principle 5: Build projects around motivated individuals. Give them the environment and support they need, and trust them to get the job done.

APM requires that management assign motivated team members on Agile projects for success and skilled in the domain. Agile team is self-organizing, and self-managing. APM identifies that management should provide them the environment and support system and processes. Further management should trust the team to complete the job at hand. Team is self-organizing. Team learns and grows through team building stages of: Forming > Storming > Norming > Performing and finally Dissolving. Building projects around motivated individuals is essential as the team needs to be empowered to make the decisions, which in-turn promotes better buy-ins and commitments. Team is protected from management interference while providing the environment to continue to flourish and deliver the features at sustainable pace. The pull model where team pulls the features to complete becomes the norm. Team members come together to help each other in achieving what needs to be done. The informal environment and collaboration keeps the team moral high too.

An important criterion of a successful agile is that the team stays together even after the project releases. The Team continues to innovate and develop products for new initiatives. Another criterion is that leadership remains intact.

Principle 6: The most efficient and effective method of conveying information to and within a development team is face-to-face conversation.

Agile principle identifies the mode of communication and team collaboration. It encourages the team members and customers to use direct communication and optimal methods to exchange project information. This supports the importance of "individuals and interactions over processes and tools." For globally dispersed teams, individuals and interactions get the support through various tools and processes like messengers, video conferencing, wiki, SharePoint sites, emails, etc. This principle highlights the fact that face to face communication is the most effective mode of communication. A lot of communication rides on the mood, expression and context than just words. Collaborative mindset with rich communication fosters agility.

Principle 7: Working software is the primary measure of progress.

Documentation is to support as reference for working software as primary deliverable. Working software is essential. Documentation is to provide help and support for the software. Yet documentation without working software is next to useless. Agile team continues to deliver an incremental product at the end of sprint. This provides a better status to stakeholders than percentage completion reports and false positive reports on progress.

Principle 8: Agile processes promote sustainable development. The sponsors, developers, and users should be able to maintain a constant pace indefinitely.

Sustainable pace of work is the essence of continuous and frequent delivery. The stakeholders, team and end clients are able to maintain a constant pace of work indefinitely. This principle addresses waste resulting from improper working style of varying load. Practices of working late hours and over the weekends near the end of project release only causes crunch and increases the possibility of escaped defects. This compromises the quality of the product, thus in turn affecting the reputation of the team, which in turn affects the expectations of the customer. Such long lasting effect has severe effect on ongoing relationships and enterprise image which no time can return. Agile teams avoid "Student Syndrome" as well as "Parkinson's law" due to the sustainable pace concept. This promotes quality of life for all stakeholders as well as the quality of product.

Principle 9: Continuous attention to technical excellence and good design enhances agility.

Technical excellence and good designs are constantly visible to allow inspection and adaptation. Thus, agile processes promote continuous inspections at various phases. Various strategies and techniques are utilized to deliver valuable software of high quality. This aspect is closely bound to next principle. Agility is achieved by providing simplicity which results in technical excellence by constant adaptation and improvement. Agile discourages gold plating.

Principle 10: Simplicity--the art of maximizing the amount of work not done--is essential.

The product development is kept simple to develop only the necessary functionality. This principle identifies that complex designs are to be avoided as they are hard to change. Simple designs allow flexibility and are easily adapted to changing environment. This is crucial to allow value-driven results and support agility even late in the development. Hence, the team works on delivering exactly what is desired and not add to complicate design to cover future enhancements. Simple designs are easy to change and enhance.

Principle 11: The best architectures, requirements, and designs emerge from self-organizing teams.

Principles manage Agile teams. Management manages and enforces these principles. Agile teams get to organize its work and development process. Thus, team orients itself to the environment and becomes self-organizing and self-managing. This allows for best architectures, requirements and design and thus, drive value-driven results. However, a team member could be wise and talented; however, the whole team collectively would have much higher talent and wisdom put together. Team works together to collaborate and deliver the best system based on principles and values for customer's competitive advantage.

Principle 12: At regular intervals, the team reflects on how to become more effective, then tunes and adjusts its behavior accordingly.

This principle ties in with previous principle as self-organizing teams are self-managing. Thus, Scrum allows reflection on process to become more effective using the three pillars for implementation of empirical process control: transparency, inspection, and adaptation. The teams perform for the processes besides the product. Retrospectives are performed at regular intervals as after regular product reviews and deliveries and at release level. Retrospectives allow the team to gather data on development process; to generate insights to improve the process and decide the process improvements for upcoming development process.

Declaration of Interdependence

Declaration of interdependence (DOI) was developed in 2005 by the co-founders of Agile Project Leadership Network, now known as Agile Leadership Network [DOI, 2005]. DOI is targeted towards Project leadership and management.

Declaration of Interdependence

Agile and adaptive approaches for linking people, projects and value

We are a community of project leaders that are highly successful at delivering results. To achieve these results:

1. We **increase return on investment** *by making* **continuous flow of value** *our focus.*
2. We **deliver reliable results** *by engaging customers in* **frequent interactions and shared ownership.**
3. We expect **uncertainty and manage** for it *through* **sprints, anticipation, and adaptation.**
4. We **unleash creativity and innovation** *by recognizing that* **individuals** are the **ultimate source of valu**e, and *creating an environment* where they can make a difference.
5. We **boost performance** *through group accountability for* **results and shared responsibility** *for team effectiveness.*
6. We **improve effectiveness and reliability** *through* **situationally specific** strategies, processes and practices.

DOI is directed towards leadership where the focus is on product planning and aligning the initiatives to enterprise vision. These six principles tie in the major challenges for leadership and identify the approach to resolve them.

Return on investment (ROI) is not realized until the product is released to the customer and starts to earn revenue. Agile addresses this though early and often delivery of value to customer. As soon as the product is release to the customer, revenue starts and also feedbacks enhance alignment of the product to market needs and trends. Thus, ROI is optimized for the product.

Reliable results are always demanded but hardly met in complex domain. The tendency to lose focus and compromise quality while delivering early or on schedule leads to escaped defects. Agile leadership utilizes frequent customer collaboration and direct interaction between the Development Team and customer during planning, review and retrospective meetings to encourage common ownership. We are seeing a trend where Agile enterprises are taking caution to take clients who are willing to collaborate throughout the product development. This is also reflected in Agile contracts where negotiation terms are focused on collaboration. Hence, frequent interactions allow reliable results as tacit knowledge is shared, acceptance criteria is determined and used during review to accept the deliverables.

Uncertainty is a characteristic of empirical process. In order to manage uncertainty, agile teams utilize short development timebox known as Sprint. An incremental product is delivered every Sprint. The product is demo and review feedbacks help anticipate and adapt the product to the needs. This allows managing uncertainty where frequent feedback and handshake occur in every Sprint.

Agile leadership recognizes that people are the most important asset. Creativity is the idea while innovation is realization of that idea as a service or product. Individual ingenuity unleashes creativity and innovation. Agile projects are built around motivated individuals with needed support and environment to foster creative ideas and build innovative products. Further the management is done through principles. Individuals collaborate as a team where self-organization, self-discipline and self-management of development occur.

Performance is ensured when collaboration and motivation runs high. Agile leadership seeks to promote group accountability and buy-in for results. Team owns the responsibility to collaborate with the customer and within the team to have shared ownership. This encourages sharing of ideas, osmotic communication, tacit knowledge to spread quickly, and collaboration to promote performance boost.

Reliability of a product runs high when right combination of processes and practices are adopted. Agile leadership allows teams to be self-organized. Scrum Master manages the Scrum process and also acts as mentor for the team in facilitating with product and development process improvements. The activities in retrospectives are planned to aim at specific situations. This allows the Team to inspect and tune various strategies, practices and processes according to the specific situations.

Summary

In this chapter, Agile manifesto and its principles are discussed. These core values and principles drive the zest of Scrum as it has continued to evolve over the last decade. This would allow a strong foundation where Scrum overview covered earlier and comparison of Agile triangle with Iron triangle would start to become clearer. While we compared Agile methodology with waterfall and iterative development, we need to be cognizant of the domain of influence of Agile methodologies. While waterfall methodology continues to drive simple projects, Agile becomes a better choice for complex projects.

Our aim is to seek the readers to get a good grasp of Agile values and how the principles seek to reinforce these values. Scrum Framework has various roles, ceremonies and product development and management aspects that tie back to these values and principles.

Starting with next chapter, we go deeper into the intricacies of each value – whether higher or lower to gain more clarity and strengthen your foundation and understanding.

Chapter 9 Individuals and Interactions

"Management is doing things right, leadership is doing the right things." – Peter F. Drucker

Introduction

Great software is delivered by individuals through successful team work and not by processes and tools. While processes and tools facilitate the development of software, they cannot deliver the great software. For instance, having a great word editor program cannot ensure a best-seller novel!

Soft skills and team player attitude is paramount. Many good practices and seeking the teams to collaborate together are discussed to help you excel through complex projects.

Agile teams

Agile teams are built on the servant-leadership values where the leadership is not enforced top-down, instead earned bottom-up.

Agile teams are oriented towards high-performance team structure, where:

❖ Team is self-organizing instead of silos based as analysts, designers, developers, or testers

❖ Team are empowered to take decisions instead of accepting directions from above

❖ Team build with teamwork as focus to achieve task at hand

❖ Team focuses on success for the team, instead of success at any cost

❖ Team decides its decisions and fully committed to its commitments

❖ Team is built on trust, instead of enforced fear, threats, and directions from above

❖ Team is consensus-driven, with full divergence and then convergence

❖ Team is in constant constructive disagreement and realizing that conflicts exist while continue to make efforts to deliver customer values

❖ Team continues to adapt and are members are cross-functional; with focus on team ownership, instead of individual ownership

Team Building

The worst form of inequality is to try to make unequal things equal. - Aristotle

Bruce W. Truckman developed the stages of team development after analyzing behavior of small teams in a variety of environments. He identified that these stages are all needed in order for order for team to achieve maximum effectiveness. The stages are: Forming, Storming, Norming, Performing, and finally Adjourning.

During the Forming stage, the team members come together as the team members are identified. Team members are generally driven by a desire to be accepted by each other. Behavior seeks to avoid conflict and controversy. Team seeks to follow the leader for guidance and direction. *Here the leadership should be directive.* Individuals are busy gathering information and impressions. Routines to understand the organizational structure of team, role of each team member, the meeting schedules, tasks to be accomplished, etc. Team seeks to agree with the leader. Individual roles and responsibilities are not clear. Not many activities are performed and hence, not much is accomplished at this stage. Leader answers a lot of inquiries and insightful questions about team's purpose, objectives, and external relationships. Team tends to ignore processes. Members tend to test tolerance of system and the leader. Though the motivation may exist, it seems to be covered by the relatively uninformed issues and objectives of the team. Team members are at their best behavior yet very focused on their own role and responsibilities. Though mature team members evolve to display appropriate behavior even at this early stage of team formation. Sharing the knowledge of "development stages of teams – Forming, Storming, Norming, Performing and Adjourning" is helpful and insightful to the team. As members get to know each other, they exchange personal information and become friends. This is a good phase to seek how each team member performs and their behavior under pressure.

During the Storming stage, different ideas compete for consideration as members of the team start challenging each other in an effort to start addressing issues. The level of conflict raises among the team members. Issues are addressed around team's purpose as to what problems the team is to solve, how the team will function independently and together, and what leadership model would prevail. Team members tend to confront each other's ideas while some may delve on details to evade real issues. This stage promotes the growth of the team. It can get contentious, unpleasant, and even stressful to the team members who cannot handle conflict and controversy. Tolerance and patience of team members and their differences should be emphasized else the team may fail. Hence, the leadership behavior should be Coaching and is marked with Highly directive and supportive behavior. Arguments arise but tend to pass rather quickly. The conflicts tend to be around the work, team's purpose, and even responsibilities of the team members. Some team members may tend to stay in the comfort of the Forming stage. In order to address conflict, the team members may believe that they are winning or losing battles and cite rules or instructions to minimize constant conflict.

During the Norming stage, the team has a shared plan and goals. In order to make the team function, some members give up their individual ideas and agree with the team goal. Team members take on responsibilities and strive to work for the success of team goals. Much clarity and acceptance prevails to the individual team member roles and responsibilities. Major decisions tend to be made with group agreement. Team shows strong commitment and unity. Discussions prevail on the processes and strategies. Leadership style is Delegating with low direction at this stage.

The Performing stage is a state of flexibility and interdependence. Not all teams reach this stage. Team functions smoothly while roles and responsibilities of the members change as needed almost seamlessly. Team unity, morale, trust and loyalty are at an all-time high. Team achieves high performance and is able to function as a unit as the members strive to complete tasks smoothly and effectively with higher trust and without much conflict or external supervision. Hence, Leadership style is Delegating with low direction and support as team members strive to be more driven, knowledgeable, and motivated. As members are more people-oriented and task oriented, the team focuses on completion of tasks and achieving the goals. The team members display high competence, and are able to handle decision-making without supervision. Leader during this phase is mostly participative. The team makes most decisions. Even most high-performing teams tend to revert to earlier stages in certain circumstances. Long standing teams tend to go through these stages as they reach to change. For instance, if leadership changes, team could revert back to Storming where the new people challenge existing norms and dynamics of the team or even to Forming stage where team members start to seek the purpose of the team under new leadership and wait on more direction. At Performing stage, team is strategically aligned for the goals. Team has a shared vision, able to stand strong with no dependency or interference from the leader. The focus shifts to over-achieving the goals, and the team makes most of the decisions against the criteria established with the leadership in earlier stages. Disagreements occur but are resolved within the team positively and necessary changes to processes and current dynamics are practiced by the team. Team members look after each other as trust and loyalty is at an all-time high. The leader mainly delegates tasks and projects to the team. Team members may ask the leader for assistance with personal and interpersonal development and growth. Mainly the leader delegates and oversees.

The final stage is Adjourning where the team disperses and the members go on different initiatives. With the team adjourning, the roles and responsibilities are also over and the team members become disengaged from their tasks, goals and project initiatives. Adjourning normally occurs as the project end which could be from successful completion, successful completion of release with transition over to another team, successful goal with team members taking lead roles on a larger program, and even in case the project has been placed on-hold or cancelled. Leadership style is Empathetic with leader being highly supportive and empathy as the team adjourns.

During the Adjourning stage, team members may enter into depressed state as they see it as closure of their relationship with other team members. Team members find it difficult to accept that the team has dissolved. They continue to move onto next project yet always miss the working relationship. The trust and loyalty built over time seems to continue much after the adjourning stage. If the team members do come together in future, the bond quickly develops and help them progress to Performing stage quickly.

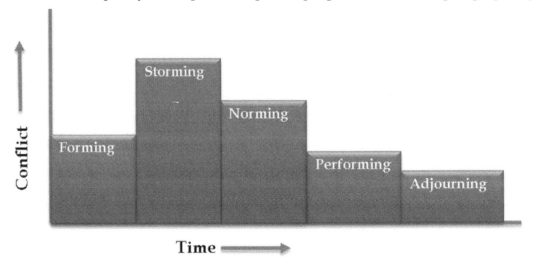

Figure 9-1 Stages of Team Development

The team development model is characterized as applicable to all team development scenarios, applicable to all industry sectors and domains, and is not time bounded. This model is utilized to help the team reach and sustain at the Performing stage as soon as possible. Hence, Agile teams also go through these stages and find their effective growth and collaboration achieved as soon as they reach norming stage. Retrospectives and reviews tend to drive a lot of insightful and dynamic behavior. Leadership starts to drive teams to higher goals and help navigate to the Performing stage where the teams attain self-managing, self-organizing and self-motivated behavior as per the model.

Team behavior and leadership tend to go through different transitions as the team transitions from one stage to another. These are evident as team dynamics evolve.

Agile promotes empowered teams. Team is self-organizing, self-directing, and self-managing in various aspects. This shows that the teams are mostly in Performing stage and seldom goes to Norming stage. Since team changes are less frequent and discouraged, efforts are made to avoid team to transition to Storming or Forming stages. While projects are completed, a successful Agile Enterprise ensures that the team continues to move on to new initiatives; without much impacting team dynamics and motivations.

When teams do adjourn, the team members tend to miss the team dynamics and performance level. Sometimes this is reflected in their behavior as they tend to take longer transitioning through stages in the new team.

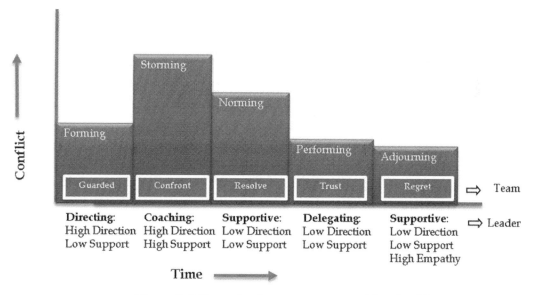

Figure 9-2 Team development stages and Leadership

Yet, mature team members with higher Emotional intelligence tend to adapt quickly to the change. An ideal way to adjourn a team is to set aside a time to debrief together to:

- ❖ How did we all work on the project? What went well and what didn't go as well?
- ❖ What did we learn as a team?
- ❖ Acknowledge the team members
- ❖ Last but not least, celebrate a job well done!

This helps the team members to come to a closure as emotions run high with feelings of victory, success, grief, lamentation, and insecurity about what comes next.

Scrum Master as Process Champion

Agile Leadership

Agile values in creating quality products and do it quickly. Ultimate customer value is delivered at the point-of-sale, not the point-of-plan. APM values principles over processes, values adapting, improving, and innovative thinking over repetition, and more environment than methodology. "*In high performance teams, the leaders manage the principles, and the principles manage the teams.*" - Carl Larson and Frank LaFasto (1989).

In essence, Agile leaders manage principles and lead teams, while non-Agile ones manage tasks. Traditional project management focuses on developing plans, creating WBS in MS Project, and then spends hours assigning and tracking tasks while following the plan to the letter. Unfortunately, they still realize that plans continue to change, as they are just that: "plans." The idea of leading the team appears indefinite, unclear, ongoing, and never definite when compared to following a definite plan. APM focuses on leading team and manage principles to build self-organizing teams. In an agile project, the team takes care of tasks and the project leader takes care of the team. Ultimately, this is difficult yet more rewarding than managing tasks. Thus, an Agile leadership style is based on servant-leadership style where the project leader removes impediments for the team, shields or protects the team from external interruptions, provides support and encouragement, and communicates the project vision. This may involve activities like:

- Protecting the team from external influences like stakeholders constant interruptions to demand features outside the scope in a given sprint or sprint

- Re-affirming the project vision for the team in regular interactions

- Providing administrative and management support for team to be able to focus on project activities focused on delivering values; rather than administrative tasks or heavy compliance roadblocks identified by the team

- Providing external help by bring SMEs and Technical Advisers in cases of difficulties in a project area or uncertain aspects

An agile leader creates self-organizing, empowered, motivated, and adaptive teams by ways to influence, nudge, facilitate, teach, recommend, assist, urge, counsel, and direct some instances when situation warrants. While non-agile leaders focus on controlling the team. They assign tasks and manage getting tasks completed as per the plan. Agile leaders realize that plans can change, so they plan to change as well. They avoid extensive plans upfront. Rather planning is taken up throughout the project and supports the team focus on delivering value. Hence, APM shows a significant shift of focus, which results in evolution of Agile Triangle instead of Iron Triangle of Project Management.

Leading teams versus Managing teams

Traditional projects are managed and not led. It's an easy trait to follow and so a project manager seems to gravitate towards managing the task, following the plan and report accordingly. Agile leadership is difficult task to perform yet provide great benefits to all the stakeholders. Leaderless teams are rudderless ones. The difference is subtle yet critical to grasp. It is essential to recognize these not as positions but rather as mindsets and personal styles of working.

Management	Leadership
manages tasks and driven by requirements	manages team and driven by value
deals with complexity	deals with change
uses plans, controls, budgets and process to manage complex projects	uses lightweight processes to drive the complex projects

Influences using power and position	influences using respect
authority is delegated top-down	authority is earned bottom-up
don't like change or adapt	like change and manages risks, uncertainty, and change with lightweight processes based on principles
Self-directing teams could drift and procrastinate under command	lead teams to be self-directing, self-organizing and self-disciplined team
No confidence with uncertainty	Confident with uncertainty. Admit and deals with uncertainty.
Tend to have extensive documentation and structure	tends to have just sufficient documentation - not too much and light-weight processes - just adequate

Agile project leaders embrace servant-leadership style as it contributes significantly to project success. They focus on providing support and environment to the team(s).

Communication effectiveness

*Communication is a mean to an end – **understanding** - and not the end itself.*

In 1967, two psychological studies reported in *Journal of Consulting Psychology* and *the Journal of Personality and Social Psychology* and later reinforced by Professor Albert Mehrabian, Ph. D. of UCLA in two books: *Silent Messages* and *Nonverbal Communications*. These seem to identify an oversimplified statistical model for the effectiveness of spoken communication; what has now commonly known as "Mehrabian Myth." Mehrabian Myth promotes a model consisting of three components of any communication to help convey information as:

- Verbal (What you say) conveys 7% of intended information
- Vocal (How you say it) conveys 38% of intended information
- Visual (body language) conveys 55% of intended information

Few factors are out of line here. Mehrabian provided useful explanatory note as he did not intend for the statistic to be used or applied freely to all communication and meaning. This aspect is commonly ignored.

First is dependency, Addition of tone to words enhances the amount of information. Further adding body language over tone and words help convey more information. However, the delivery of the message and ability of recipient are ignored here. The context and the two parties able to focus on the context with intentions and impact need to be added for proper transfer of information.

Words are essential aspect as they contain bundle of information. If this was not the case, books would not serve any purpose. Yet we know that it is not true. A lot of information is conveyed in words – verbal or written. We certainly get more than 7% of information from radio talk; if we still do listen to radio or audio channels.

Context of discussion is with both parties participating and active listening help information exchange.

Alistair Cockburn proposed another communication effectiveness graph based on the type of communication modes. This seems to be closer to reality, yet continues to propagate similar myth as that of Mehrabian Myth. As the richness of communication increases, the effectiveness seems to increase. Cockburn contends that most effective communication is via face-to-face, in-person and it appears to decline as the richness declines. Though most of the part hold true, it ignores the aspect of interest, context and ability of the recipient to be able to grasp varies. Modeling options listed in declining order are: face-to-face at whiteboard, face-to-face conversation, video conversation, phone conversation, Videotape and lastly, email conversation. Documentation options include Videotape, Audiotape, and lastly, paper written communication.

Additional aspects would be context and focus of communication. There have been survey results of varying level but they do imply that when individuals are communicating using various modes and with other factors being equal, the mode of communication does have the richness reflected.

Summary

This chapter described the importance of individuals and interactions. This topic is addressed in detail in our book: *Solving Problems – The Agile Way*. While communication is the key, it is only a mean to an end – understanding. If the two parties involved are not able to attain the desired understanding, no matter what communication media is used, it'd be ineffective. On the other hand, if the two parties are ready to collaborate and build understanding, even an ineffective communication media could be useful. Rich communication will, no doubt, enhance the collaboration.

Communication is directed towards understanding the objective that fosters collaboration. Next chapter discusses the essential five Agile business objectives.

Chapter 10 Agile Business Objectives

"Leadership is the art of getting someone else to do something you want done because he wants to do it." - Dwight D. Eisenhower

Introduction

It is imperative that we need to be clear on objectives before we start to dive deep into Agile Project Management details. We simply describe Agile business objectives in simple terms: *Adapting to change is part of planning. Only objective of planning is to deliver.*

This concept is further expanded into multiple dimensions of impact as: building innovative products, product evolution, meeting market needs, development strategy, and finally, the delivery of reliable product. Jim Highsmith describes these as the five key business objectives [HIGHSMITH, 2009] for Agile Project Management (APM) as:

1. *Continuous innovation* – to continue to adapt and improve delivery. on evolving customer requirements, for customer's competitive advantage
2. *Product adaptability* – flexibility and adaptability to deliver on future customer requirements
3. *Improved time-to-market* – to meet market trend, timelines, and optimize return on investment (ROI)
4. *People and process adaptability* – To quickly adjust to external change factors like product , market, people, and business values
5. *Reliable results* – to support growth and profitability; thus, maximizing ROI and adapt to changing market

APM is more than just developing a product in changing market conditions. It promotes the product evolution through adaptation to various external needs. It is not to build a product without having any idea of the product. That would be a chaotic approach. APM addresses complex product development with changing needs. Hence, it helps to understand each object in detail.

Continuous Innovation

An adaptive culture, promoting self-organization and self-discipline, fosters continuous innovation. Today a product development involves meeting the changing user needs which is reflected in changes propagated through the market-trend, user needs, technology, growth, and creativity. Thus, a mindset and attitude change is required to be able to foster to these needs. Various principles like ones of self-organizing, self-discipline, constant adapting, staying flexible, simplicity and value driven approaches are required to generate innovative ideas. Innovation cannot be promoted through blindfolded following of traditional structured, prescriptive and authority driven management. A definitive, plan-driven, and inflexible management approach can only work on simple development projects.

Product Adaptability

As discussed in Continuous innovation, product adaptability builds on the need of changing needs. Needs continue to evolve and having waterfall approach that tries to discourage changes to a product by enforcing a change management process and thus, even putting a high price tags for each change at times has failed to meet these needs. With the rate of external factors influencing the needs, only pathway to success is to adapt to such changes quickly and allow flexible design and simplicity. Thus, product development has taken a flexible, lightweight, and adaptable approach over prescriptive processes, roles, and artifacts driven practices of the past.

Improved Time-to-market

Improved time-to-market is achieved in three ways: product focus, value streamlining, and skill development. Product focus is to be able to prioritize product features and deliver the features of higher value early and often. This also helps realize revenue and optimize ROI. Iterative process with constant revisiting and prioritizing features is essential to optimize on greater value to customer, revenue growth, meeting needs, and optimize ROI for the organization. Value streamlining allows the development process to be lean and remove any waste caused by various factors like overhead, wait, rework, and so forth to optimize the duration of development of features. Selecting a team of right skills for members of the team is essential. This reduces any learning curve. Further working with customers allows business knowledge to build over time to expedite implementation.

People and process adaptability

People and processes need to adapt, just as product adaptability case discussed earlier. For product to be adaptable, it's critical for people to be flexible to adapt to the changing needs and processes to be lightweight as well to allow enabling changes in expedited manner instead of resisting any change. Processes should be adapted to the product needs to maximize value and provide the features of highest value early and frequently. This also incorporates the feedback mechanism so any important change can be considered and focus is maintained for value as priority.

Reliable results

Agile focuses on people and process adaptability to deliver reliable result. Enterprises need to adapt to meet the frequent and continuous delivery of incremental product with value priority to the users. This need is higher than achieved through repetitive strategy; as is common in assembly line and production oriented process. The repeated processes are prescriptive, structured, specific, and address the aspects of iron triangle. Agile advocates adaptive processes which work better for product adaptability. The strategy is to allow adaptation to product using a consistent strategy. The strategy does not need to change. Strategy needs to allow adapting to product innovation, changing needs, and allowing change in direction. Agile methodologies introduce various practices and processes to enable these. Continuous integration and continuous delivery help integration and delivery of product. Development processes and practices like Test Driven Development (TDD), pair programming, estimation techniques, and iterative development allow delivering reliable results, time and again. The strategy does not need to be different every time while delivering reliable product. A suitable strategy that promotes adaptation works best.

Summary

In this chapter, we explored Agile Business objectives with insight on various aspects that tie back to Agile values and principles.

In subsequent chapters, we shall explore Agile estimation and planning aspects. User stories and estimation techniques as some are borrowed from XP methodology since 2001 are also now considered part of Scrum Framework.

Chapter 11 Agile Project Management

"The cautious seldom err." - Confucius

Introduction

Four broad topics are covered in Agile Project Management (APM): Opportunities, values, frameworks, and practices. Further, there exist five major topics in APM are: Agile values, scaling agile projects, advanced release planning, Project governance, and Performance management. These provide a distinction from the prescriptive (aka assembly, well-defined, industrial) lines of product development strategy. Agile contracting, frameworks, practices and development provide alternatives for this. Agile manifesto, Agile principles, and The Declaration of Interdependence (DOI) focus on customer, values, and projects as we shall discuss further.

Opportunities

APM provides opportunity for products that are innovative, research based, thoughts provoking, creative, enticing, and defining new services. The SDLC (waterfall methodology) is applicable in simple scenarios where the complete set of product requirements are known upfront (in software development, to know everything to know at the start? who are you kidding, really!), non-changing during the development, a defined process with defined phases is identified with resources and skills already mature and available. This applies mostly to assembly line products where the different pieces are built, assembled, and "Voila! We have the product ready to market." This requires hardly any creative thinking as all pieces are well defined. However, with evolving market we need new methods and practices for complex projects. Yet Agile project management is within the domain between well-defined and chaotic. Chaotic projects for product development are the other extreme where things are continuing to evolve and resulting in much waste and priorities keep changing over time. Such projects are also out of reach as no process can be defined to contain chaos. History has proven that chaotic projects either dwindle away or come to the level of complex projects where they can be handled and managed.

Values

Agile is all about value driven delivery. APM focuses on delivering value to customer while being flexible to adapt to future customer needs. Traditional project management has failed on managing this as they require the time, scope and resources be defined upfront. In reality, the plan is set in stone and is followed with minimum changes. Customers have to pay high prices for any change in requirements. There have been many instances of vendors bidding under the cost for a project to win it and count on high costs for changes to make the profit. Further the process is to raise prices and constrain the customer within the original concept. Back and forth negotiations continue with neither parties coming to clear consensus. Most projects end up failing - a lose-lose scenario. APM comes to help such projects to change it to a win-win scenario.

Traditional projects are fixated on requirements and focus on delivering on scope, schedule, and cost. Further changes to requirements are discouraged as all requirements are defined upfront and configuration process is identified. Reality holds that product needs to be adapted to changing trends that include users need, market trend, technology and so forth. While in reality, Product success indicators and thus, project success indicators include product vision, business objectives, and product features (capabilities - high level product functionality), not requirements. These indicators define a releasable product of value to the customer and the quality is defined by easily adaptable and reliable product that works now and is easy to adapt to growing needs. Hence, value is the primary focus on agile projects and managing scope, cost, and schedule is secondary. Most agile projects experience schedule as a major constraint and hence, is tracked via team velocity and timebox, in sprints, while the scope varies. More will be discussed on this later.

Frameworks

Agile frameworks are driven to allow teams deliver consistently high quality and high value products reliably to customers in the wake of continuous change, changing directions, technological advancements, market changes and ambiguity (though still not in chaotic domain).

Practices

Agile practices promote core values and principles over processes. The practice could be by breaking the silos to participatory and constant interactions for a value-driven product development. It identifies various ways for team to continue to deliver value while allowing customers to have constant insight into the development progressively. Thus, allowing customers and development team to work hand-in-hand for the best product at hand.

Agile values

Agile values are around three value statements [HIGHSMITH, 2009]:

1   Value delivery over meeting constraints (Value -over- constraints)
2   Leading the team over managing tasks (team assignment -over- task assignment)
3   Adapting to change over conforming to plans (Adapting changes -over following plans)

These values are fully supported by Agile Manifesto and Declaration of Interdependence discussed later. Agile Manifesto is written for software developers while Declaration of Interdependence is for project leaders. Hence, these values are also referred to as: *"Agile Leadership values."*

A good agile leader focuses on adapting to changes and is self-organizing. Unfortunately, traditional project manager is not good at adapting as focuses on confirming to plan and also need risk management practices. Practices can indicate mindsets but cannot determine mindset for the key agile values. Agile is all about mindset, not just practices.

Project governance

With the expansion of APM taking over software development industry, a common discussion prevails on comparing project governance from waterfall versus iterative versus agile project management approaches.

Executives are interested in mainly two aspects for project governance; viz. investment and risk.

Governance pertains to making decisions in uncertain environment with varying market conditions, demands and needs of customers, and so forth. Executives hence seek to assess ROI, associated risks, and probability of success on early payback on the investment. We will discuss the calculations in detail later. Currently, the comparison with transition from waterfall to iterative to agile is essential to grasp. An essential aspect is the fact that for research based exploration projects, risks are not identified by specifying requirements upfront. Risks are reduced by exploring, analyzing the problem domain, investigating, creating simulations, prototypes or research and development efforts.

Waterfall approach assumes that when all the requirements are defined, the risk is reduced. Also, it sets the criteria for return on investment. However, reality is that the value is recognized at delivery of product to the customer and not at requirement definition. Unless we have a production line project where the problem domain and solution domain are both known which allows clearly defined requirements and plan on developing the product as if in production-line, waterfall model fails to manage risks and investments; and thus, in turn fails to manage returns on investments. Hence, for an exploratory project, with higher level of uncertainty and complexity, waterfall methodology experiences an inherent shortcoming as not everything is known at every phase.

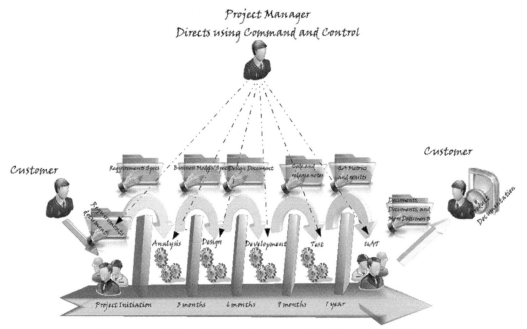

Figure 11-1 Waterfall Development (Traditional SDLC)

While an iterative approach breaks development in multiple iterations. Breaking into smaller cycles enhances delivery of value. It does not realize empirical process control. The ability to inspect and adapt is not attained due to the limitations and restrictions imposed by the processes. Further, methodologies like RUP are heavyweight due to being prescriptive. It is tightly coupled with a set of artifacts and comprehensive documentation to result from different user roles and processes in a workflow.

 RUP faces the drawback and gets overburdened by the artifacts, processes and roles involved. The transitions from one phase to next phase goes through a phase-gate progression where decision of go/no-go are made and the project continues to progress further.

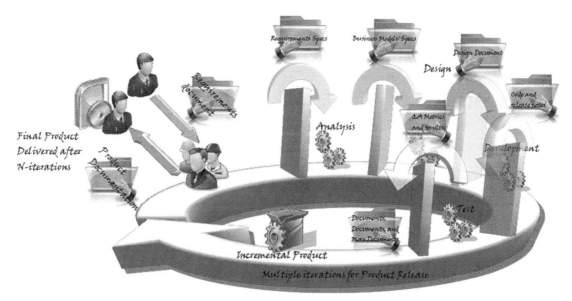

Figure 11-2: Iterative Development - uses silos

Agile methodology provides the phase-gate progression where the governance and operational modes operation separately in parallel. Executive perspective is a series of linear phases while operational mode is a series of iterative planning followed by delivery. With delivery a constant approach to review the product and the process of product development provides the essential feedback loop to be able to inspect and adapt to optimize the value driven while managing and maintaining the quality of the product.

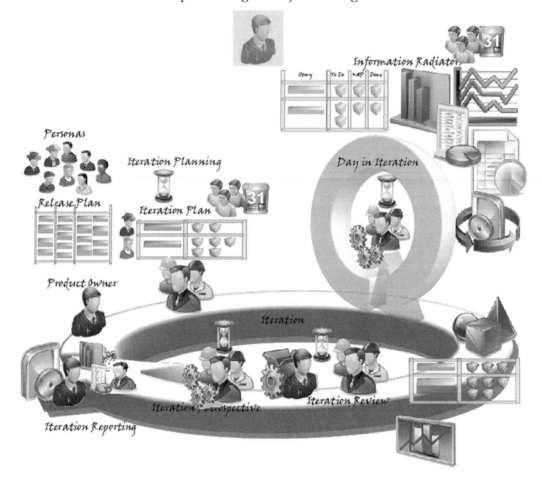

Figure 11-3: Agile Development uses Empirical process control

Performance management

Quality is not an act, it is a habit. - Aristotle

Agile brings a new perspective to performance management. Traditional project management measures performance by strict adherence to the Iron triangle: scope, budget and schedule. APM measures team performance by new triangle called "Agile Triangle" that consists of value, quality, and constraints.

Often Traditional Project management and Governance body do not take value into consideration. They are focused on scope to be met within time and cost constraints.

Value has been ignored as if it'd be self-managed if time, resources and cost constraints are managed. For traditional project managers, the assumption is that delivering on scope, schedule and cost equates to delivering value. This is hardly true if practices are not promoting the value factor. APM addresses this by bringing in Value and Quality as major factors while time, scope, resources, technology, and other limitations as constraints.

Change, adaptation, and flexibility are the trademarks of agile projects. While conforming to plan is the trademark of traditional projects. Hence, APM streamlines the performance management to meet the set goals as per development and practices.

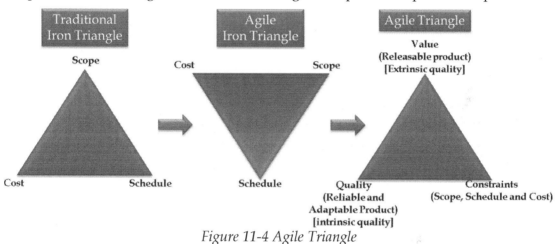

Figure 11-4 Agile Triangle

In traditional project management, Iron triangle is followed consisting of scope, schedule, and time. Mostly scope is primary driving factor due to false assumption of knowing the scope early. Thus, cost and schedule vary to meet the scope; while plan was devised to lock all three down early on and even refactored periodically.

The second – Agile Iron triangle evolved during early agile development where schedule was fixed as end date of delivery (timebox) while scope was allowed to vary and time was a fixed constraint. This still had plans define success by identifying schedule and tasks and not to adaptive nature of agile projects. This brings us to the Agile triangle. The factors of Agile Triangle are: Value (to the customer), Quality (attain to deliver value to customer), and constraints (scope, schedule, and cost). The primary factor in APM is value and constraints need to be adjusted as project progresses to maximize value. Schedule (timebox) may still be a constraint, yet scope and cost are managed to deliver highest value. Hence, adjusting constraints to meet value or quality helps organization meet the needs. In an Agile Triangle:

1 *Value goal*: Build a releasable product
2 *Quality goal:* Build a reliable, adaptable product
3 *Constraint goal*: Achieve value and quality goals within acceptable constraints

Agile triangle recognizes the fact that the value of a product is recognized at the point of sale or release to the customer instead of the scope defined at the point of inception.

For agile values, the measurements systems that support these values need to evolve to support and measure the success. The success factors are seriously impacted as we set the bar for value delivery. Sometimes project goals are set low just to meet the success factor and then at times a project is driven more like a production unit with stable yet outdated technology to meet the demand. These projects can very well be driven in waterfall methodology while following a plan, yet the difference is set when a project is in complex domain with uncertainty, cultural factors are imposed and it is hard to find the skilled and experienced personnel would force a project to be more suitable to accept agile methodology to be successful. This is due to the value driven product delivery while maintaining high quality and managing the constraints. Further toppled with the compliance and regulatory demands, it may appear that agile methodology is not suitable. That is not normally is the case. When there are compliance and demands, say extensive testing requirement, it is easier to still follow agile methodology but provide delivery of product in releases or even at roadmap levels when extensive testing has been performed. A project recently done had two sprints lag in a release to meet the extensive compliance without development teams stopping to do the testing. This was achieved by different environments where the code was delivered with extensive testing was performed by automated tests before they completed the phase-gate transition to the next level.

Summary

In this chapter, we covered Four broad topics are covered in Agile Project Management (APM): Opportunities, values, frameworks, and practices. Further, there exist five major topics in APM are: Agile values, Scaling agile projects, Advanced release planning, Project governance, and Performance management. All these tie closely to Agile values and principles. Product planning structure breaks away from the Sprint and allow exposure to product roadmap, release, wave and sprint planning aspects.

In subsequent chapters, we shall explore Agile Project Management model, Agile estimation and planning aspects.

Chapter 12 Agile Management Model

"Good leadership consists of showing average people how to do the work of superior people."
- John D. Rockefeller

Introduction

Declaration of Interdependence (DOI) identifies that APM is not about best practices. Rather situationally specific strategies, processes and practices are employed to support the underlying values and principles. Agile methodologies provide a common framework for decision making strategies that are applicable to large enterprises.

An agile enterprise framework model is identified to provide guidance at enterprise level as shown in Figure 12-1. Portfolio management requires adaptation to provide measurement parameters based on value instead of scope as traditional approach. Besides, it would also provide checkpoints and thus would be feeding into Project Management layer. Project Management layer provides guidance to projects and management strategies based on values, constraints and quality. Sprint Management encompasses management of sprints which collectively could be feeding into Project Management layers for releases and roadmap. Sprint management includes daily activities to focus on delivering functionality at the end of sprint. These activities include technical practices like pair programming, refactoring, continuous integration, etc. Thus, each layer feeding into above layer for providing a sustainable Agile enterprise framework.

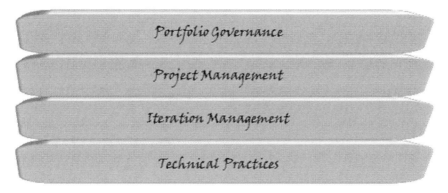

Figure 12-1: Agile Enterprise Framework

APM model focuses on execution and adaptation consists of 5 phases – Business need analysis, Estimation, Execution, Inspect-and-Adapt, and Project Closure. An Agile development provides insight to the common methodology that exists and provides iterative delivery of valuable software product features to the customer. These are depicted in Figure 12-2. This aspect goes through further transition as discussed in Chapter 25: Planning layers.

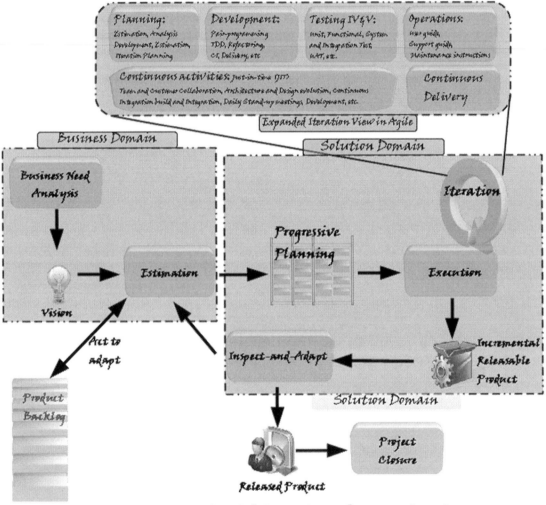

Figure 12-2: Agile Development with Domains, Phases and cycles

Agile delivery approach is in five phases, each with supporting practices:

1   ***Business Need Analysis***: Phase of defining well-articulated product or service need with market analysis

2   ***Estimation***: Phase of deriving vision and various estimations on ROI and high-level effort, product specifications and initial product planning and Backlog generation

3   ***Execution***: An iterative phase where product features are implemented based on value as priority

4   *Inspect-and-Adapt*: The product features implemented and development processes are reviewed and adaptive actions are incorporated in the next sprint. This leads to updates to the Product Backlog to keep it DEEP

5   ***Project Closure***: The project concludes and knowledge transfer is done. A closure ceremony follows signifying sharing of appreciations and easing the adjourning of various teams on the project.

This is shown elaborated in relation to Scrum Framework as:

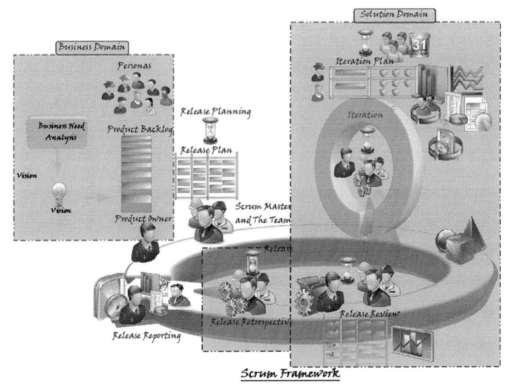

Figure 12-3: Scrum Framework with domains

Further there are two cycles: Business domain cycle that includes Vision and Planning phases and Solution domain that includes Execution and Inspect-Adapt phases; as shown below in Figure 12-2 and Figure 12-3.

In recent times, this model is getting further refined. Customer collaboration aspect is gaining significance. The planning is further explained

Business Need Analysis

Business need analysis results in product vision that is defined by product vision box and elevator statement; as discussed individually in this section.

Product Vision Box

Front of the box contains 3 items:

    1   Product name
    2   A Graphic
    3   3 or 4 bullet points to sell the product

Back of the box contains:

    1   Detailed feature description
    2   Operating requirements

Figure 12-4: A Sample Product Vision Box

Elevator Pitch or Elevator test statement

As a product vision model, elevator speech, pitch or elevator test statement is developed besides the Product Vision Box. Elevator test statement is so called as it comes from the idea of passing an elevator test as you are in the elevator with CEO of your company and you have just two minutes to describe your product and pass the elevator test. The statement addresses three aspects: the target customer, key benefit(s), and competitive advantage.

The format for elevator pitch comes from Geoffrey Moore's book "Crossing the Chasm" 1991.

Template of Elevator pitch is:

for (target customer)
who (statement of need or opportunity)
the (product name) *is a* (product category)
that (key benefit, compelling reason to buy)
unlike (primary competitive alternative)
our product (statement of primary differentiation)

Creating a product vision statement helps teams remain focused on the critical aspects of the product, even when details are changing rapidly. It is very easy to get focused on the short-term issues associated with a 2-4 week development sprint and lose track of the overall product vision.

Project Data Sheet (PDS)

Project Data Sheet (PDS) is a summarized visioning practice of a product that identifies the project objectives and constraints. PDS is only a single page document that covers the key product objectives, its capabilities and project management insight. The single page aspect is attractive to all stakeholders and helps ascertain the vision of the product. Sample PDS is illustrated in Figure 12-5.

Project Data Sheet contains information pertaining to the Business Domain as well as Solution Domain with initial planning of the strategies for marketing, Project Objective statement, Business objective, Trade-off Matrix, Capabilities, Milestones, Issues and Risks. It does contain many aspects, like Quality and Performance, which are intrinsic in Agile and are always upheld.

Project Data Sheet	
Name: Karaoke Recorder	Project Champion: Jim Walsh
Start Date: July 4th, 2012	Project Manager: Andy Wen
	Executive Sponsor: Ann Miller
Clients:	
Marketing	
Music Industry	
Sales and Accounting	
Project Objective Statement:	**Quality Objectives:**
The objective is to build a web-based Karaoke	All server and critical defects be fixed
song builder application that includes easy	Comprehensive test automation
integration of mp3 songs with text and time	
based synchronization between the text highlights	
Total cost: less than 1 M	
Business Objectives:	**Performance Guidelines:**
Innovative product	User should be able to integrate songs with text
Easy of operation	in less than 10 minutes for a song with 100 words
Greater accuracy and performance	

Trade Off Matrix:					Architecture Guidelines:
	Fixed	Flexible	Accept	Target	Integrate effectively for web display
Scope	X			300 SP	
Schedule		X		13 weeks	
Cost			X	$1 M	

Project delay cost/month = $50K	
Exploration factor = 10	Maximize reuse and ease of use
Capability:	**Major Project Milestones:**
Recorder functionality be web based	Initial recorder by August 1st, 2012
Downloadable modules be PC or Mac based	Customers account management by Sept 1st, 2012
Upload of MP3 or linking from online allowed	Integrated downloadable player by Nov 1st, 2012
Storing and sharing of resources allowed	
	Issues and Risks:
	Web interface module technology is unstable
	Development cost is unpredictable at start time
	Varying priorities between Marketing and Sales

Figure 12-5 Project Data Sheet

Estimation

At surface the word "estimation" appears to indicate guessing while dictionary definition is "approximate calculation." Approximate calculation refers closely to address planning around the uncertainties using empirical control process and continuous need to inspect-and-adapt throughout the project. Estimation phase follows the Execution phase that builds the product based on its vision. Estimation phase consists of the following:

- Gather requirements as they pertain to at the moment with unknowns
- Product Backlog definition or enhancement based on the gathered requirements, costs, effort estimates, and risks
- Release plan development with prioritized backlog
- Estimation of cost and product development in releases

Output of Speculate phase is a risk-normalized Release plan. Conceptually, a mini-speculate phase occurs during Sprint as well that results in a Sprint plan.

Execution

Execution phase focuses on product feature development and delivery planned for the release. These are carried out mainly in Sprint while planning aspect continues to be managed at higher levels along with customer collaboration and team collaboration, intra-team collaboration, Release and Sprint planning and execution including the development practices. This is discussed at length later as part of Release and Sprint in Scrum.

Inspect-and-adapt

Inspect-and-adapt phase focuses on reviewing the product and its features developed during the Execution phase and the development process used for developing the product features.

Besides, In Retrospective ceremonies, the core team focuses on reviewing and optimizing the development process that includes inspection and tuning of development practices, processes and resources.

Product Review is conducted at Release, Wave and Sprint levels. During product review, the product demo is conducted to the customers and stakeholders. After the demo, further feedback is taken from the participants. This allows the Product Backlog to be updated based on the feedback that can again be updated and prioritized during the Estimation phase.

Project Closure

Every project has a start and hence, correspondingly a closure. Project Closure phase is essential as when not defined when the project ends seem to send the project into never ending cycle of continuum. The "mini" closures at release and sprint levels allow the learning measures to be incorporated in the next iterative cycle.

Often there is a confusion regarding Project Closure phase. Project Closure phase applies to the project, and not the product. Project ends while the product continues to live. Team would then transfer knowledge to project support and maintenance teams that can continue to support and maintain the product while the development team moves on to the next project.

Most important activity at this phase is Project Retrospective. The lessons learned are gathered and passed onto the next project (support) team. The project closure is normally marked with recognition and celebration to mark the project end.

In an Agile enterprise, the project teams move to next project but continue to be the cohesive group. This also reduces the team formation and development phases.

Summary

In this chapter, we explored Agile Project Management model with insight on detailed analysis of phases and activities in Business and Solution domains.

In subsequent chapters, we shall explore Agile estimation and planning aspects. User stories and estimation techniques as some are borrowed from XP methodology since 2001 are also now considered part of Scrum Framework.

Section III
Scrum Backlogs –
Heart of Scrum

Chapter 13 Backlogs

"It is a bad plan that admits of no modification." - Publilius Syrus

Introduction

Scrum framework uses empirical process control to help deal with complex projects where uncertainties, unknowns, and risks are present. The product evolves with JIT decision making when new information is available. Besides, in Scrum, highest value product feature is always addressed earliest. These aspects make it essential to manage all the known and unknowns in a single bucket. This is achieved using backlog. Backlog is a prioritized list of all types of requirements of a product. Each item in the backlog is referred to as Backlog Item (BI). This was covered briefly in earlier chapters. In this chapter, we shall explore the details on why and how the different backlogs are created, groomed, and evolved over time.

Product Backlog

Product Backlog is a list of all product requirements including functional and non-functional, features, updates, defects, and changes. Product Backlog constantly emerges based on requests from the stakeholders. The Product Owner manages, prioritizes, regularly updates, and owns the Product Backlog. The Product Backlog is the single artifact for complete development effort. Figure 13-1 shows a prioritized backlog where the vertical height of each backlog item equates to effort estimate; the color hue corresponds to details; and position reflects relative value of the backlog item. Terms like 'ordered' and 'ranked' are frequently used interchangeably with prioritized. The essential aspect is to ensure that it is value

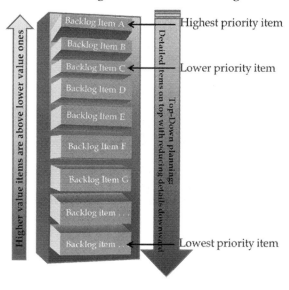

Figure 13-1: Prioritized Product Backlog

driven stack with highest value items on top, listing items top-down in declining value and the lowest value item is at the bottom.

Scrum Framework requires Product Owner to own the Product Backlog. The Product Owner needs the Development Team to provide the effort estimates for BI. The market analysis and stakeholders provide the other insight to value of each item.

Good Product Backlog

Product backlog is regularly groomed to ensure highest value item is at the top. The

backlog items are progressively elaborated top-down allowing the items on the top (highest value) be detailed at greater length so that unknowns are minimized and can be considered for development during the planning session. Good Product Backlog is Detailed appropriately, Emergent, Estimated, and Prioritized (DEEP) [Roman Pichler and Mike Cohn, 2010]. It is sorted with highest value item on top.

Figure 13-2: DEEP Product Backlog

Detailed Appropriately

Items are detailed top-down as and when new information is available or discovered about the item. The items on top are detailed progressively during grooming sessions. The Product Owner collaborates with stakeholders and the Development Team to detail Backlog items on regular basis. Top level Backlog Items must be appropriately detailed for the planning session for the Development team to consider them for the Sprint.

Emergent

Product Backlog continues to emerge throughout the project lifecycle. There are new findings from Business domain like user preferences, trends, and technology that continue to affect the Backlog. The Product Owner frequently collects details on Backlog items and then collaborates with the stakeholders to identify dependent details like market analysis, ROI, and effort estimates. During the Review sessions, further inputs are received from stakeholders who can further update Product Backlog. Progressive elaboration is an essential concept driving the detailing and emergence nature of Product Backlog.

Estimated

The Product Owner collaborates with the Development Team to collect effort estimate to complete a Backlog Item. In order to estimate the level of effort, the Development Team requires the Backlog item to be sufficiently detailed with acceptance criteria. Product Backlog Items are estimated using various techniques as: User Stories, ideal days or ideal hours; as is further detailed in Chapter 16: Estimation and Planning. A smaller backlog item is easier to estimate than a large one.

Prioritized

To avoid scenario where all requirements are Priority 1, Scrum enforces prioritization of Backlog items in Product Backlog. The Product Backlog is prioritized top-down based on value. The item on top is of higher value than the item below. Thus, the list is prioritized from highest value on top to reducing in value as we move down.

Cost has a direct impact on value. For instance, if we have Backlog Item A that can sell at 10K and another Backlog Item B that can sell at 8K; it is still not enough information to prioritize them. When we estimate the effort involved and say Backlog Item A has effort estimate cost of 5K while that of Backlog Item B is 1K, we derive that ROI for Backlog Item A as 5K and that of Backlog Item B is 7K. This makes Backlog Item B a higher value than that of Backlog Item A.

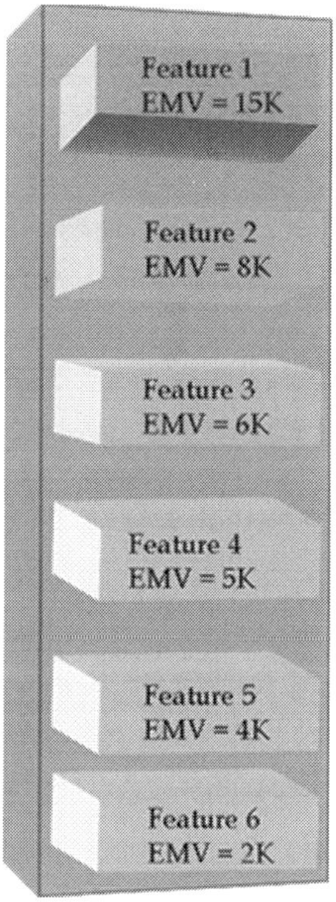

Risk prioritized backlog

Agile projects require product backlog to be prioritized based on value to the customer. Risk

Figure 13-3: Product Backlog with Features and EMV values

severity provide the value in EMV terms due to the significance of risk occurring. Hence, the product backlog, initially setup to include the product features, can also include risk based on risk impact.

Note: In examples, currency symbol is ignored to keep the analysis simple.

Based on initial analysis, the Product Backlog is prioritized based on functionality along with the monetary value provided for each feature and then prioritized based on value. Here, Feature is a type of Product Backlog item.

Feature 1 has expected monetary value of 15K,

Feature 2 with expected monetary value of 8K

Feature 3 with expected monetary value of 6K

And so forth.

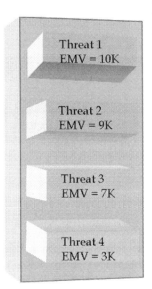

Risk management allows the risks to be listed for the project. In this example, let the following risks be identified:

Threats are listed as:

Threat 1: Technology driver

Risk Severity = probability X impact

= 0.5 * 20K = 10K

Risk Threat 2: Loss of resource

Severity = 0.9 * 10K = 9K

Figure 13-4: Risk Prioritized Backlog

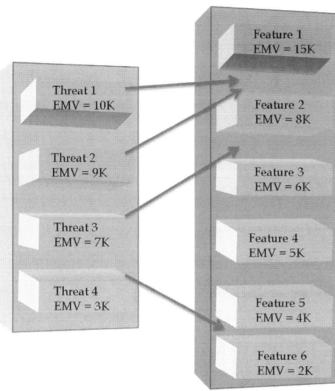

Figure 13-5: Mapping risk items in Product Backlog

Risk Threat 3: production support

Severity = -.5 * 14K = 7K

Risk Threat 4: Infrastructure support

Severity = 0.3 * 10K = 3K

Now, the risks are also merged in the Product Backlog to derive the risk prioritized backlog with risks also prioritized in the backlog based on the value:

The risk prioritized backlog would appear with features and threats identified in the value prioritized backlog. Agile projects allow the risks based Product Backlog items (PBIs)

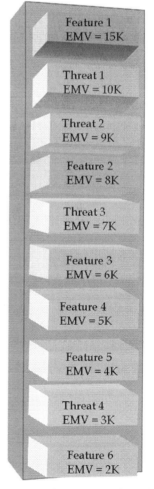

Figure 13-6: Risk Prioritized Backlog

to be assigned to a given release.

MoSCoW is a common strategy identified to allocate PBIs to a release.

Here, the product backlog could be viewed in the following perspective:

Features are the opportunities (to satisfy the end needs) and functions of the software.

Threats are the risks that can impact the project adversely.

Another important aspect is the compliance factor as there are normally government compliance factors on documentation and extensive quality assurance that must be met. These compliances when not 'done' have an adverse on the project. In these cases, respective PBIs could be added with respective EMV based on the penalties imposed for non-compliance. They can then be added to the Product Backlog. The Product Backlog is then prioritized periodically.

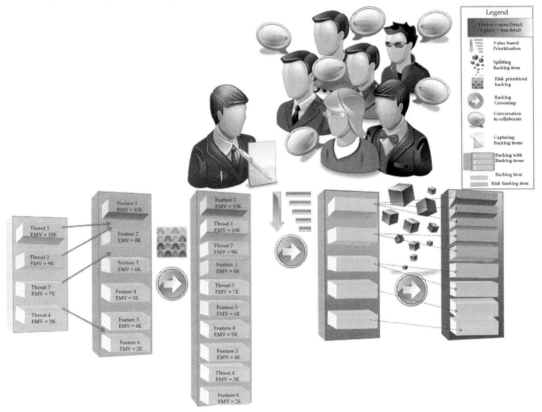

Figure 13-7: Risk-prioritized backlog with customer collaboration

Risk Burndown Graph

Risk Burndown Chart could still be tracked beside Release Burndown Chart. Risk Burndown chart is just tracking the severity of the risk over a period of time.

Note: The risk prioritized backlog allows the risks to be included as PBIs in the product backlog and thus be assigned to a release and addressed accordingly.

Risk Burndown Graph is to track the threats (risks impacting the project negatively) mainly. Let's consider a project with the following risks as discussed above as Threat, Risk probability, Risk Impact and Risk Severity at the start of the project:

Threat (Negative Risk)	Risk probability	Risk Impact	Risk Severity
Threat 1: Technology driver	0.5	20K	10K
Threat 2: Loss of resource	0.9	10K	9K
Threat 3: production support	0.5	14K	7K
Threat 4: Infrastructure support	0.3	10K	3K

where,

Threat: Threats are the bad risks that can pose a hurdle for the project. This could cause delay or even impact project seriously. For example, loss of an architect to project deliverables, management interference in case of changing organization, decline in market demand due to another competitive product launch are all examples of threats to the project. Risk management plan is devised to reduce the probability of such threats to the project.

Risk impact: Risk impact is the loss the project could incur in case of the risk occurs

Risk probability: Risk probability identifies the chances of the risk event to occur on the project

Risk severity: Risk severity is the significance of the risk in quantitative risk analysis. It is expressed in *Expected Monitory Value (EMV)* and is derived as:

Risk severity = Risk impact * Risk probability

Now, tracking the threats over sprints is reflected in the table below for risks and their corresponding severity value over sprints:

Threat	Sprint 1	Sprint 2	Sprint 3	Sprint 4
Threat 1: Technology driver @ 20K	10K	8K	5K	0K
Threat 2: Loss of resource @ 10K	9K	5K	5K	1K
Threat 3: production support @ 14K	7K	7K	7K	7K
Threat 4: Infrastructure support @ 10K	3K	3K	1K	0K

Note:

1. Risk impact is assumed to be a constant value here. This value could also change due to various factors but simplified in the above example for simplicity.
2. Interesting to see that Threat 3 did not undergo any change in the four sprints. This could be due to the fact that it was no assigned or if assigned, the probability could not be reduced due to multiple factors.
3. Threat 4 reduced in severity even though it may not have been assigned to a sprint backlog.
4. Another limitation of Risk Burndown graph is that it does not show whether the risk was assigned, being worked on, or just left out as down be in lower priority in the Product Backlog.

Risk Burndown graph in this case would be cumulative risk graph across time can thus be viewed using simple excel graph:

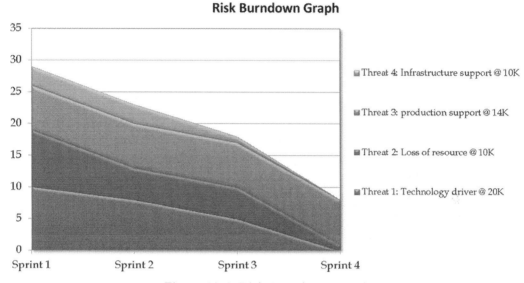

Figure 13-8: Risk Burndown Graph

One important aspect presented by Risk Burndown graph is the view showing how the threats have been managed during the sprints. This along with Risk prioritized backlog also identifies risk spikes that need to be taken up to address major risks. Risk Burndown graph is oriented towards threats reduction. Similar Risk Burn-up chart could be developed to address the opportunities.

To be able to assess risk management aspect, the risks related PBIs need to be tracked in the Risk prioritized backlog for product development.

Fail Fast

Failing fast appears to be an alarming concept at first sight. While every project would seek to be successful, trying to seek a project for fail-fast scenario seems like CLM (Career Limiting Move). Besides, the Standish Group published Chaos report does not look at "Fast fail" based risk spikes to be beneficial to a project. That is due to the short-sightedness in measurements. This in reality is a blessing in disguise. Fail fast approach identifies the addressing risks using risk based spikes. Adopted from XP, a spike is a small exercise to learn something new about the issue or goal.

Agile methodologies promote fail fast to address risks and uncertainties associated with the project early and often. Fail fast surfaces the risks and uncertainties early. This is by TDD and coding complex tests early and exposing bugs where it is easier to fix in early stages. Also applicable to planning, Fail fast concept is used where it saves investments by exposing risks by executing spikes and saving future investments that could have been lost had the limitations not been exposed early.

During quantitative analysis, risks are identified on the project for their significance. These risks need to be managed proactively. Risk prioritized backlog provides the initial insight and allows a serious risk to be addressed early. If the risk spike exposes a "fast fail" scenario, then the project can be stopped early, and further investment can be reinvested in another project with higher success rate. Let's look at this in an example:

Project A has been incurring an expense of $100K per month and is expected finish in 6 months. However, during risk management, a serious threat is identified. Let's consider two scenarios:

On an agile project, a risk spike is executed in the beginning of second sprint to address a serious threat. The risk spike performed identifies that the project should be stopped as a threat imposed by a federal quality compliance factor would have severe impact and could incur an overall loss of $500K to the project.

On another project, the risk is not managed and avoided as it appears to be too hard to handle and managed by the enterprise. Management continues to play hide-and-seek until the last month when the threat exposes itself and the project incurs a penalty of $500K. At this point, the project has already invested a total of $600K (6 months * $100K/month). Further, the penalty causes a loss of $500K and the project is cancelled in failing to meet the compliance.

In this case, the total loss of $1.1 million is reported for the project. Everyone pointing fingers to others and the organization is in trouble. While for an agile project, allowing the risk spike to identify "fail fast" only incurs $100K expense and $500K expense is saved by terminating the project early. Now the organization can look at other initiatives where they expect better ROI. Teams are directed towards the new effort and opportunities are explored for better outcome. In this case, "fail fast" is a favorable scenario. In both the cases, the Chaos report would list project A as failure by the Standish Group but the company would have saved and hopefully directed its effort and teams towards a more successful initiative.

Hence, as displayed, risk spikes are often performed on agile projects to allow "fail fast" scenarios:

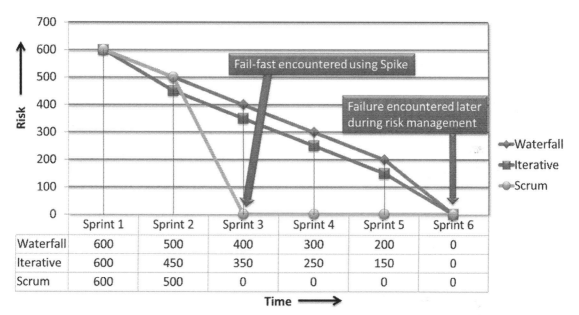

	Sprint 1	Sprint 2	Sprint 3	Sprint 4	Sprint 5	Sprint 6
Waterfall	600	500	400	300	200	0
Iterative	600	450	350	250	150	0
Scrum	600	500	0	0	0	0

Figure 13-9: Fast fail using Spikes

Sprint Backlog

Product Backlog may have Backlog Items that may take months and even years to complete. Sprints are short timebox of 1 week to 4 weeks. In order to determine the Backlog Items that can be completed in a Sprint, backlog items are discussed and identified for the Sprint. The set of selected Backlog items, for the Sprint, forms the Sprint Backlog.

In Sprint planning, the team collaborates with the Product Owner to identify the Product Backlog items it can deliver in the Sprint. The two sessions of Sprint planning are shown in Figure 13-16.

During the first part of Sprint planning, the Product Owner starts explaining the Product Backlog items at the top. The team inquires on various aspects to build a clear understanding of the backlog items. This helps with estimation updates, identifying any risks, unknowns, etc.

Figure 13-10: Sprint Backlog built in Sprint Planning

The scope of work relates to the number of most valued backlog items team can commit to for the Sprint. This is dependent on various factors like team calendar, effort estimate for each backlog item, how detailed the backlog item is, any unknowns and uncertainties, any associated risks, etc. Then once the team has identified the backlog items to commit to, the team identifies tasks required to complete each backlog item. The list of backlog items and related tasks form the Sprint Backlog. Then the team members own various tasks in the Sprint Backlog. This is displayed in Figure 13-17.

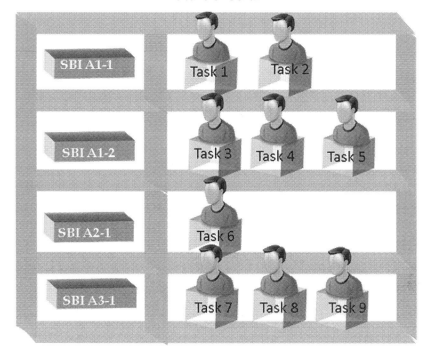

Figure 13-11: Sprint Backlog

Summary

This chapter describes Scrum artifact. Backlog is at the heart of Scrum Framework and is instrumental in supporting highest value delivery to the customer. Product Backlog, Sprint Backlog, Risk Backlog and Risk-prioritized Backlogs were discussed at length. Also, essential aspect behind Backlog Item (BI) has been discussed for clarity.

Chapter 14 Backlog Item

"The more time you spend contemplating what you should have done... you lose valuable time planning what you can and will do." - Lil Wayne

Introduction

Backlog item is a single item in a Backlog. Each Backlog item is of value to the customer. The Product Owner works with the customers and end-users to write these and use these to represent all types of requirements.

Sashimi concept

Sashimi is a Japanese dish made from thin slices of raw fish. Each slice is complete in itself. It's a kind of gross metaphor. Another way to sashimi is Sieving concept. Where you can take a larger rock and break into smaller. The estimation and related aspects match Sieving concept much better; as we shall discuss later. This practice of having a complete functionality is one of the ingredients in Scrum.

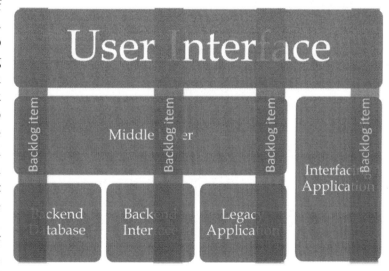

Figure 14-1: Backlog Item as Sashimi – a complete vertical slice

In Scrum, a backlog item is requirement pertaining to functionality to the customer or end-user. Each completed backlog items provides a complete functionality that the end-user can value. There are other metaphors that are befitting metaphors for conceptual description of backlog item: slice of Cake or Pizza. A cake slice where each slice contains a vertical cut across with all its surfaces and provides a complete taste in itself. These backlog items are then stacked based on their value and ranked to derive the Product Backlog.

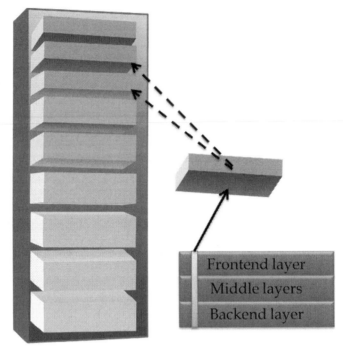

Figure 14-2: Sashimi > Backlog item collection to build Product Backlog

Common hierarchies of Backlog items

As part of progressive elaboration, as the details are known, the backlog items can be split into smaller units. Features and capabilities are normally the high level item types. These are further broken into smaller units. There are many versions of Backlog item hierarchy in-effect and three of those are:

- ❖ Features > Epics > Stories (most commonly used)
- ❖ Features > Theme > Epics > Stories (now gaining popularity with Story maps; discussed later in Chapters 37 and 38)
- ❖ Capabilities > Epics > Stories

The most common hierarchy is the first one. A feature is a large vertical slice, epic is considered a comparatively smaller one and a user story is yet smaller than an epic. These are depicted in Figure 14-3.

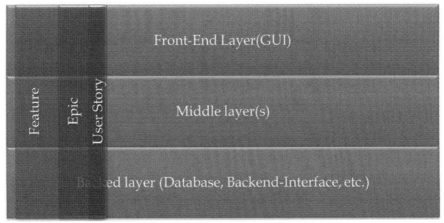

Figure 14-3: Sample Hierarchy of Backlog Items

In this hierarchy, Feature can be split into epics. Epics, in turn, can be split into stories. The stories are then accepted in Sprint for development. This aspect is depicted in Figure 14-4.

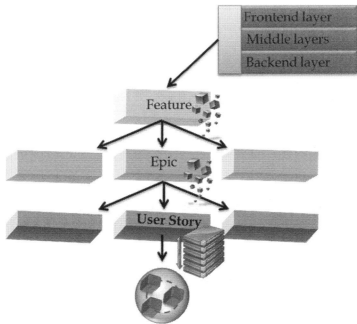

Figure 14-4: Backlog item - Hierarchy

Product Backlog items are refined in backlog grooming ceremonies. The Product Owner is responsible for facilitating the grooming sessions and ensuring that the

Product Backlog is DEEP. Figure 14-5 shows a Product Backlog where PBIs are identified as different types. As the detailing is done top-down, stories are small sized backlog items as they are frequently visited and detailed. Epics are detailed and then split into stories. As the backlog items rise to the top they are split into smaller sizes, are more refined with details and acceptance criteria. This enables the team to estimate effort. A well-defined backlog item can then be taken up for development in a Sprint.

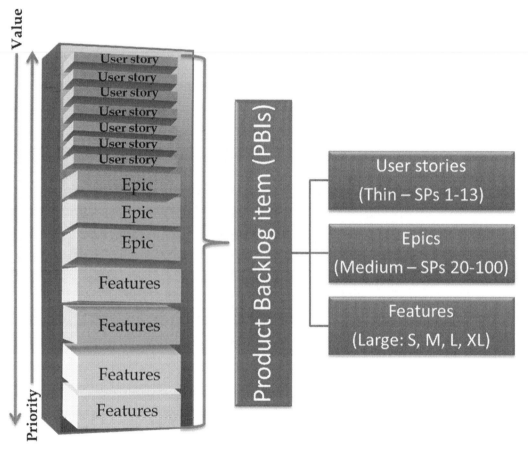

Figure 14-5 Sample Product Backlog Item Hierarchy

Features

Features correspond to the functionality at Product Vision Box level. Features are fairly large units of functionality and require many Sprints. Besides, it is not a good idea to implement one feature completely in a Sprint as the details may be varying in different aspects of the feature. Hence, features are normally broken down into epics.

Theme

Combining stories is done when stories are too small. Sometimes developers feel that fixing would be faster than documenting such stories. Common approach for such tiny stories is to combine these into a story from half-a-day to several days of work. This can be done by stapling or clipping the index cards with a cover card. This set is treated as a single story for estimation and planning. Such a set is known as a theme. An epic is often also a theme.

Epics or capabilities

A story that is too large is called an *epic* or *capability*. Normally an epic is too big to be assigned to iteration and would need to be broken into smaller stories, but not always the case, as an example: "A buyer can view information about each item that matched in a search." Such a large story is valid, realistic, and does not have to be broken into further stories.

Epics typically fall into two categories: The complex story and compound story. A compound story is one that can be split into multiple shorter stories. Unlike a compound story, a complex story is inherently large and cannot be disaggregated into a set of smaller stories. A story is identified complex due to uncertainty can be split into two smaller stories: an investigative story and another developing the new feature. For example, developers analyze a complex story: "A buyer can pay for the sale item with a credit card" and they have not done credit card processing ever; can break this into two stories:

1   Investigate payment processing using credit card - a spike
3   User can pay for the sale item with a credit card

In this case, the first story would be a spike. Adopted from XP, a spike is an investigative story identified for learning. Spike is timeboxed though they may be hard to estimate accurately. When complex stories are split in this way, always specify a timebox around a spike. Spike should be put in different iteration when possible and developing story in the following iteration. This allows easier estimation of developing story in case the spike is successful.

User story

User story is a technique borrowed from eXtreme Programming. A user story is written on an index card (aka note card) that acts as most visible representation of customer requirement rather than documenting them. Conversation is engaging the Customers and development team uses these story cards and then recorded in Confirmation.

Next Chapter #15 focuses on user stories in detail.

Grooming Techniques

Splitting

Simple splitting of larger BI into smaller BIs in progressive elaboration is as shown:

A little more complex scenario where intermediate stages are identified:

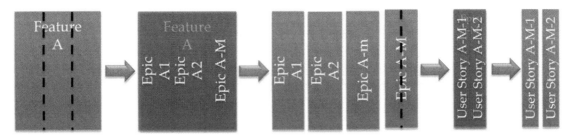

Figure 14-6: Splitting with intermediate steps

MoSCoW

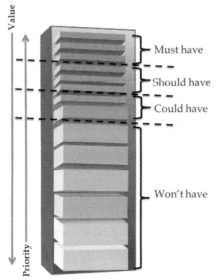

DSDM, another agile methodology, utilizes a release planning estimation technique known as **MoSCoW**.

MoSCoW is an acronym for:

- **M**ust haves - fundamental and critical features for the system
- **S**hould haves - important features but have short-term workarounds
- **C**ould haves - these could be left out of the release if time runs out
- **W**ould not haves - desired features but acknowledged as needed for following release

Figure 14-7: MoSCoW'ed Backlog

Team commits to the estimates which are still coarse. However, team commits to "Must haves" and makes effort for "Should haves" provided no time constraints encountered, and provided that there is still time, team would make best effort to complete "Could haves." The stories in these three stacks are considered for a release.

Summary

This chapter describes Backlog Items which constitute various types of Scrum Backlogs. These backlog items are regularly detailed, estimated, elaborated and prioritized based on their value. There are prevalent hierarchies of Backlog items types that enable easier management of Backlog Items. We briefly looked at the various techniques like Splitting and MoSCoW as prioritization techniques of Backlog.

Next chapter we describe 'user stories' – a Backlog item type that has gained wide acceptance from XP to Scrum communities over the years.

Chapter 15 Backlog Grooming

"Leadership is solving problems. The day soldiers stop bringing you their problems is the day you have stopped leading them. They have either lost confidence that you can help or concluded you do not care. Either case is a failure of leadership." - Colin Powell

Introduction

To maintain a DEEP Product Backlog, it is essential to groom it proactively. Managing Product Backlog is an activity that is at the heart of Scrum and can make difference between an outstanding, mediocre or failure project. The aspect that iterative development seeks to deliver value while Agile development delivers highest value speaks to this fact. Scrum projects focus on Backlog grooming to ensure that highest value Backlog Items are at the top, are elaborated in sufficient detail, so that they can be estimated and taken up for development early. Delivering highest value is dependent on how well a Product Backlog item at the top of the Product Backlog is detailed.

Grooming is an activity to detail the backlog top-down to ensure items are sufficiently detailed to be committed to; in a Sprint. This requires the items to be small enough for the Sprint as large items would not be good candidates and may have unknowns hidden.

Backlog Grooming for items more than 2-3 Sprints or over two releases is also undesirable in complete details. As spending effort so far in future could be a waste as priorities may change. On the other hand, only grooming to have just one Sprint worth of Backlog items is also undesirable as there is no scope if the team could take up more items within the Sprint. During planning meeting, the team seeks to understand enough stories that it could consider for the Sprint. This allows the team to also understand what could be the next set of stories to own if it finishes the items in Sprint Backlog early.

Backlog Grooming: A continuous activity

The Product Owner collaborates with stakeholders to identify the value of each product backlog item. The detail is defined using various factors like value, cost, ROI, details, and risks. Items are frequently added, deleted, updated, and moved to a different location in the Product Backlog based on their value.

Backlog Grooming involves four major sets of activities carried out top-down:

1. Creating Backlog items: Story Writing workshops and during the project
2. Refining Backlog Items: progressively elaborate details of Backlog Items
3. Estimating Backlog Items: Estimating effort level required for completing the backlog item
4. Prioritizing Backlog: Prioritizing Backlog items based on the estimates, EMV, risks, unknowns, and details

The Product Owner collaborates with stakeholders and Core team to groom the backlog. Anytime new information is available, backlog is prioritized JIT.

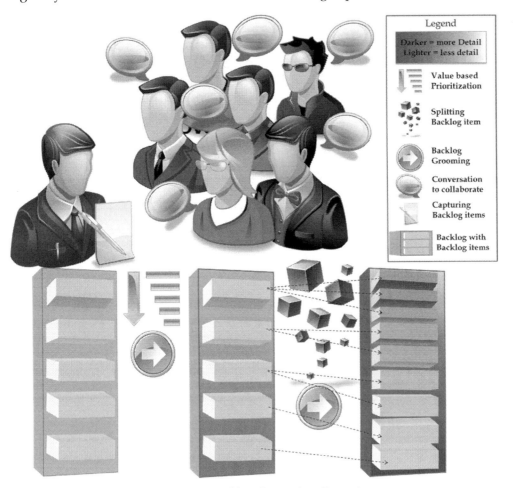

Figure 15-1: Backlog Grooming Overview

As shown here, the initial Product Backlog may just start with a list of backlog items which are then prioritized based on value. Then splitting of backlog items results in generating smaller sized backlog items. The top-down detailing results in the Product Backlog items on top to be detailed as they are of interest due to the inherent high value vested in them.

Prioritizing and splitting are continuous activities performed on Product Backlog to ensure high value items are detailed earlier and often.

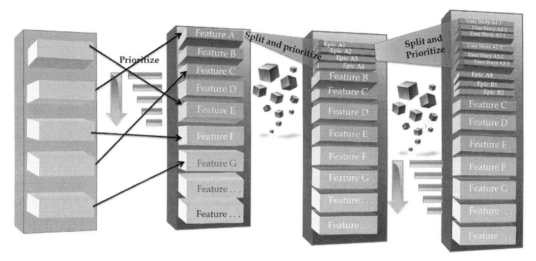

Figure 15-2: A Sample layout of Backlog stages during grooming session

Relative sizing is simpler and preferred than absolute sizing of effort and value. It is easier to know that Backlog item A is larger than Backlog item B than identifying exact effort level required for either. This aspect is further discussed in Chapter 16: Estimation and Planning.

Variety of steps in Backlog Grooming

Four major steps involved in Backlog Grooming are further illustrated here in Figure 15-3. Product Backlog is groomed with domain focus: Business domain and Solution Domain. First three activities are carried out in Business domains while the third activity can be carried out in Solution Domain. The fourth activity of prioritizing Product Backlog is comparatively lightweight and can be done even independently. Reviewing an independently prioritized Product Backlog is essential to understand the perspectives and considerations taken.

Figure 15-3: Four essential Backlog Grooming activities

Product Owner collaborates to various stakeholders for specific areas of their ownership in helping with refining of Backlog Items. For instance, Product Owner works with customer and end-users to determine MMFs, works with Marketing and sales team to derive EMVs for ROI analysis, Acceptance criteria, and runs pilot programs to seek further inputs. Product Owner collaborates with the Scrum Master and the Development team to collect information on effort estimates, any technical Backlog Item refinement, determines relationships between different Backlog items and associated risks/unknowns to further follow-up with appropriate owners. The Product Owner is constantly grooming the Product Backlog to fill in appropriate details.

Creating Backlog items

Backlog items are created initially in a Backlog/Story Writing workshop. These workshops are also conducted at regular interval during the project. The Backlog items are initially gathered during this session and then they are prioritized using techniques to derive MMFs/MVPs. Common techniques are: Innovation games, MoSCoW, and Kano Analysis. The backlog items are then prioritized with the identified values. This session may also be split into multiple sessions as the Product Owner may need to collect inputs from the Scrum Master and the Development Team regarding effort estimates and dependencies prior to prioritizing based on value. Stakeholders need to know the cost to identify value as well.

Figure 15-4: Writing Backlog items from user needs in Business domain

Refining Backlog Items

Adding details to Backlog Items is conducted during Refinement sessions. Scrum Framework uses progressive elaboration process where additional details are added to the Backlog items. The details for a backlog items are multi-facets and are needed to be of value to the customer. The refinement of Backlog Item includes: Detailing the description, parameters, functional and non-functional aspects, acceptance criteria, end-to-end navigation flow, its relationship with other backlog items, any unknowns to identify related risks, any compliance requirements, and so forth. Refinement of

Backlog Item at times allows the Backlog Item to be further split into smaller backlog items. Progressively elaborating and refining Backlog Items resulting in splitting into smaller Backlog Items provide inherent advantage as it is easier to estimate and quickly deliver small Backlog items than a large one. This also allows the MMFs to be optimized with essential high priority smaller Backlog Items to be grouped together and plan an effective delivery strategy.

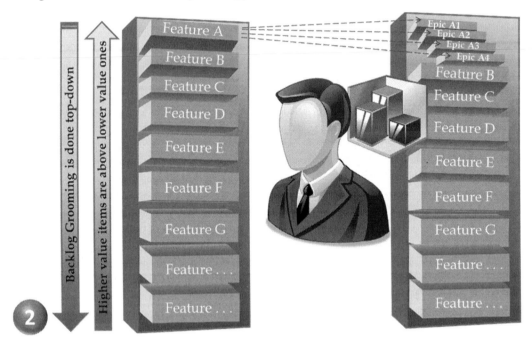

Figure 15-5: Refining (elaborating) Backlog items

Estimating Backlog Items

Estimating effort level required for developing and delivering valuable functionality corresponding to a backlog item. Effort estimates are done not just in planning session. The Product Owner can collaborate with the Scrum Master and the Development team in independent Backlog Grooming sessions where these details are discussed. The effort estimates provided can further feedback into Innovation games with the stakeholders to optimize MMFs and priorities. The Development Team needs refined Backlog items to be able to estimate accurately. The unknowns result in Spikes – experimental Backlog Items that need to be addressed fast-fail scenarios and test out various options and alternatives to discover and unveil the unknowns and test alternate solutions before the real value effort can be estimated. The Development

Team can split complex Backlog items that may be too large and also create composite Backlog items by combining many related small Backlog items for optimal delivery.

Figure 15-6: Estimating Backlog Items

Prioritizing Backlog

Prioritizing Backlog items based on the estimates, EMV, risks, unknowns, and details of Backlog items. This is the most essential activity and must be done at least once in Sprint. Prioritized Product Backlog is needed in Sprint Planning to ensure that the Scrum Master and The Development Team can help with the Sprint Planning for next Sprint.

Figure 15-7: Prioritizing Backlog based on Value

Backlog Grooming is recommended to be performed at twice the frequency than other Scrum ceremonies; once for each domain. The Product Owner performs major Backlog Grooming after Review ceremony to incorporate review inputs from the Stakeholders and the Team as well. This grooming session is essential as the next ceremony is the Planning ceremony where the Product Backlog must be DEEP enough.

Backlog Grooming Session

As is evident that these four activities occur in overlapping fashion where output from one activity results in input to another and the resulting output further feeds into the previous activity. Due to the complexity of this, Product Owner is the accountable to be the interface between the Business Domain and Solution domain.

Preparation for Grooming

Preparation to Backlog Grooming requires an up-to-date Product Backlog with agenda item to specific domain: Business domain or Solution domain.

Timebox

Backlog Grooming is arranged as timebox to keep from going overboard. The items are detailed top-down, split, then estimated sufficiently and finally prioritized. The first two activities take up the first half of the session where Brainstorming and generating insights and action items with unknowns are covered. In the later session, the items are estimated and the backlog is prioritized.

Attendees

Product Owner facilitates Backlog Grooming ceremonies. Business domain sessions include customers, end-users and stakeholders like marketing and sales teams and clients.

Inputs

Current Product Backlog and any new information or request for information discovered or collected in earlier reviews or planning sessions.

Value stream mapping

Value stream mapping in Product Backlog pertains to Business domain. While lean principles seek to ensure the development is efficient, here the focus is on business needs. Value stream mapping of user needs are performed to ensure that the valuable software helps the end-user in deriving optimal value with full set of functionality. MMF or MVP aspects play major role in this aspect. The whole is more than the sum of its parts – holds true as collective set of features to complete user tasks in a workflow can derive higher revenue than individual features which may still leave gaps in ability to achieve user goals.

Stakeholders' inputs

Customer and end-users provide much insight from the business domain. Input on the backlog items to detail them is essential.

Miscellaneous

During Product Backlog Grooming, many new unknowns, risks, constraints and product analysis action items may be identified. The Product Owner needs to ensure that these are captured on a Parking Lot and addressed sufficiently in an ongoing basis. Various members may also own some of the parking lots and it is essential to collaborate with the Product Owner to include any detail to keep the Product Backlog evolving and up-to-date. Progressive elaboration technique needs to be followed. The Product Owner continues to groom the Product Backlog even outside the grooming sessions. Grooming sessions allow brainstorming and generating insights to determine derived information to sufficient detail where the items can be split to sufficient size and appropriately estimated.

Outputs

DEEP Product Backlog where the current information is reflected top-down.

Summary

Product Backlog is a powerful artifact in Scrum Framework. Backlog grooming is one of the essential activities to keep the highest value software delivery to customer frequent and continuous. This chapter describes the concepts and details of Backlog Grooming.

Backlog Grooming is essential for the backlog items to be sufficiently estimated for consideration in the next Sprint. The Product Owner collaborates with the Team during the planning session. User stories enable this collaboration and allow the Team to converse and confirm the details. User stories are addressed in the next Chapter.

Section IV
Scrum Requirements
& User stories

Chapter 16 User stories

"Creativity is just connecting things. When you ask creative people how they did something, they feel a little guilty because they didn't really do it, they just saw something. It seemed obvious to them after a while. That's because they were able to connect experiences they've had and synthesize new things." – Steve Jobs

Introduction

XP, on the other hand, brings, specific to situation, effective practices to each of the areas where waterfall seems to fail. XP projects are story-driven projects which focus on three aspects of Card, Conversation, and Confirmation known as 3C's [JEFFRIES, 2001]. A user story is written on an index card (aka note card) which acts as most visible representation of customer requirement rather than document them. Conversation is engaging the Customers and development team uses these story cards and then recorded in Confirmation. Hence, the three aspects of Card, Conversation, and Confirmation are discussed next.

Card-Conversation-Confirmation

A user story addresses production functionality of value to the customer. A Customer could be a user, purchaser, or a stakeholder: someone with interest in the product. A user story has three aspects known as 3C's [JEFFRIES, 2001]:

1   A written description of the story that can fit a 3″ * 5″ index card or post-it note; later used for planning purpose and reminder for later conversation
2   Conversations that help refresh and flush out the details of the story
3   Acceptance criteria and documentation details to help determine the acceptance criteria for development; to know when the story is complete

Good user stories

A good story has six attributes designated by **INVEST** [Bill Wake, 2003]:[1]

---

[1] *Extreme Programming explored and Refactoring workbook* by Bill Wake 2003

❖ **Independent** - Dependency between stories causes prioritization and planning issues

❖ **Negotiable** - by developers and users; as they are not contracts or requirements that the software must implement

❖ **Valuable** to purchasers, users, or customers

❖ **Estimable** - developers, with domain and technical knowledge, are able to estimate the effort

❖ **Small** - Ultimately, story size is based on the team, its capabilities and technology in use

❖ **Testable** - stories are written to be testable; so developers can ensure when they finish coding

Three common reasons why a story may not be estimable are:

1   Developers don't have required domain knowledge
2   Developers don't have required technical knowledge
3   A large story or epic

User Roles and Personas

A user story is written in business terms by the customer, not in technical terms. It represents functionality that will be of importance and valued by the users. Connextra, one of the early adopters of Extreme Programming, incorporated roles into their stories by using a format template of three phases. This template for user stories is getting very popular industry-wide. The story template popular is:

I as a *<user role>*, I want *<function>*, so that I can *<business value>*

Alternatives to this template paraphrase similar layout and are as follow:

As a *<user role>*, I can *<what>*, so that I can *<why>*

As a *<type of user>*, I want *<capability>* so that *<business value>*

As a *<user type>*, I want to *<goal>* so that *<reason>*

This concept has also evolved from Unified Process where Use Case Modeling encourages the identification of Actors interacting with the product. Identifying user roles bring the product functionality in perspective as to how the end user intends to use it. This information is lost when long tedious, and wordy requirement documents are prepared in waterfall projects.

When we talk about the retail website to buy and sale products, we intend to know how the users intend to use the product or services. Thus, it is critical for us to get user's perspective to discover what their end goal is. We need to know what the users intend to do, what is the value driven features, what is their background, and when do they are driven to visit and so forth. Perhaps we are conversing about a user – Let's call him Sam - who likes to visit the website daily to find a great deal and is always on a lookout for a cool electronic gadget or Perhaps we are discussing about Pat who does not want to worry about managing a retail store and uses the site heavily to sale and track inventory of products. In essence, a user directly interacts with the system to derive some value. "A *company* is buying a product for employees to use" or "*someone* is purchasing the product for resale" are not good user roles. Hence, we can identify user roles for the retail website as:

❖ Buyer
❖ Seller
❖ Administrator

Role modeling steps

Role modeling steps are identified to identify a useful set of user roles as:

1   Brainstorm an initial set of user roles
2   Organize the initial set of user roles
3   Consolidate the user roles
4   Refine the user roles

If real users are on-site, it helps to discuss the stories and their values directly. However, when users are not easily accessible, these techniques provide substantial insight.

Brainstorm an initial set of users roles

This is done in a brainstorming session where the customer and as many developers and stakeholders gather around a white board with a stack of index cards. During the brainstorming session, everyone is encouraged to write as many user roles on index cards. No round robin or calling is done. Participants just write and paste the card with the new role on the white board and no discussion or evaluation is held during the brainstorm. This session is not timeboxed. However, rarely does it exceed fifteen minutes duration. Not all user roles need to be identified; yet we can get close enough. For retail website, an initial set of roles could be: Distributor, Dealer, Retailer, First time buyer, Seller, Buyer, Administrator, Power Seller, Deal Seeker, Gadget Seeker, and Frequent Buyer.

Figure 16-1: Initial set of user roles

Organize the initial set of user roles

Once the initial set of user roles, on index cards, is identified in the brainstorm session, these need to be organized. Organize the roles, the cards are moved around for related grouping and relationships. For overlapping roles, the cards are placed overlapping based on the degree of overlapping. If roles overlap little, the cards overlap little and if the roles overlap completely, then cards overlap yet show the user roles clearly. This activity can be completed in fifteen minutes. For retail website, it could be arranged as:

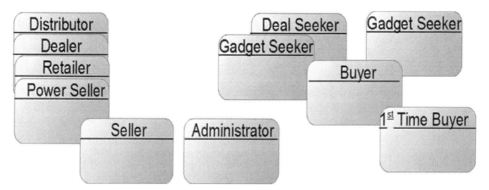

Figure 16-2: Organize User role set

Consolidate the user roles

Consolidating the user roles involve condensing the roles. First the complete overlapping cards are described by their writers. After a brief discussion, the equivalent roles are identified and consolidated in a single role. This activity can be completed within fifteen minutes.

Figure 16-3: Consolidate user roles

For retail website, Distributor, Dealer, Retailer, and Power Sellers are overlapping. These could be consolidated into one role: Power Seller. Though there appears to be an overlap between Deal Seeker and Gadget Seeker, the group decides that the experience could differ as Gadget seeker is searching for latest gadgets and cool features besides the deals; while Deal Seeker is seeking deals among different categories of products. First time Buyer could still be of importance to the team to customize the advertisements and suggestions based on the user preference and setup of user profile. This is to improve user's experience based on interests and recent searches and browsing on the website. Yet the group may add new user role: Inactive Buyer and Inactive Seller to represent a buyer and seller, respectively, who has not visited the site for 180 days or more and may need to be deactivated. Consolidated list of user roles for retail website would then be listed as shown in Figure 16-3.

Refine the user roles

Once consolidated and understanding the relationship between the roles, the roles can be modelled with attributes and details. A role attribute is a characteristic or behavior about the user that fulfill the role. Any information that differ one role from another can be a role attribute. This activity can be completed in fifteen minutes. Some of the attribute pertaining to retail website user roles are:

❖ The frequency at which the users utilize the site for transactions, searches, browsing, etc.
❖ The user's familiarity with the website layout and ease of use
❖ The user's primary goal of using the website
❖ The user's familiarity and usage of various features on the website

These above four steps could be done within the hour, no more.

A sample user role card for retail website:

User Role: Deal Seeker

Computer Savvy and adept at using the website. A frequent visitor and performing searches on various types of products, seeks cheapest deals of popular items and best sellers. Very familiar with navigation and searches frequently. Saves searches and sets email notifications for specific search criteria. Profile setup completed with contact details and credit card provided.

Figure 16-4: Sample User Role: Deal Seeker

Two additional Role Modeling Techniques

Personas

While identifying user roles is essential, identifying the user as a persona with various personality traits helps during user story discussions. A persona is an imaginary representation of a user role. Yet as close these personas are to the real users, it helps to understand how the user would be using the product and identify value features. For retail website, a Persona could be:

Persona: Sam – a Gadget Buyer

Sam is a real estate agent at Agile Reality Inc. - a premier real estate firm in the nation. He's worked for 10 years and likes to keep latest electronics gadgets, luxury cars, lives in an estate home, and is single with a strong interest in video games. Sam is a power user of computers and is web savvy. He is constantly like to upgrade his gadgets and appliances. He is working on becoming a CPA to expand his domain and make more income. He goes on vacation every month to exquisite places.

Figure 16-5: A sample Persona - Sam - Gadget Buyer

Extreme Characters

Another technique is to use extreme characters when considering a new product. For example, in case of retail website, an extreme character could be someone trying to sell products out of country to make higher profits, escape taxes, utilizing low shipping and handling cost, letting default transactions, no refund, and managing multiple accounts on the website.

Extreme characters are useful in leading to stories that may have been missed otherwise. They bring various important aspects of the system to consider. It is worth to experiment with extreme characters - especially ones who are notorious and do not like to follow the rules.

Advantages of User Stories

User stories provide many advantages over alternative approaches; such as[2]:

- ❖ User stories are perfect for planning; as it represents a function user would do in a single sitting
- ❖ User stories emphasize verbal conversation rather than written documentation
- ❖ User stories work well in an iterative development process
- ❖ User stories capture main concept while differing details until later when the customer has best understanding of what the users really need
- ❖ User stories are comprehensible by the customer and development team, both
- ❖ User stories encourage differing details; thus promoting continuous planning instead of planning upfront
- ❖ User stories support opportunistic design
- ❖ User stories promote participatory design
- ❖ User stories help build up tacit knowledge

User stories that are worked on in next few sprints should be small enough to be completed in single sprint. While ones that are further away can be left as epics of themes.

Summary

This chapter describes user stories – a concept borrowed from eXtreme Programming and is now commonly used in Scrum.

We shall understand further aspects of estimating user stories which results from the elaboration, refinement, and feeds into their prioritization.

---

[2] Details on each advantage of User story - Chapter 13 – *"User Stories Applied"* by Mike Cohn, an author, thought leader, and Agile evangelist.

Chapter 17 Agile Estimation

"Again, you can't connect the dots looking forward; you can only connect them looking backwards. So you have to trust that the dots will somehow connect in your future. You have to trust in something - your gut, destiny, life, karma, whatever. This approach has never let me down, and it has made all the difference in my life." - Steve Jobs

Introduction

Estimation involves effort estimates required to deliver a backlog item. Estimates measure complexity level and not delivery time. It is easier to estimate an item when compared to another item. For instance, it is easier to say that the complexity of item A is twice as that of item B while very hard to state how long it would take to deliver either items. This simplicity keeps estimating light weight and hence, relative estimations are preferred over absolute ones. Further it is necessary to identify that estimates are not commitments; as is normally understood. It is a planning technique and not deterministic in nature.

Measure helps identify capacity of work team can undertake and commit to finish in a timebox. For Sprints, team capacity is measured in story points for "done" stories that have been accepted during the Sprint review.

Estimating user stories

User stories are estimated based on the following approach:

- ❖ estimate can be updated when we have new information about a story
- ❖ estimate works for epic as well as small stories with different levels of precisions
- ❖ provides progress and remaining work insights
- ❖ imprecision in estimates applies using appropriate techniques like Fibonacci series.
- ❖ provide planning of release and sprint

The law of diminishing return states that it is very hard to exactly estimate a story. While sieving is a defined analogy, the size estimate differs for different individuals. Stories be estimated, with just sufficient time, but avoid analysis-paralysis.

Estimates are shared by the team even though it's best known that better estimates are provided by the ones developing the story. The estimates are not assigned by individuals for two reasons:

1   On agile teams, we don't know who would be assigned to a task on the story
2   estimates done by team may avoid any short-sightedness by individuals

The three common estimating techniques are:

1   *Expert opinion*; where expert relies on intuition or gut feel to provide an estimate (quick approach) e.g. Delphi technique
2   *Analogy*; where relative sizing against a set of relatively sized stories technique also known as *triangulation*
3   *Disaggregation*; where a story is split into smaller or more stories easier to estimate. This is similar to sieving analogy where the pebble be crushed/broken to smaller pebbles

Planning Poker

Planning poker is an estimation technique that combines all three estimation techniques viz. expert opinion, analogy, and disaggregation; and turns it into an interesting game for the team. In the beginning, all developers are provided a set of different size cards for estimation. Product Owner picks out the top story and discusses it with the development team. Developers can ask questions to gain clarity and understanding of the scope for the story. Then each of the developers selects a card reflecting their estimate and keeps it faced down. Then they turn over all cards at the same time. It is possible for them to diverge in estimation. Outliers then discuss their reasoning of estimating the story so. Then another round of estimate is done similarly and so forth until the convergence occurs. The goal is for the estimators to converge to a single estimate. However, at times the outlier agrees to the estimate from majority of developers. Seldom does it take more than three rounds. Point is to be reasonable instead of being precise in the estimates.

Planning poker has the following advantage over the individual estimation technique above:

❖   Planning poker results in multiple expert opinions from a cross-functional team from all disciplines in software development project

❖ It promotes team collaboration and collective discussion for higher accuracy as the user stories are often intentionally vague and context free

❖ Studies show that averaging individual estimates and estimates from group discussions are better. Planning poker promotes group discussion which leads to converging the individual estimates over the rounds

❖ Finally, planning poker is fun!

Minimum Scrum plan should contain: Vision and Product Backlog [SCHWABER, 2011]. Together they provide a Story Map; discussed in detail in Chapters 35 and 36.

Estimation techniques for user stories

There are three common types of estimation techniques for backlog items:

❖ Ideal days
❖ Ideal hours
❖ Affinity mapping

Story size estimate in ideal time

Stories can also be estimated in ideal time like ideal days or ideal hours. It is easier to estimate in ideal time versus elapsed or actual time. If we are asked to estimate how long a football match is, it'd be 4 quarters of 15 minutes each. This in ideal time is easy and accurate time period. While in actual time, there are many interruptions during the game and an average football game lasts for approximately 3 hours and could extend to as long as 4 hours. This actual time taken is referred to as actual hours. When working in ideal time, assumptions are:

1 The developer will only work on story estimated
2 Everything needed will be on hand from the start
3 There will be no interruptions or distractions during the development of the story from start to end

When estimating a story in ideal time, one aggregate estimate must be assigned to the story. For example, for a story, if designer will take 4 ideal hours of estimated effort, two programmers will take 3 hours of estimated effort each, one ideal hour for a DBA, and three ideal hours from a tester, then the estimate of the story would be 14 ideal hours (4 + 3 * 2 + 1 + 3). Do not provide individual estimates for the story written down in different colors or initials for team members. However, there are exceptions to this rule when we have resources that are not cross-functional and need to capture the estimates for each role on each story.

Ideal hour vs. actual hour

Ideal hour is defined as an hour of work duration where work can be performed without any interruption, impediments, distraction, or breaks. While actual hour is the time in reality where, besides performing tasks, activities include checking emails; having conversation; taking coffee breaks; reading documents; and preparing for meetings and discussions. At times, we see that team is bound to commit to ideal hours while management pushes on them if it falls below one. Story point, a brilliant introduced concept in Extreme Programming (XP), is used to also curtail that aspect.

We have personally experienced this on various projects. When we start with requirement analysis, discussions with customers, preparing a prototype, demo and follow-up discussions, getting details on user goals, and final delivery of simple product may take a month. Sometimes customer inquiries another independent consultant showing the end product as to how long it'd take him to develop this product. Everything is done and ready, so a response of couple of weeks raises customer and management expectations. Many projects have suffered due to such switching of context and feedback where difference between ideal hours and actual hours are not well understood. Management and leadership should be wary of this aspect.

Story points

User stories are estimated in *story points*. One great feature of story points is that a team can determine the criteria of story points based on their preference. A team can define a story point as ideal days, while another can define a story point as an ideal hour, and yet another team can define a story point to be an ideal pair programming hour which is actually two ideal man hours. Fractions are avoided when determining story points as it tends to complicate matters. Simplicity is the key. Thus, story points are represented as "Nebulous Units of Time, or NUTs"[3].

Story points provide a comparative reference to the effort for developing a story. If there are two stories with 2 story points assigned, it'd mean that they would take identical effort to develop. However, since different teams can identify their story point based estimation criteria differently, their performance cannot be measured based on the story points completed in each sprint or release. However, one or more sprints or releases within a project for the same team can be compared with another on the project. A story point defined for a project must stay as such for the life of the project. Changing the definition would distort the release management. Team members define this criteria based on their preference.

Story size estimate in Story points

Story points are relatively sized. The raw values assigned are unimportant. *The relative values are important.* Due to relative sizing, a story assigned two story points should be twice the size (where size is a combination of the effort, complexity, risk associated, etc.) of the story assigned one story point. Hence, the relative values identify the amount of effort required to develop the story. The relative sieve size is of importance and not the specific magnitude of each sieve net!

Story points vs. Ideal time

Estimating stories in story points instead of ideal time is favorable as:

1. Story-points help derive cross-functional behavior
2. Story-point estimates hold as they are based on relative sizing
3. Story-points are a pure measure of size
4. Estimating in story points typically is faster
5. My ideal days are not your ideal days; for example, an expert developer could finish a story in 3 ideal days while another average developer would take 5 days.

While estimating stories in ideal days instead of story points estimation is favorable as:

---

[3] Joshua Kerievsky on *Extreme Programming yahoo group*, August 5th, 2003

1   Ideal days are easier to explain outside the team
2   Ideal days are easier to estimate at first
3   When team cannot accept a benefit if separating estimate of size and duration
4   When the team is struggling with estimating, based on large sizes and ambiguities. Affinity estimation could be more suitable here. For instance, T-shirt sizes: XL-Extra-large, L – Large, M – Medium, and S – small. Later, refinement and splitting could allow to gradually switchover to story points.

Advantage of Effort based estimating

Hence, estimating in story points completely separates the estimation of effort from the estimation of duration. For example, For a 100 story point estimate, for product to finish the project in 5 sprints, an average velocity of 20 points is needed. However, if the team only achieves 10 story points, do not go back to re-estimate all the stories to twice the size. Even if the team doubles the size of stories; the total sum of all stories will now be 200 points and it'd still take 10 sprints instead of 5 sprints (100 stories/10 points per sprint).

Normal variance vs. Special variance

Other interesting concept for second half of Scrum Planning session:

Estimates of effort vary per individual - Just as a professional runner vs. new athlete learning to run would have difference. Similarly, someone experienced in skills, knows the problem domain well, or familiarity with technology will have edge over others. Even within these three categories, there would be differences. Thus, the estimation should be based on ownership of various tasks and ownership of the tasks to derive better estimates - even planning poker can work well if owners are earlier identified.

This is especially true, if a new member joins a team that is in Norming or Performing stage. The new member would take time to get on board and starts performing at the level others are performing.

Caution: Team should be consistent and any new member should be brought in with that perspective.

Concern by Product Owner and stakeholders: The same story would take different level of effort even though it could be comparable to other stories with different effort. In order to keep consistency with norm, it helps to identify the effort-level of new resource as low as it includes learning curve. Thus, the team capacity as average/person would drop even though team could be expected to deliver consistent velocity. Thus, in practice it is seen that sometimes the team velocity either stays consistent or even drops. This is caused due to special variance as team pulls in efforts to bring the new member up-to-speed.

Thus, even though the story points would be consistent, the effort level required for tasks would be different based on ownership and could reflect differences in the total of effort for cumulative set of tasks to complete the story. This is expected to converge over the sprints as all team members perform and KT enables them to optimize their individual efforts. Normally, it has been seen that it takes 3-4 Sprints for team to become more consistent. Planning poker becomes more effective at this point as it starts to match the actual effort!

Agile estimation - JIT with retrospection on planning aspects (top-down)

Say that in Product Backlog the epics and stories are estimated with effort of 100 story points each.

While backlog grooming and planning sessions, if an epic of 100 story points breaks into a collection of stories (say 7) of 50 points each, then the epic totals to 350 story points. Thus, all stories of comparable size need to be increased to 350 points else the Burndown or Burnup charts will show skewed aspects.

Further, as spikes simplify the solutions, the level of effort would change based on findings and reduced risks. Thus, a risk-based backlog needs to be adjusted. A backlog with no risk identified would still need to be revised to reflect the new effort estimates as more information is now available.

For instance, Story A - split into Spike A1 and sub-stories A2 to An - Spike A1 could be say 5SP, and then A2 to An could be 1 Story Point - This would also reflect the estimates more accurately

Planning is indispensable and backlog needs to be groomed regularly to reflect the estimate periodically.

Summary

This chapter describes agile estimation techniques and their respective advantages. It is essential to understand this for effective planning.

Agile planning utilizes estimates and team capacity to deliver these in a Sprint for schedule planning. Thus, it is essential to grasp the aspect for sprint planning which escalates to feed into higher planning layers.

Chapter 18 Team Velocity

"Whenever the work is itself light, it becomes necessary, in order to economize time, to increase the velocity." - Charles Babbage

Introduction

Velocity is a measure of a team's progress rate. At the end of sprint, team reviews and calculates the velocity as the sum of story points of completed stories. There are no partial story points to claim for incomplete stories at the end of the Sprint. **It is either 100 percent or zero percent!**

When viewing velocity, it is always best to use a range or average value. Velocity is only a single term used in Scrum to help derive schedule. Velocity is taken as metaphor from physics. Considering velocity as an independent term is a common mistake. It is not independent and is rather just one parameter of a more expanded metaphor. Let's consider this metaphor in proper perspective in detail. When driving from point A (start) to point B (destination), there are various factors acting as expanded metaphors like:

- ❖ Route from point A to point B which is the complete scope to be traversed
- ❖ Types of routes for example, local versus highway or interstate which is the type of domain
- ❖ traffic lights and stop signs (unknowns, constraints and risks),
- ❖ time of day (technology, skills, business domain or market trends)
- ❖ time of day (rush hour vs. non-rush hour)
- ❖ state of traffic like traffic jam due to accidents (external factors like recession, job cuts, corporate culture)
- ❖ weather conditions (rain causes everyone to slow down
- ❖ Icy conditions, snow, torrent rains, and/or sleet increase chances of accidents, or at least cause bumper to bumper drives, etc.(external factors like market conditions and pressures)
- ❖ Number of lanes (parallel development routes – cross-functional teams and skilled/motivated professionals)
- ❖ Velocity is the combination of speed and direction towards the destination

When travelling to a known destination, it is easier to give an average time or use a range than trying to find an absolute time. This is common sense. Asking and demanding to provide an exact value and holding the other party to that deadline is immaturity; yet it is a common practice.

A travel of 10 miles on highway is much faster than travelling on local road where there are traffic lights in every other block. These traffic lights need much effort and are time consuming. Just as not every traffic light turns green it is futile to expect every risk and unknown to just be resolved on its own. Effort and time are required.

Not every team member is skilled to the same level. It pays to have skilled professionals in the long run to get the job well done – efficiently and effectively. When trying to run two athletes: an Olympic runner and an average high school student would not give equal performance. Similarly, skilled and novice professionals would not perform equally. Even same person on two different projects with different environment, domain, skills requirements, technology, or business domain shows different performance levels. Comparison between two teams when any of these factors differ is like comparing apples and oranges. The other metaphors should be compared.

Our experience shows that just as 10 miles of local took us 35 minutes while 25 miles of highway also took us 35 minutes; they are like metaphors for two very different projects. Local route represents a project that has a lot of unknowns, constraints and risks. These factors cause interruptions and delays. Interstate route appears to move fast yet even the traffic patter could differ during the different time of day. When a project has heavy turnover due to recession or reorganization, this is evident. Agile encourages keeping the development team for the whole project for that matter.

Apply the complete metaphor and keep the navigating the route perspective with different factors as metaphors when analyzing schedule. This would allow you to understand the complete picture. It helps to look at team velocity as a range or average pertaining to a specific environment.

Benefit of velocity

Further, velocity corrects any estimation errors. Over a few sprints, team's velocity prevails over estimated velocity or predictions. Velocity is not desired or enforced. It starts as an initial estimate. However, it stabilizes when the team runs a few sprints. While the estimate could be 25 points, if the team's velocity at the end of sprint is 20, then team's velocity is 20 story points. The team cannot be criticized for its velocity. For example, a team of estimated velocity of 15 story points is expected to deliver total of 120 story points in eight sprints. However, when the team runs a few sprints, the velocity achieved is ten story points. This means that the team will deliver in 12 sprints; instead of 8 sprints.

Also, two teams within the organization cannot be compared on the velocity as the raw values assigned to stories are meaningless and only the relative values count.

Initial Velocity

Initial velocity can be determined in any one of these three ways:

1   Use velocity from past or previous project
2   Execute a sprint and use the velocity of that sprint
3   Estimate a velocity based on specific criteria (For this, road trip metaphor helps)

Each of these is applicable in specific situations. Remember the various metaphors that work beside velocity as it can help you in using the best strategy. Even in the best possible scenario, it would be harder to specify exact time or effort it would take to complete any project. It would be like saying that we would over 35 miles in precisely 42 minutes and 21 seconds. That could be precisely wrong and a recipe for disaster.

If the project is identical in all respects, it is like taking the same route as taken in the past. Use historical values in this case as the current project is identical to the project whose historical value from another identical project.

Running sprint is good for new project with new set of parameters. However, as experienced, little is known in the beginning of the project, team may be new to the project and building on the tacit knowledge, the customer and users may seek many changes, may not be easily available, and other factors. Expect the team to learn as it becomes familiar with the business domain and pick up velocity later. Uncertainty and ambiguity is high in the beginning so continue to use average velocity from past sprints instead of taking precise values.

Guessing at velocity should be done based on specific criteria that can be supported. However, this can be done based on the Estimating user stories exercise covered earlier. If we identify the ideal hours, then we need to identify how many actual hours would it take to do an ideal hour worth of work. Since the sprint duration is known, it can be used to derive the initial velocity. For example, if we estimate that an ideal hour of work can be done in 2 actual man-hours. Story points are defined as one point for four ideal hours. Then, for a sprint of two weeks (10 actual days), we can cover for a team of 5 developers, total of 80 * 5 = 400 actual hours which is equivalent to 200 ideal hours, which in-turn is equivalent to 50 story points. Hence, the initial velocity would be guessed as 50 story points.

Calculating Velocity

Velocity is the number of story points the development team delivers at the end of a sprint. At the end of a sprint, team delivers stories to the customer. Story points are assigned to user stories. Hence, velocity is defined as the sum of story points of the stories completed by the team. For example, a team completes the following stories for the sprint:

Story	Story points	Status
Story A	6	Finished
Story B	7	Finished
Story C	2	Finished
Story D	4	Not Finished
Story E	4	Finished
Story F	6	Half finished
Story G	0	Not started

The velocity for the sprint would be sum of the story points of each "completed" story. Hence, the velocity (implied measurement unit: story points) would be: 6 (Story A) + 7 (Story B) + 2 (Story C) + 4 (Story E) = 19 story points. Only completed stories count. Even half-finished story does not count. In above case, 3 stories were completed: Story A, Story B, Story C, and Story E. Another instance, find the velocity of the sprint for the following outcome of Sprint review:

Story	Story points	Status
Story A	0	Finished

Story B	7	Half finished
Story C	0	Finished
Story D	6	Not finished
Story E	3	Finished

The velocity for the sprint is: 0 (Story A) + 0 (Story C) + 3 (Story E) = 3 story points. In above case, 3 stories were completed: Story A, Story C, and Story E.

Sometimes, knowing the definition of story points would add further complexity. For example, if team identifies that an ideal day is one story point. Then , after the sprint review, what is the measured velocity and how many ideal hours of effort completed for below case?

Story	Story points	Tasks ideal hours completed	Status
Story A	0	0	Finished
Story B	7	6	Half finished
Story C	0	0	Finished
Story D	6	5	Almost finished
Story E	3	3	Finished

Again, though the effort ideal-hours completed is: 0+6+0+5+3 = 14 ideal hours of effort, the velocity is still 3 story points as earlier: 0 (Story A) + 0 (Story C) + 3 (Story E).

In next sprint, what is the velocity and ideal task hours completed based on outcome from the review:

Story	Story points	Tasks ideal hours completed	Status
Story B	7	1	Finished
Story D	6	1	Finished

Story E	4	4	Finished
Story F	0	0	Finished
Story G	1	1	Not finished
Story H	2	1	Half finished
Story I	3	2	Finished

Story I assigned story points and task hours are not a typo. It was to identify that story points are just an estimate. The team may take longer or shorter at times. Sometimes teams go and revisit the Story points for such case. However, there are many cases seen in real projects where the customer accepts a story as it meets the "done" criteria, more insight during the review, or some other reason.

Here the velocity for the sprint would be: 7 (Story B) + 6 (Story D) + 4 (Story E) + 0 (Story F) + 3 (Story I) = 20 story points.

However, remember that story points are estimates and can be updated based when something new is discovered. Here, new discovery is the fact that the story took 2 ideal hours, hence, the story would have been updated to 2 story points. Then the velocity would be 19 story points based on this new realization. Yet it has not occurred as may be 1 hour of ideal hour work worth task may have been completed in one of the earlier sprints.

Ideal hours of task effort completed is: 1(Story B) + 1(Story D) + 4(Story E) + 0(Story F) + 1(Story G) + 1(Story H) + 2(Story I) = 10 ideal hours.

Management is always excited when they here that we have made substantial improvement in our process. This misinterpretation creeps into velocity analysis where we have not even introduced complex matters, as will be the case later. Here, savvy folks can claim substantial improvement to have completed 20 story points with merely 10 ideal hours of effort vs. previous sprint with just 3 story points with 14 hours of ideal task hours.

Hence, even comparing velocity between sprints is not as clear indicator of progress. Normally this aspect is not addressed, yet it is of interest for a serious practitioner.

Planned vs. Actual velocity

To track deviation from predicted path, it helps to track actual velocity against planned velocity for different sprints of a release. This can be shown on the following scale:

Velocity type	Sprint 1	Sprint 2	Sprint 3	Sprint 4	Sprint 5
Planned	5	4	3	5	8
Actual	6	4	3		

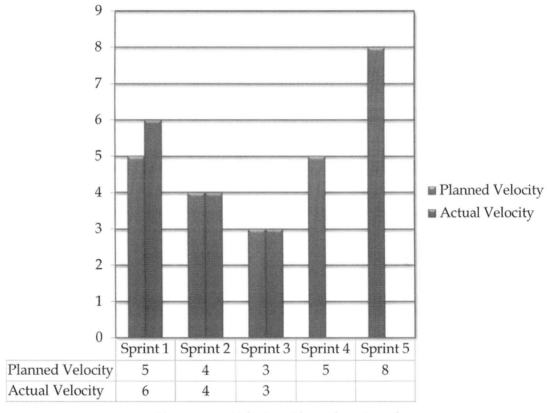

	Sprint 1	Sprint 2	Sprint 3	Sprint 4	Sprint 5
Planned Velocity	5	4	3	5	8
Actual Velocity	6	4	3		

Figure 18-1: Velocity - Planned vs. Actual

In Figure 17-1, Sprint 4 is currently in progress and hence, the estimates are known and actual velocity will be determined after the Sprint Review ceremony. The team would be misleading if using the cumulative planned and actual story points is used to specify that they are exceeding planned velocity and could move up the delivery date. For this they need either: the cumulative story points graph or the velocity graph.

While Mike Cohn, an author, thought-leader, and Agile evangelist, refers to the velocity graph, it is not needed; as velocity graph can be derived from the cumulative story points graph and vice versa!

The cumulative story points help compare the planned vs. actual progress for team to report progress.

Cumulative User Story Points type	Sprint 1	Sprint 2	Sprint 3	Sprint 4	Sprint 5
Planned	5	9	12	17	25
Actual	6	10	13	-	-

Deriving Schedule

While story points and ideal days help with the relative estimation of effort of a user story and deriving team velocity, velocity can be utilized in deriving schedule. Normally, other texts follow an assumption that there are no holidays, vacations, sick days or unanticipated events in life. So, they propose that a team attains consistent velocity after a few Sprints. This is hardly a reality as observed. Projects have unexpected occurrences all the time. While not all can be anticipated, incorporating the effect of team calendar can provide better estimates when seeking out a planned velocity.

Figure 18.2 illustrates an example where planned velocity was identified for a team using team calendar and team's consistently high velocity of 40 story points from the past. As is anticipated, Sprint 4 and 5 are impacted due to X-mas and New Year holidays. Similarly, there can be other external factors, like:

- ❖ Vacations, holidays, sick days and personal days
- ❖ Spikes and risk stories to address uncertainties, constraints, and risks
- ❖ Events that demand time for team like tradeshows, events, and reorganization
- ❖ External dependencies on other teams, operations, and technology

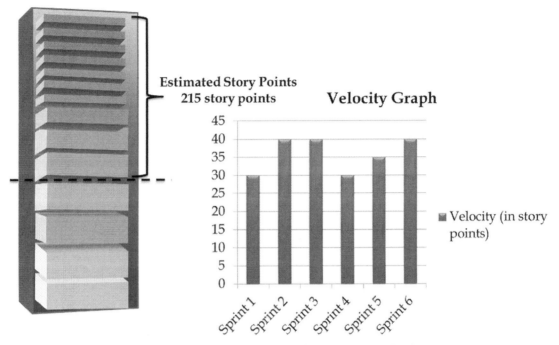

Figure 18-2: Estimating total points across Sprints

Tracking Velocity on Product Burndown Chart

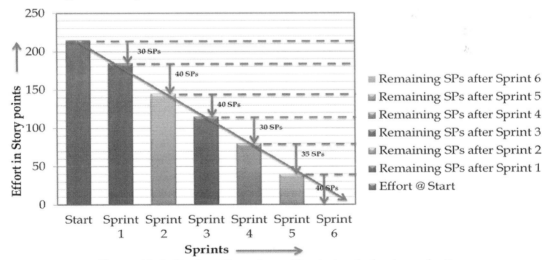

Figure 18-3: Product Burndown Chart - tracked using velocity

In Figure 18-3, the total remaining story points for Figure 18.2 are reflected in Burndown chart above. The remaining story points reduce with every sprint. Another graph shows planned vs. actual velocity driven Burndown Chart; as illustrated in Figure 18-4.

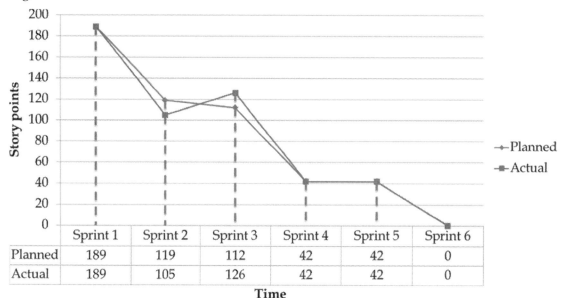

	Sprint 1	Sprint 2	Sprint 3	Sprint 4	Sprint 5	Sprint 6
Planned	189	119	112	42	42	0
Actual	189	105	126	42	42	0

Figure 18-4 Product Burndown Chart: planned vs. actual

Reflecting Velocity on Product BurnUp Chart

Figure 18-4 shows same information in BurnUp chart where the product release is shown over six Sprints. The velocity in each Sprint is accumulated and at the end of sixth Sprint, 215 story points worth of progress has been made.

Velocity is here expressed in terms of story points. The velocity of each sprint is just accumulated with every consecutive Sprint timeline to report the total accumulated progress. This is a basic BurnUp chart to grasp initial concept.

The BurnUp graph becomes complex with changing scope and backlog grooming updates with refining backlog items, splitting, value prioritization and so forth. The concept is expanded further in chapter 20 – Information Radiators.

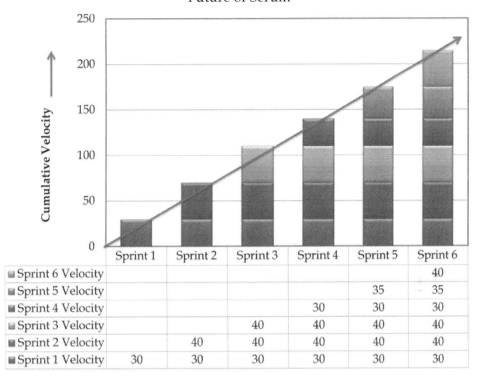

	Sprint 1	Sprint 2	Sprint 3	Sprint 4	Sprint 5	Sprint 6
▪ Sprint 6 Velocity						40
▪ Sprint 5 Velocity					35	35
▪ Sprint 4 Velocity				30	30	30
▪ Sprint 3 Velocity			40	40	40	40
▪ Sprint 2 Velocity		40	40	40	40	40
▪ Sprint 1 Velocity	30	30	30	30	30	30

Release BurnUp Chart

Figure 18-5: Product BurnUp Chart - tracked using velocity

Common challenges in determining team velocity

It is a common misconception to use same value as team velocity value for planning of future Sprints. Experience has shown that such assumption leads to constant variance. It is essential to look at two major aspects of such variance:

1. Team calendar: When the team members are on
2. Domain knowledge pertains to Business as well as technical domain
3. Uncertainties and unknowns resulting in Spikes

It is better to identify an average velocity with percentage deviation or simply a minimum and maximum range instead of a precise value. When it is not possible to precisely identify the time it would take to take a road trip to a frequently travelled destination, there is no reason to expect it for a complex project.

Misuses of Velocity

There are many misuses of velocity prevalent in the industry. Most are generated due to limited understanding of velocity as a standalone metaphor and not considering all other parameters where schedule itself is a metaphor of a road trip. Some of the common ones are:

1. To compare velocity of one team to that of another team to establish credibility
2. To expedite the schedule
3. To show greater performance gain
4. Trying to measure relative sizing on absolute scale
5. Misunderstanding the effort level to demand overtime
6. Estimates taken as contract terms or set in stone
7. Expecting teams to maintain velocity in new business domain
8. Expecting team to take on additional responsibilities
9. Multi-tasking and expecting velocity to increase over time
10. Letting go the essential aspect of sustainable pace

These are common misuses and hampers team growth during the execution phase. The Team provides estimates where two user stories of 8 points may be comparable. However, these do not need to be identical in their individual demand of time, skills, personnel, etc. While Scrum seeks to incorporate change, overloading the effort basis on past measures result in overtime and results in technical debt. The user story delivered should be of full quality, not partial quality incurring technical debt. Technical debt is the gap in quality of the deliverable product.

Adjusting velocity in each Sprint

Estimates from planning are best when looking at the stories in Product Backlog of unfinished stories. There is a tendency of Product Owners, Scrum Master and the Development Team to look at finished stories to compare the new user stories. We learned it from our experiences that such estimation is inaccurate as the new story may have unknowns while the 'done' story has all unknowns uncovered and in hind-sight may not have been so easy.

Summary

This chapter describes estimation techniques for Backlog Items in user stories and Ideal time units, and schedule planning using velocity. These are essential aspects and should be considered as tools to provide foresight for planning.

When the tools are misused to cause undesirable impact resulting in overtime, burn-out of team members; it normally results in technical debt. Technical debt is described in the next chapter.

Chapter 19 Technical Debt

"Wilt thou seal up the avenues of ill? Pay every debt as if God wrote the bill."
- Ralph Waldo Emerson

Introduction

Technical debt [CUNNINGHAM, 1992] is the lack in quality of deliverable. When software of lower quality is delivered, the customer feels a direct impact. This results in lowering customer satisfaction as the customer fails to realize full potential value of the delivered software. The customer may seek for alternative ways to meet the needs, first with the use of the low quality product if there is perceived value and then later seeking another product in the market that address the need and has the desired quality as well.

Agile Triangle identified that quality is intrinsic and should not be compromised. Any compromise of quality affects the success rate of the product. Technical debt is a reflection of missed quality goals and must be met to ensure retaining customer.

Technical debt is not due to loss of process, practices or development resources. These factors may act as contributing agents to technical debts but they are not technical debt in themselves.

Need to pay Technical debt

Delivering valuable software frequently and quickly to the customer is the highest priority. This may result in some compromise on quality. This lack of quality is referred to as Technical debt. Just as any debt accrues interest, technical debt also accrues interest and result in reduction in value and if not paid time, loss of value.

Building software on top of low quality has inherent impact. This results in the quality to be compromised and makes it harder to go back and fix the code. The longer technical debt stays, more it impacts the quality of existing and newly added functionality.

There are instances where the refinement of Product Backlog also brings forth information that needs us to inspect-and-adapt; requiring the change of direction. When the Development team fails to change its direction and continues to move forward, ignoring the new information, technical debt accrues and impacts overall value of delivered software. This type of technical debt may not have resulted from deliberate effort. Yet it needs to be addressed timely.

Last Responsive Moment (LRM) as discussed before shows this in direct relation with technical debt. When technical debt is not taken care off and farther we go from the last responsive moment, harder it becomes to fix the causes, debt increases and thus, requires more rework cost. Figure 18-1 shows the relationship of rework required from both cases of technical debt – too early implementation and then failing to change the direction and too late after much is known. As early information is known, it is imperative that the debt is paid.

It is hard to identify LRM looking forward. It is easier to plan with hindsight in this case. We discussed couple of strategies to help with responding to making decisions at last responsive moment. Below graph helps identify proper response based on the cost it would take to respond and possible influence and impact.

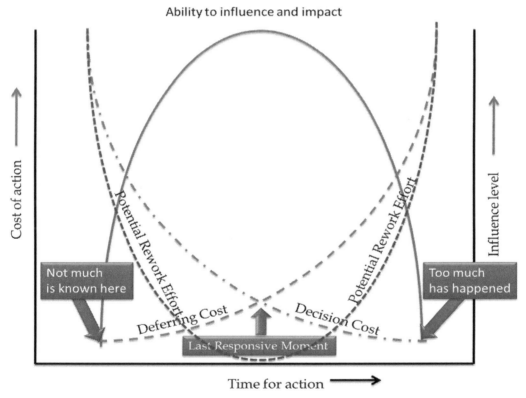

Figure 19-1: Technical Debt - Rework Cost relation with Last Responsive Moment

Even in traditional Waterfall development, it is known that every time a fix needs to be made, the later it is addressed, the higher the cost. The cost increases by a magnitude at every successive phase. So, if something takes $1 to fix at analysis would take $10 in design phase, $100 in development and $1,000 in test phase to fix. The cost of fixing early is not just the effort but also the time spent. Fixing early allows the time and effort to be utilized efficiently for value delivery.

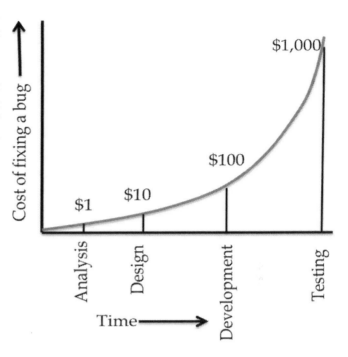

Figure 19-2: Technical Debt - Cost of fixing a bug increases exponentially in time

Similarly in Agile software development, this is reflected where longer it takes to pay back the debt, harder it is to fix and higher the cost. It is essential to address technical debt as early as possible. This approach, to pay off any residual technical debt early, enhances agility, simplicity and encourages intrinsic quality. Just as interest accrues on debt and if not paid timely, the interest becomes additional debt and cycle goes on.

It is a realized fact in agile software development that

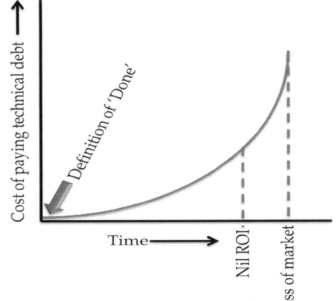

Figure 19-3: Effect of Technical debt over time

when quality is compromised, the following effects are visible:

- ❖ Loss of Simplicity: Simplicity is lost as the code tends to become spaghetti code and harder to change as new features are added on the existing design and code
- ❖ Loss of agility: The resulting design and architecture introduces inflexibility and agility to change direction as time passes and quality is not upheld
- ❖ Workarounds: Instead of deriving optimal design, the new code is required to circumvent to avoid being tied to the buggy code
- ❖ Spaghetti code: The design becomes convoluted and coding becomes complex in time
- ❖ Bugs multiply over time: The rate of bugs seem to escalate over time as the buggy code starts to show its effect
- ❖ Longer Development cost: Cost increases to address resulting bugs
- ❖ Longer Development Time: It takes longer to code simple functionality
- ❖ Increase in complexity: The code becomes harder to maintain
- ❖ Loss in value: ROI continues to reduce as more time is spent on trying to fix bugs arising due to underlying software. These bugs are symptoms and the root-cause need to be fixed
- ❖ Market loss: Delays in delivery to customer due to longer development efforts have a direct impact as it becomes harder to respond to external stimuli
- ❖ Customer satisfaction declines: Customer needs remain unaddressed while the team is focused on working around technical debt to meet the current demands. In the long run, this reflects with declining satisfaction levels and loss of market share.
- ❖ Infected sick software: The quality weakens as the customer starts to see the loss of value over time when the quality is not upheld
- ❖ Individuals and interactions downfall: Finally all these results in people to feel frustrated and seek other avenues. Resources turnover increases, blame game becomes common, and losses escalate

Types of Technical debts

There are types of technical debts that need to be addressed as soon as new information is available. These include:

- ❖ Ill-defined definition of 'done'
- ❖ Incorrect analysis
- ❖ Predictable yet incorrect design
- ❖ Complex code
- ❖ Insufficient IV&V
- ❖ Gaps in Acceptance criteria
- ❖ Failure to understand the needs

Causes of Technical debt

While initially any lack in quality could be the result of faster development, soon this starts to slow down the successive Sprints. The common causes of technical debt are:

- ❖ Ill-defined definition of 'done': Definition of done needs to be well defined to avoid any loss of acceptance criteria to allow technical debt to accrue
- ❖ Resisting to be agile when new information is revealed
- ❖ Pressure to deliver early: time constraints and market demand for early delivery is probably the most common cause
- ❖ Pressure to realize velocity: At times, the team may need to realize story points to upkeep the show of high performance or expectations
- ❖ Previous Technical debt: Debt builds on more debt over time as new features are developed on current debt
- ❖ Predictable upfront work: In empirical process, uncertainties are common. When team builds a feature around uncertainties, it is necessary to realize the unknowns and the need to be able to revisit when information becomes available and need change. Agile planning incorporates the need to adapt plans based on new information.
- ❖ Gold plating: At time teams try to put in features that may not have been desired. This is an attempt to excite customers as favors. These may normally result in a quick and dirty fixes which were not part of planning and reflect back later as technical debt.
- ❖ Limited skilled resources and processes: These limit the ability if time is not provided to learn the domain knowledge and skills required. Tedious processes also result in frustration and shortcuts become common escape.

❖ Reduce testing: Addressing testing to cover limited scope lets bugs escape and come back to haunt as customers' dissatisfaction.

❖ Skip testing: Eliminating testing is failure to meet definition of 'done.'

❖ Creating new Backlog items for defects: There is a common tendency to create new Backlog items as defects to be handled later. A better approach is to create Backlog Item related to unknowns so when new information is available, it can be addressed. Defects have the tendency to stay lower in priority and infect system wide over time.

❖ Insufficient Backlog grooming: Last but not the least, a Backlog not DEEP passes on the work and resulting technical debt from the Product Owner to the Development Team. This results in rise of cost by many magnitudes.

Summary

This chapter describes technical debt to identify the serious impact on the value-driven approach. It is essential to pay off technical debt as soon as it is visible.

Chapter 20 Information Radiators

"Technology is nothing. What's important is that you have a faith in people, that they're basically good and smart, and if you give them tools, they'll do wonderful things with them."
- Steve Jobs

Introduction

Information Radiators are used to communicate progress in highly visible area. These mainly consist of big charts and graphs placed on corridors for visibility. Passersby are able to see these and can quickly know the progress. Further it reduces constant inquiry to the development team to report their progress. Various tools now support dashboards which provide similar aspect as stakeholders visit the site and can see the graphs on project dashboard to give them quick insight into team's progress.

Team vision statement

"Vision is the art of seeing what is invisible to others." - Jonathan Swift

Vision statement expresses a desired goal in one sentence statement that describes a clear, precise, and inspirational sustainable change resulting from an entity's effort. Some examples of real vision statements are:

Human Rights Campaign: *"Equality for everyone."* **(Vision in three words)**

Feeding America: *"A hungry-free America."* **(four words)**

The characteristics of vision statements are: **CLIMB**

1. **Clear**: Vision statement needs to be distinct and easy to understand.
2. **Lasting**: Vision statement needs to identify a lasting desirable goal – something that is sustainable and motivational.
3. **Inspirational**: Vision needs to instill with worth, purpose and value.
4. **Memorable**: It should be easy to remember and make its mark as soon as it is introduced.
5. **Brief**: It should be easy to grasp quickly. Concise and to the point statement is effective.

A vision statement could change but only by a better one to provide CLIMB to greater height. A leader generates commitment to an organization's vision. This requires sharing the vision in ways that matters to people. People in the organization must believe in the vision and to pass it on to others. Thus, vision needs to be embraced vertically in a hierarchy as well as horizontally among peers. Thus, the energy flows and stays connected with constant open channels in an organization. This builds teams, in-turn building the complete organization as a whole.

To create a vision, a leader takes on the following roles:

Observer: Be an astute observer of the surroundings. Immerse into watching, listening, inquiring, seeking, questioning, probing, brainstorming, discussing, generating, gathering and collecting information in organized manner.

Reflector: Respond to the flow of information with internal reflection. Connect the events in life, work, organization, and social and economic. Reflect with your own stories, lessons, and metaphors to help build the vision. Seek the end goal in mind. It is hard to get others to drive, when you cannot show them light at the end of the tunnel.

Writer: Be a writer before becoming a spokesperson for your vision. This is an essential step. Many visions are shot down as the writings are skipped. With past pace and changing facets, it's easy to skip writing. Writing down the vision help assert the ability to CLIMB to the goal.

Speaker: As a final step, share the motivation and inspiration you get from the vision. This is contagious. It helps to inspire and motivate others. Thus, building trust, support and acceptance, the vision spreads through like wildfire.

Sometimes elevator statement is taken as vision which work as short term goals and phase out as soon as the product is outdated. A true vision does not.

Team calendar

Team calendar helps with strategic and tactical alignment of team goals. The calendar helps team during the Sprint execution with tracking the commitment and how a given Sprint velocity may be impacted. Also, time-off needs to be accounted for vacations, holidays, etc. These have direct impact on team configuration and hence, on the velocity.

Working agreements / Ground rules

Working agreements are essential to maintain a stable environment. The core team works together to come up with the working agreements at release and higher levels. At Sprint level, the development team identifies the working agreement for their development work. The working agreements should be in line with Scrum values and Scrum Master helps the team to avoid pitfalls. When a member violates a working agreement, it is presented to the team where the members being directly responsible to the team can express their views. Scrum Master regularly helps the team to revise the working agreements. The development team can review and update the working agreements at any time.

The scope of working agreements is focused on all development activities and Sprint ceremonies. The core team maintains working agreement for wave, release, and product level ceremonies.

Sprint level information radiators

Iteration is referred to as Sprint in Scrum. Sprint level information radiators keep the development and ceremonial processing transparent to everyone. This helps as the stakeholders do not have to disturb the development team members to assess the progress.

Sprint Burndown chart

Sprint Burndown chart records the progress at daily basis for the sprint. Daily all team members report the number of ideal hours' worth of work achieved. This shows the plot for daily basis and how close we are to completing the work. Simply sum all the hours once per day and report it on the graph.

An example of Sprint Burndown chart is illustrated in Figure 20-1. It shows the coverage on daily basis. Metaphor of a burning candle resembles where it takes a while for the candle to burn down over time. The effort, as expressed in actual hours, contributes to bringing down the total amount of work effort down every day of the Sprint. Hopefully the effort comes to zero at the end of Sprint.

Sprint Burndown Graph

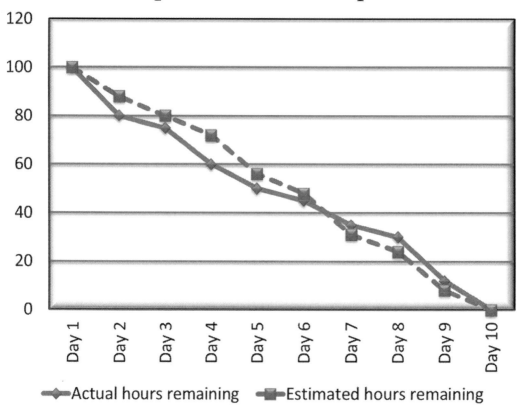

Figure 20-1: Sprint Burndown chart

Sprint Burn-up chart

Sprint Burn-up chart records the progress at daily basis for the sprint in identical transformed manner as was discussed between Release Burndown and Burn-up charts. Further Sprint BurnUp charts provide additional insights for process improvements as shall be discussed at length later in Kanban section.

An example of Sprint Burnup chart is as shown in Figure 20-2.

Sprint BurnUp Graph

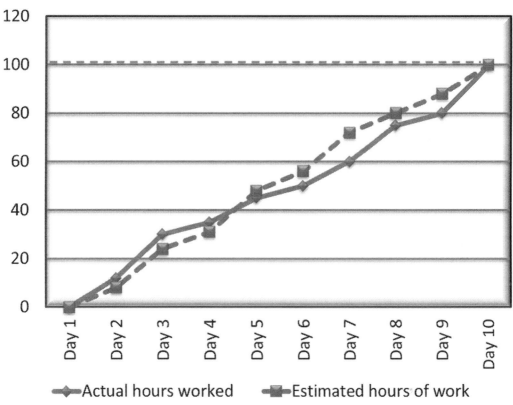

Figure 20-2: Sprint Burnup chart

Story Board

Story board shows story to task mapping for a Sprint and could expand to show Story Map as well. Story mapping is discussed in Chapters 37 and 38.

Task board

Task board is also known as Kanban, a Japanese term where kan means "signal" and ban means "board." The concept has come from Lean principles.

A sample task board is shown in Figure 20-3 with Work-in-progress (WIP) identifies the tasks currently in-progress. This allows an easy assessment in streamlining the work and looking at potential bottleneck to optimize the value stream.

A simple example as discussed in Kanban method is:

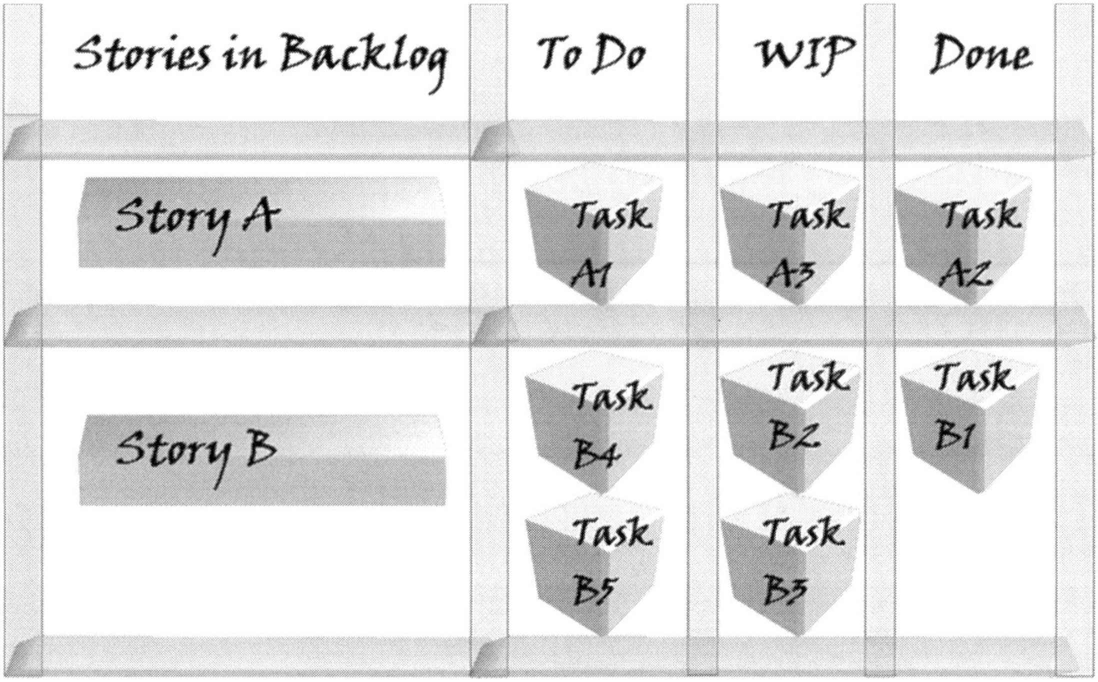

Stories in Backlog	To Do	WIP	Done
Story A	Task A1	Task A3	Task A2
Story B	Task B4 / Task B5	Task B2 / Task B3	Task B1

Figure 20-3: Kanban or Task board

This can further be expanded to different phases to manage complete deliveries from start to end. Kanban method seeks to look at the complete process instead of each phase.

Kanban or Task board when provides insight on the progress with identified work that can be taken in each phase. The capacity required for Kanban can be derived using Cumulative Flow Diagrams (CFD) as had been discussed briefly in Kanban methodology earlier.

Figure 20.4 illustrates that when all the tasks for a user story are completed, the user story is 'done.' This simple graph is expanded later to identify individual stage for CFD analysis in Figure 20-5 and as taskboard in Figure 20-6.

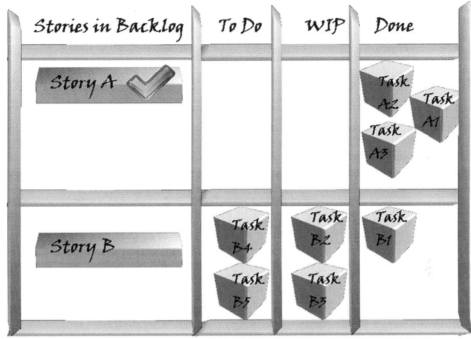

Figure 20-4: Kanban – in-progress

Above distribution could also be represented as shown in Figure 20-5. However, it would not convey as much details as Kanban or taskboard with real tasks.

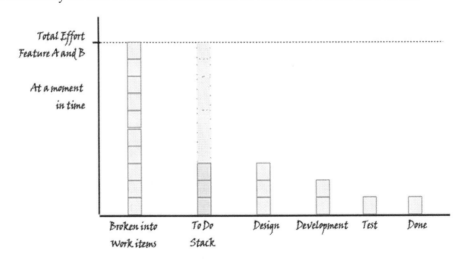

Figure 20-5: Kanban or Taskboard analysis graph

Though when this same information is reflected in Burn-up chart for a sprint, it would provide further insight.

In XP terms, a similar presentation based on story and related tasks at a given date can be represented as:

Story	Tasks To do	Test Automation	Implementation	Test	Done	Effort
Story 1	S1 Task 7	S1 Task 5	S1 Task 3		S1 Task 1	24 hours
	S1 Task 8	S1 Task 6	S1 Task 4	S1 Task 2		
	S1 Task 9					
Story 2	S2 Task 3	S2 Task 2	S2 Task 1			16 hours
	S2 Task 4					
Story 3	S3 Task 1					8 hours

Figure 20-6: Kanban or Task board example

Kanban is a Japanese word which means sign, signboard, doorplate, poster, or billboards. Kanban is also commonly referred to as "signal card" or task board. It is based upon Lean [4]manufacturing. Kanban is a scheduling system for Lean and Just-in-Time (JIT) production. Kanban development process was developed by Taiichi Ohno at Toyota for Just-in-Time (JIT) production. Kanban was devised to maintain high rate of improvement as a scheduling system that helps determine what to produce, when to produce it, and how much to produce.

---

[4] http://www.eudict.com/?lang=japeng&word=kanban

Release plan information radiators

Release level plans are updated constantly throughout the project. Release level plans are impacted by Sprint level plans which are in-turn impacted by daily plans. This provides constant insightful updates and allows the team to check and adapt to align with the project vision. Key difference between this plan is that it does not list tasks that are needed to complete a story. Rather it lists the stories and hierarchy between stories as stories are split into smaller stories. This allows a feature completion based reporting instead of traditional Gantt charts where value delivered is hard to interpret.

This "feature breakdown structure" is much more informative than the work breakdown structure (WBS) with tasks and resource allocations in traditional project plans.

Team Velocity graph

Velocity is tracked for each sprint of the release. A sample velocity graph is:

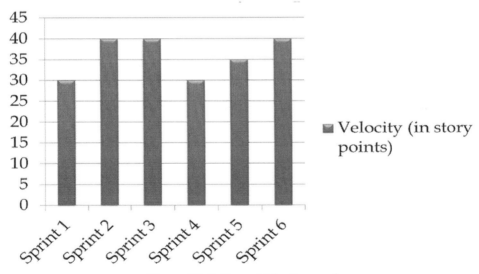

Figure 20-7: Team Velocity graph

An important aspect seen is that representing velocity graph as bar-graph is better represented than line graph. However, as realized in release burn-up chart, the progress is derived from cumulative velocity. As shown below, it can be derived that 300 story points would be attained in 9 sprints based on current progress.

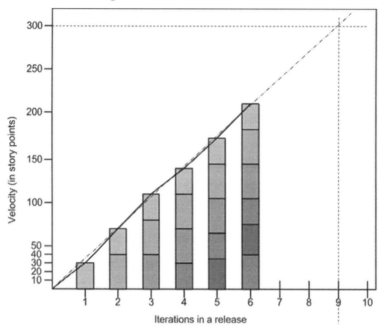

Figure 20-8: Release Burn-up chart with velocity analysis

Release Burndown chart

Release Burndown chart as discussed earlier shows the current progress and helps derive schedule. Let's say that the total story points for the project are: 300. Looking at the graph, it is possible to know the schedule when 300 story points will be delivered from above as:

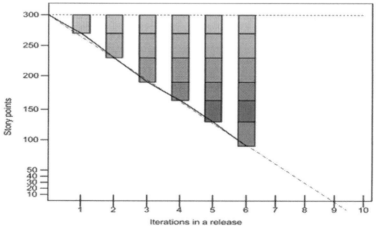

Figure 20-9: Release Burndown Chart with velocity analysis

Here at start the total of 300 story points of effort is identified. In sprint 1, 30 story points are delivered which brings down the remaining effort to 270 story points. In sprint 2, 40 story points are completed; bringing total remaining effort to 230 story points. In sprint 3, 40 more story points worth effort is completed which brings remaining effort to 190 story points and so on. An average line drawn on the slope with different values via connecting line of remaining effort after each sprint crosses around 9th sprint. This helps derive the schedule as we expect to complete the original estimate of 300 story points around 9th sprint. The Burndown graph is actually shown without the bars as below:

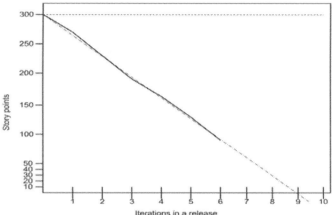

Figure 20-10: Release Burndown graph

Release Burndown chart for below table could be a little more complicated. There are four simple rules to follow for Burndown chart for such case:

1   Top is lowered by the amount of work completed in a sprint
2   When team re-estimates the work, the top moves up if there is increase in the story points and moves down if the story points decrease by the amount of change
3   When new story points are added, the bottom of the graph is lowered by that amount
4   When story points are removed, the bottom is raised by that amount

Sprints >	Sprint 1	Sprint 2	Sprint 3	Sprint 4	Sprint 5
Story points at the start of sprint	100	90	100	61	35

Completed story points during sprint	35	35	35	35	35
Story points due to new stories	6	35	0	16	
Estimate changes by team during sprint planning	19	10	-4	-7	
Sprint velocity	90	100	61	35	0

Let's see for sprint 1, starting story points is 100, team completes 35 story points which brings down the level to 90 story point. However, new stories are added, which pushes the bottom zero mark to -6 story points. Team changes the estimates during sprint planning which moves the top marker from 90 story points to 109 story point.

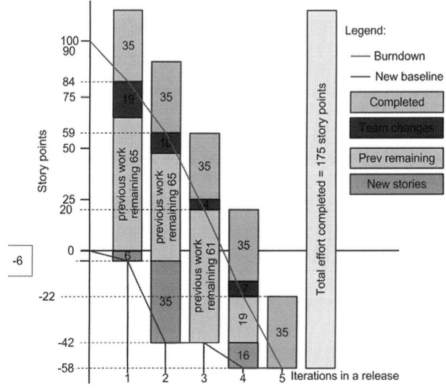

Figure 20-11: Release Burndown chart with project updates from table

Similarly, for sprints 2, 3, 4, and 5, the graphs have been plotted with blue line showing the movement of new baseline from zero to downward as new stories are Below graph is shown with different bars to provide the relationships on Burndown efforts and baseline changes.

As we can see, it gets complicated. Become aware of these rules to be able to identify if the graph will move up or down based on the changes by the team effort, team estimation, and new stories added by the customer. Since the baseline move causes this calculation to become complex, Burnup chart is recommended as it reflects the effort above and provide true reflection for simpler analysis of various factors.

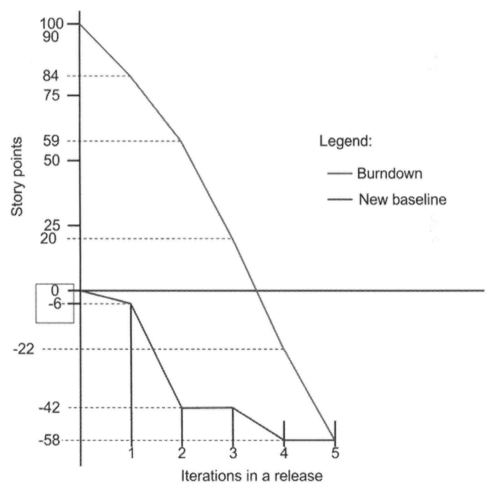

Figure 20-12: Release Burndown chart with project updates

Release Burndown chart for above graph is displayed without the bars is shown in Figure 20-12. The graph shows the change in scope using the line below the x-axis and brundown of effort arising due to completed, team changes and remaining estimate from previous sprint.

Release Burnup chart

Release Burndown chart gets complicated as the baseline also moves with Product Owner adding new stories and removing stories to the Release Backlog. This is much simplified in Release Burnup chart. The chart starts with displaying the total story points at start. The effort starts from zero and grows cumulatively to progress to meet the total story points of effort desired. As the changes to baseline can be reflected by moving the total story points at start, this graph is much simpler to understand.

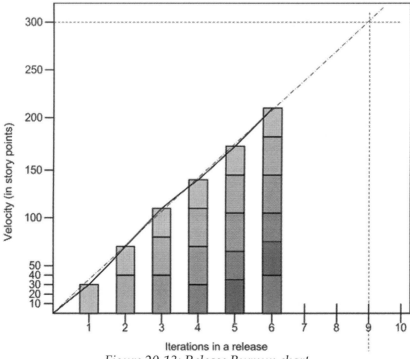

Figure 20-13: Release Burnup chart

For Burnup chart the following four rules apply:

1   Bottom burn-up line is raised by the amount of work completed in a sprint

2   When team re-estimates the work, the baseline moves up if there is increase in the story points and moves down if the story points decrease by the amount of change

3   When new story points are added, the baseline of the graph is raised by that amount

4   When story points are removed, the baseline is lowered by that amount

A Simple release Burnup chart, as shown in Figure 20-14, corresponding to the earlier table identifies schedule estimates and outstanding work effort at each Sprint.

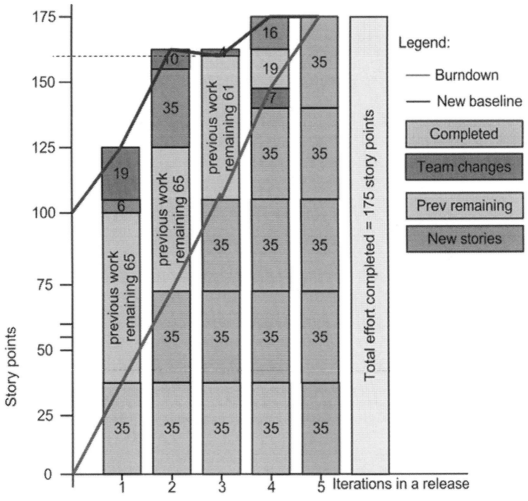

Figure 20-14: Release Burnup chart with project updates

actual burn-up chart is shown without the bars, as follow in Figure 20-15. This graph shows all the values above the x-axis and differentiates it with the progress to the Backlog over the period. A close observation reveals that the BurnUp chart is a vertical flip of Burndown chart where the Burndown starts from origin (0, 0) and all other values are relative to the origin.

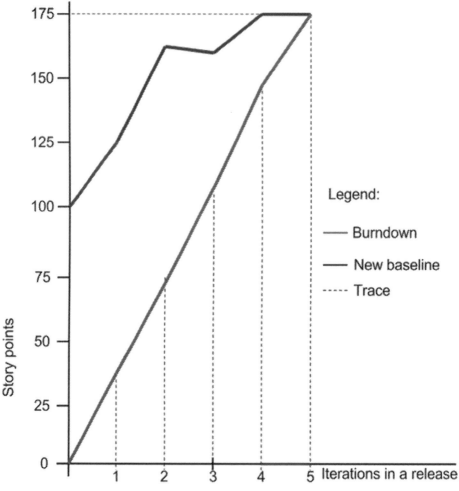

Figure 20-15: Release burn-up chart

Communicating with plans in MS-Project

A clever way to identify agile planning in MS-Project is to list the stories for a sprint in a given release. Since team owns all the stories in the sprint, team is collectively allocated as resource. This allows a plan which represents a graphical Gantt chart and stories are estimated with story points to identify the effort level involved.

Release Burndown Analysis

Release Burndown charts is another way of assessing progress. It shows the amount of work, expressed in story points, remaining at the end of each sprint.[5] This shows total user stories planned as well as changes to the number of user stories for the remainder of release. An example is:

Sprint >	Start	Sprint 1	Sprint 2	Sprint 3	Sprint 4	Sprint 5
Remaining User stories	25	17	12	9	5	0

However, even Burndown charts could be misleading due to various factors including:

    1   Customer could have added/removed more stories in a sprint

    2   Team could have changed estimates and added/updated tasks and effort levels

    3   Since planning is done at rough estimates at release level and sprint level details are covered in planning, estimates for the stories may change during sprint planning

Hence, managers and stakeholders should not get upset just by viewing the Sprint Burndown chart. For example, below is example over 5 sprint release progress:

Sprints >	Sprint 1	Sprint 2	Sprint 3	Sprint 4	Sprint 5
Story points at the start of sprint	100	90	100	61	35
Completed story	35	35	35	35	35

---

[5] Mike Cohn, author, thought leader, and evangelist, states in: *User stories applied.*

points during sprint					
Story points due to new stories	6	35	0	16	
Estimate changes by team during Sprint planning	19	10	-4	-7	
Sprint velocity	90	100	61	35	0

Product level information radiators

The original implementation had a change report which would reflect the deliverable against the product level. With Sprint and Release level radiators, these seem to be phasing off. However, they come into play when progress need to be tracked across multiple releases.

Product Backlog Burndown chart

Product Backlog Burndown chart is simply the chart showing Burndown across releases. Since Product development could be spanning multiple releases, the graph would display accumulated display of Burndown for each Sprint in each Release.

Product Backlog -up chart

Product Backlog Burndown chart is simply the chart showing Burndown across releases. Since Product development could be spanning multiple releases, the graph would display accumulated display of Burnup for each Sprint in each release.

Summary

This chapter describes various information radiators utilized and the corresponding information they represent. These information radiators help reflect the progress. Further the visibility of the current progress allows inspection and adaptation to be able to flexibly adjust planning and actions to optimize the result.

The next section discusses Scrum Roles and their respective responsibilities.

Section V
Scrum Roles

Chapter 21 Product Owner

"Effective leadership is not about making speeches or being liked; leadership is defined by results not attributes." - Peter Drucker

Introduction

In Scrum, Product Owner drives project success. The Product Owner creates product vision and iterates it to the Team and stakeholders as a common binding force. The Product Owner creates and manages the Product Backlog and keeps it DEEP. The Product Owner collaborates with the Development Team to ensure understanding of requirements and support them in Business domain. The Product Owner collaborates with stakeholders in Business Domain and facilitates activities like Innovation games, Story writing workshops, Backlog grooming, and Scrum Reviews. The Product Owner participates in Scrum ceremonies and helps the Team with support and environment to foster development and delivery of valuable software. The Product Owner is alone accountable for the success of the Product. The Product Owner must be authorized to take actions to ensure ROI and overall success of the product.

In this chapter, we describe the many essential responsibilities, characteristics and qualities of what make an effective Product Owner. Further we explore how the Product Owner role can be combined with other roles and scaled up effectively.

Characteristics

In Scrum, Product Owner is the Product Champion. The Product Owner is a central role in Scrum Framework. The Product Owner is a common interface between the Business domain and the Solution Domain; acting as an internal representative for the stakeholders including customers and end-users, and the Scrum Master and the Development Team.

As shown in Figure 20-1, the Product Owner facilitates collaboration between the Scrum Master, the Development Team and the Business or Problem Domain. The Product Owner acts as internal representative of the customer and end-users to express the needs to the Development Team. The Product Owner identifies what is to be built, the priority as to when to build, and the acceptance criteria to determine as definition of 'done' to know when it is built. On the other hand, the Product Owner becomes the voice of the Development Team to inquire and progressively elaborate the Product

Backlog and facilitates various ceremonies with the customers and the end-users and other essential stakeholders.

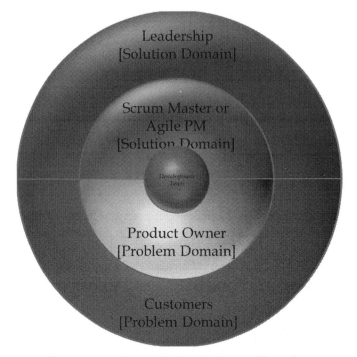

Figure 21-1: Scrum Project Roles and Interfaces

Good Product Owner

A good Product Owner is CRACK [Boehm and Turner 2003]:

- ❖ **Committed** to the work and fully engaged
- ❖ **Responsible** for the outcome of the project
- ❖ **Authorized** to make decisions about product under development and knows the decisions to be made with others vs. solo
- ❖ **Collaborative** as interacting with others
- ❖ **Knowledgeable** about the business purpose and the business domain

Responsibilities

Product Owner is a central role with significant responsibilities. As evident with the impact and level of influence required, it appears to be a full-time role. At times the responsibilities require the depth that the Product Owner has his own team of professionals comprising of testers, business analysts and market analysts. On large projects, there could be multiple Product Owners collaborating together towards a common goal under a chief Product Owner.

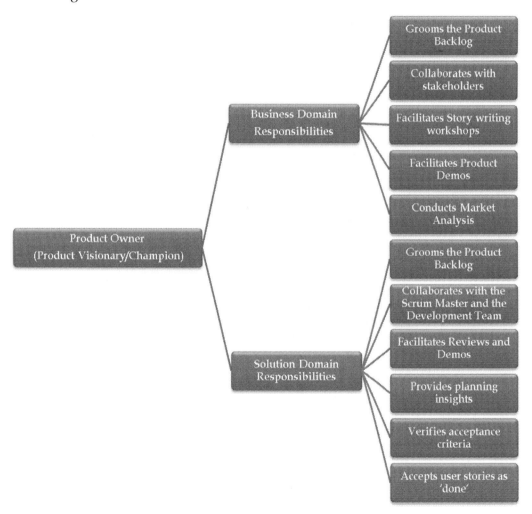

Figure 21-2: Product Owner's Responsibilities

Product Owner is active as soon as project is awarded. The Product Owner builds a project vision and uses it as driving force for all involved on the project.

Business Domain responsibilities

Conduct Market Analysis: The Product Owner performs market analysis with ROI, rough effort estimates, planning and influencing various factors and drawing a common product vision.

Groom Product Backlog: Product Owner is accountable to keep the Product Backlog DEEP.

Collaborate with Business stakeholders: Product Owner collaborates with Business stakeholders to gather requirements; build Product Backlog; identify MMFs/MVPs; organize activities like innovation games to identify priorities; and seek resolutions to various unknowns and market analysis.

Facilitate Story Writing workshops: In the beginning of the project, Product Owner facilitates 'story writing workshop' to generate user stories and other backlog items for the Product Backlog.

Facilitate Product Demos and reviews: Product Owner facilitates Scrum Review ceremony and coordinates with the team for product demo.

Solution Domain responsibilities

Grooms Product Backlog: Product Owner is accountable to keep the Product Backlog DEEP.

Collaborate with the Scrum Master and the Development Team: Product Owner collaborates on daily basis and frequently during the day to ensure that the Development Team has the required support and environment to develop and deliver.

Facilitate Reviews and Demos: Product Owner facilitates Review ceremonies and carries out pilot demos and other reviews for business client long after the Sprint is over.

Provide planning insights: Product Owner provides market analysis and manages ROI optimization to ensure effective planning.

Provide and verified acceptance criteria: Product Owner provides acceptance criteria for each backlog item to provide as a basis to know when the work is done.

Accept user stories as 'done': After a backlog items is completed and all acceptance criteria met, the Product Owner accepts the backlog item as 'done.'

Ownership

The Product Owner owns the Product Backlog – the heart of Scrum. It is the single most important artifact besides the vision to help direct product success. The Product Owner carries out and facilitates different sessions for Product Backlog Grooming and ensures that it is DEEP at all times.

Shu-Ha-Ri levels of Product Owners

Product Owners stay at Shu level where the Scrum Master helps them become acquaintance with the workings of Scrum Framework. The Scrum Master helps provide many insights to the Scrum Framework. As the Product Owner follows the rule and brings the many faceted responsibilities info workings, the familiarity with the Scrum Framework starts to settle in. This normally results in transition to Ha-level where the Product Owners are familiar with the Scrum Framework. One way to ascertain a Product Owner at Ha-level is to see their successes on multiple projects as Product Owner. Product Owner functions independently at Ha-level. At Ri-Level, the Product Owner transcends the normal workings and able to juggle the responsibilities seamlessly. It is like a conductor at work where the complete role seems to bring the complete product development appears like a nice musical concert where everything plays in sync with the rhythm and brings forth the vision to reality.

Mix with other Scrum roles

Product Owner can also be a member of the Development Team. There lies a conflict of interest when someone assumes the role of Scrum Master and Product Owner. Hence, it is not recommended for someone to take up both the roles on a Scrum project team. However, Product Owner on one Scrum team can be Scrum Master on another Scrum team even when the two teams are tied in client-vendor relationship.

Summary

This chapter describes the Product Owner role and responsibilities. Further addresses the qualities of a good Product Owner.

In the next chapter, we cover the Scrum Master role and responsibilities.

Chapter 22 Scrum Master

"A leader is best when people barely know he exists, when his work is done, his aim fulfilled, they will say: we did it ourselves." - Lao Tzu

Introduction

Scrum Master upholds Scrum Framework – its core values, principles, rules, processes and practices. Scrum Master teaches, mentors, and coaches people on various Scrum roles and related responsibilities. As a Change Agent, utilizes opportunities to foster growing and nourishing environment for the Scrum Core and Extended teams to push for change using various activities, trainings, and acting as a model. Scrum Master acts as Servant-Leader for the Team and the Product Owner. For the Development team, the Scrum Master removes impediments, protects the team, and provides support and necessary environment to be able to develop and deliver. For the Product Owner, the Scrum Master trains and coaches the Product Owner on various aspects of Scrum including yet not limited to Product Backlog Grooming, Market and Project analysis, and provide guidance when needed. Scrum Master facilitates Scrum ceremonies like Planning, Daily Scrums, Scrum of Scrums for multiple-team project, and Retrospectives ceremonies.

Scrum Master manages principles and the principles manage the process and various roles. Acting in Servant-Leader role, Scrum Master acts as proxy of Product Owner in his absence and interfaces with the Management and Leadership teams to ensure support and environment for product development.

Characteristics

In Scrum, Scrum Master is the Process Champion – an agent of change. Scrum Master acts as agile coach for the core team – the Product Owner and the Development Team. Scrum Master collaborates with the stakeholders in Business domain as well as Solution Domain to help foster support and environment to support vision. Scrum Master fosters proper understanding and practice of Scrum Framework for the organization.

As Servant leader to the Development Team, Scrum Master removes impediments, acts as a bouncer to safeguard team from outside interferences including those of the Product Owner, and serves to provide and fosters support, environment and resources needed for product development and delivery. Scrum Master follows leadership style and helps the Development team and the Product Owner with knowledge and guidance so that they can carry out their roles and responsibilities successfully. Scrum Master follows situational leadership style indirectly where the focus is on "helping people -help themselves" (HPHT) [SINGHAL, SP, 2013]. Scrum Master does not do the function of the Team or the Product Owner. Rather the Product Owner and the Development Team are guided in various situations and are even let them fail to learn from the failures.

Responsibilities

The responsibilities of Scrum Master are listed in Figure 21-2. Scrum Master is not normally a full-time role and a person could be member of the Development team and Scrum Master or be Scrum Master for two or more teams.

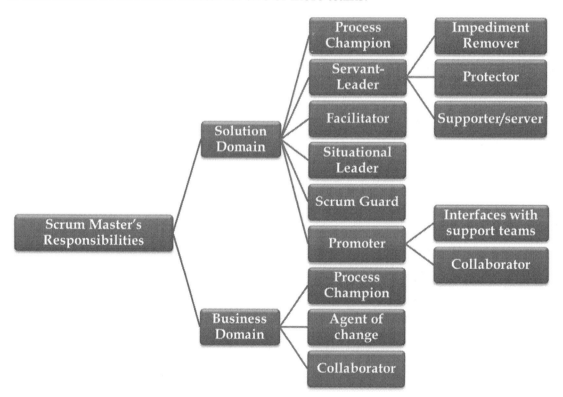

Figure 22-1: Scrum Master's responsibilities

Solution Domain responsibilities

Process Champion: Scrum Master is the agent of change and is responsible for ensuring the Scrum framework, its practices, values, and principles are understood and followed. Scrum Master mentors, trains and coaches the Development Team and the Product Owner on Scrum Framework.

Servant-Leader: Scrum Master acts as Servant-Leader for the Development Team. As Servant-Leader, Scrum Master removes impediments, safeguards the Development Team from external (as well as internal) interruptions. Our observation shows that there are more interruptions erupting internally than externally and it goes to prove the security theory also correct – there is more chances of breaches from within than without.

Facilitator: Scrum Master facilitates Scrum ceremonies and other sessions. Scrum ceremonies include planning, Daily Scrum, Scrum of Scrums, Retrospectives and other sessions include activities and agile games to help team meet a specific agenda or learn a specific lesson.

Situational-Leader (Coach): As the Development Team progresses through the different developmental stages: Forming, Storming, Norming, Performing, and Adjourning, Scrum Master takes on different situational leadership style. Besides, the Scrum Master focuses on team in the beginning and near the end of each Sprint and provides individual-level focus during the Sprint execution.

Scrum Guard: Scrum Master guards Scrum Framework from various influences. This requires a lot of diplomatic dealings and strong leadership skills when adverse environment or dealing is encountered. Collaboration and principled negotiation style with Consensus based analysis (CBA) are employed to safeguard interests.

Promoter: Scrum Master focuses on promoting Scrum Framework. Scrum Master acts as a model of scrum and teaches by example.

Business Domain responsibilities

Process Champion: Scrum Master is the agent of change for the enterprise and extended teams. Scrum Master is responsible for ensuring the Scrum framework, its practices, values, and principles are understood and followed. Scrum Master mentors, trains and coaches the Extended Team and the Product Owner on Scrum Framework.

Agent of Change: Scrum Master acts as an agent of change where the responsibility is owned to introduce and promote Scrum practices, values and principles across enterprise and business domain. While safeguarding the Development Team and the Product Owner, Scrum Master gets many opportunities to help the extended team members understand the values and principles. Besides, Scrum Master helps other teams interested in Scrum and Agile methodologies.

Collaborator: Scrum Master collaborates with the extended team to promote collaboration and consensus based analysis (CBA). The focus is on promoting solutions around interests and not positions. This requires effective leadership style in helping the extended team realize the advantages.

Process Ownership

Scrum Master owns and manages the Scrum Framework processes and practices. This is attained using, coaching, and mentoring others on Scrum rules, its core values, and principles.

Summary

This chapter describes the roles and responsibilities of Scrum Master. Scrum master upholds Scrum Framework, be a Servant-Leader, mentor, facilitator, Collaborator and overall Scrum promoter as a model.

More information on collaboration, negotiation styles, and leadership is covered in our books: Solving Problems – the agile way and

The next chapter addresses the role and responsibilities of the Development Team. The Development Team is the Development Champion.

Chapter 23 The Development Team

"Coming together is a beginning; keeping together is progress; working together is success."
- Henry Ford

Introduction

The Development Team is treated as a single entity in Scrum Framework. In Scrum, the focus is on team ownership instead of individual ownership. The Development Team displays this attitude in its development efforts. Development Team is self-organizing and does not need external interference in managing its internal affairs. Development Team is accountable to developing the incremental deliverable product in every Sprint. The Team collaborates with the Product Owner, the Scrum Master and the extended team throughout the project. The Development Team owns and manages the Sprint Backlog and Information Radiators for Sprint progress tracking. The Development Team is a major player in all Scrum ceremonies. The Development Team collaborates with the Product Owner daily and frequently to ensure a DEEP Product Backlog and provide insights as and when needed.

Development team is also commonly referred to as: the Team, the Delivery Team, The lifecycle Team, and the Project Team. The Development Team is one of the three roles in Scrum core team (committed) where the other two are: the Product Owner and the Scrum Master.

Characteristics

The Development Team is the Project Champion. The Development team is autonomous in nature, which means that it has all the skills required to deliver a user story from concept to delivery to customer. Members of the Development Team possess broad understanding of the complete development lifecycle while they may have specialization in one or more domains.

Scaling Development Team

On a small project, team size of 7 ± 2 (5 to 9) works to have an autonomous, self-organizing team of motivated individuals collaborating together. However, for enterprise teams working on a large project, multiple teams work together. This can occur in two levels:

1. Self-organizing teams of motivated individuals can structure to evolve multiple teams where some of the members could lead specific business domains
2. Explicit organization where an initial team of highly motivated and skilled professional starts on the project and gain expertise in different domains. As the domains expand, the team partitions and continues to collaborate moving forward.

The second structure is adaptive and evolving. Collaboration is achieved easily when skilled professionals see it as opportunity of growth in worth and purpose. We have observed the second structure to succeed more often. The first option where the team is expected to be self-organizing leads to a lot of conflicts. Team members seeking growth start to work against each other instead on the highest priority – delivering valuable software to customer. During training also we heard of similar occurrences on other projects at client enterprises. This shows that self-organizing aspect only relates to organizing the work within the team and not in showing the leadership when there are possible conflicting interests.

Many times scaling of Scrum is implemented with teams built technical domains instead of business domains. That is also not favorable as it results in building up silos and slowly the process degenerates into iterative development with agile overhead. Many of these catastrophic scenarios are discussed in our book: *"Get Fragile out of Agile."* [SINGHAL, TFOOA, 2013]

Responsibilities

The Development Team commits to the Sprint Goal in Sprint Planning meeting, developers the incremental product during the Sprint with daily inspection-and-adaptation during Daily Scrums and demos the product features in Sprint Review ceremony and last but not least, the Development Team inspects the development process (Processes, resources and people aspects) during the Retrospectives to tune and improve. Figure 22-1 lists various responsibilities carried out to be able to meet these.

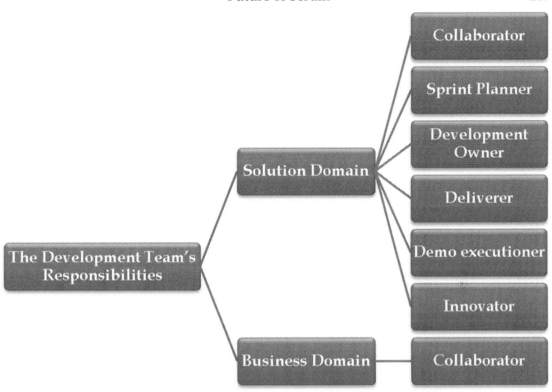

Figure 23-1: Development Team's Responsibilities

Solution Domain responsibilities

Collaborator: The Development Team collaborates with the Product Owner, the Scrum Master, Extended- support teams like Infrastructure, MIS, and network teams, vendors and other enterprise teams including management and leadership teams.

Sprint Planner: The Development Team plans out the strategy and development process to delivery Sprint Backlog Items. The Development Team owns and maintains the Sprint Backlog. Tasks are added, deleted, updated and managed as team desires.

Development Owner: The Development Team is in the best position to identify what is needed and how the development of each Sprint Backlog item would be carried out. The extended team members, the Product Owner and the Scrum Master should not impose any directives to the Development Team to follow. Suggestions are welcome but non-binding for compliance. Only compliance criteria are the acceptance criteria for each Sprint Backlog item.

Deliverer: The Development Team is accountable for the Sprint delivery. If the Team feels that Sprint goals cannot be accomplished, the alternatives and options must be quickly explored and provided to the Product Owner at the earliest.

Demo executioner: During the Sprint Review, members of the Development Team run the demo and provides insights. The Product Owner addresses Q&A sessions and provides preliminary feature insights in the beginning of the session. Collaboration with the Product Owner may show up as shifting of these responsibilities back and forth.

Innovator: The Development team is responsible for innovative ideas, creativity and brings creative ideas to reality – innovation.

Business Domain responsibilities

Collaborator: The Development Team collaborates with the Product Owner, the customer, end-users, marketing and sales teams and other stakeholders to understand the business domain and provide options and alternatives to meet the needs.

Team configurations

Each Scrum team consists of required skilled professionals to deliver the product from concept to reality. This aspect is commonly reflected in sizing the team to 7 ± 2 (5 to 9) team members in each Scrum Team. With scaling of the project, a common question asked is how Scrum teams are formed to provide appropriate scaling. The answer lies in understanding the way all other aspects are scaling. This could lead to many configurations yet are evolving based on themes to provide focus on individual domain. Then there are other aspects like how these teams work with shared responsibilities, release ownership, product ownership and so forth. Such questions are outside the scope of this guide and are addressed in detail in our book: *Coaching Agile Enterprises and Leadership teams.*

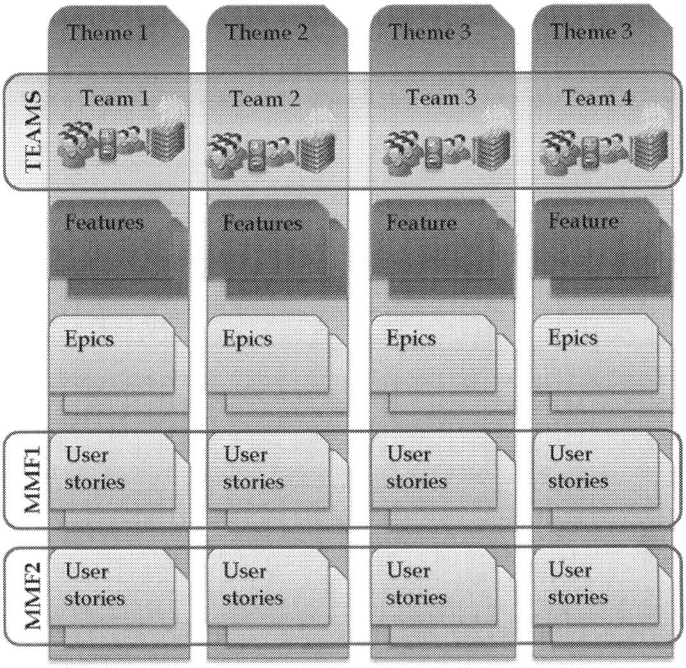

Theme 1 Theme 2 Theme 3 Theme 3

TEAMS Team 1 Team 2 Team 3 Team 4

Features Features Feature Feature

Epics Epics Epics Epics

MMF1 User stories User stories User stories User stories

MMF2 User stories User stories User stories User stories

Figure 23-2: A basic team configuration based on themes

Ownership

The Development Team owns the development process and related artifacts including Sprint Backlog, Development artifacts, Kanban or Task board, Working Agreements or Ground rules, Sprint Burnup or Burndown graphs, and progress tracking reports. The ownership is at team level as a single entity and not at individual member level. The Development Team collaborates, self-organizes and manages its internal affairs to deliver the incremental product in every Sprint.

However, in needing circumstances, the Product Owner can cancel a Sprint as the Product Owner determines what is to be built and when it is to be built with order prioritization of the backlog items is determined. The Development Team determines and owns how to build aspect.

Shu-Ha-Ri levels of Development Team

All Development Teams start at Shu-level: Follow the rule. The Scrum Master guides mentors and coaches the Team to learn the various aspects of Scrum Framework.

Besides, the Scrum Master helps the team to learn to take on the lead on becoming taking on all essential responsibilities to be an effective team. Thus, the Team can become self-organizing, self-managing, self-directing besides being autonomous.

The cross-functional aspect also expands where the team members learn to share responsibilities over time. This aspect takes the Development Team beyond the individual specialized aspect to be able to optimize value delivery for optimized task management through much dynamic value streaming through the development process. At this level, the Development Team has become well acquainted and comes to Ha-level where the concepts, principles and values are evident and practiced seamlessly. It is hard to say when a team is at Ha-level and depends on the Team members taking lead to improve. Motivation and attitude are two critical factors to enable this transition. We have seen some teams to come to Ha-level in as small as 3 sprints while other teams to not come even close after 25 sprints. Ha-level means to detach or break away where the values and principles are upheld and following the rule is not necessary as essence is attained. Sometimes in zest to get to Ha-level, we have even seen some teams take to the opposite route. Scrum Master and Agile Coaches play a major role in such cases to ensure that reverse routes are avoided and bring back the Team to progressive path.

Ri-level is where the Development Team transcends and a lot of improvements occur. Many improvements are introduced through process tailoring; which are normally identified during the retrospectives.

Team workspace

Team workspace is an area protected from external influence. However, it should have sufficient room to contain the team comfortably. The information radiators are posted as big charts on the wall. Collocated team members working in an open environment gain tacit knowledge through osmotic communication. This enables the members to gain common perception and understanding. Thus, the discussions and ceremonies are more effective. Efficiency is achieved within the timebox. Agile coaches leverage these factors to promote team members and customers to build stronger relationships by encouraging effective communication modes and practices. Osmotic communication does have a drawback – it can cause noise which could be distracting to some team members. Team is self-organizing and establishes working agreements to ensure noise is kept down and workspace is enhanced to promote effective communication.

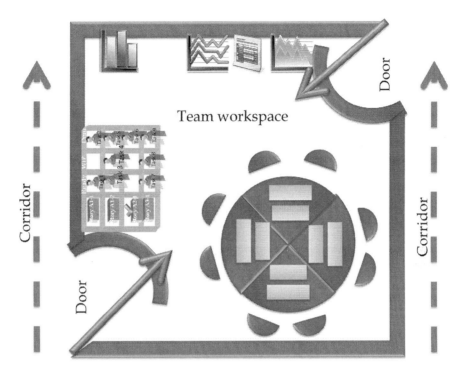

Figure 23-3: Team workspace - sample configuration

Caves and commons

Team workspace is cave area and is characterized as open, visible, big enough for team seating with ability to conduct Sprint ceremonies. Team workspace seating should be so that it allows sharing of information. The information radiators are placed in clear vision on the wall as big charts. The team sits together in the team workspace area. This promotes collaboration. Yet there is a need to ensure that team members can take their private matters and not have to disturb others or be disturbed by others presence. For this, there are isolated workspaces provided as separate rooms where the doors can be closed for privacy. This allows the team members to take personal call, conduct personal discussions and one-on-one reviews.

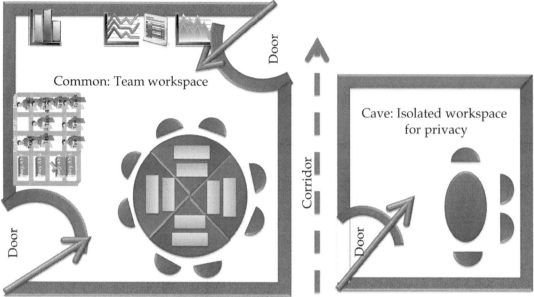

Figure 23-4: Example of Caves and Commons

Summary

This chapter describes the Development Team roles and responsibilities. The Development Team acts as Project Champion and determines how to build the incremental product in every Sprint.

This is the end of current Section. Next section addresses Scaling of Scrum for Enterprise applications and large projects. Next chapter is on Agile planning concepts.

Section VI
Scaling Scrum

Chapter 24 Agile planning concepts

"A leader is one who knows the way, goes the way, and shows the way." - John C. Maxwell

Introduction

There are essentially three types of projects:

1. A research oriented exploratory project
2. A simple production line project
3. A chaotic project highlighted by unmanageable aspects leading to chaos

APM addresses complex projects which are highlighted by three factors:

1. An unknown problem with a known solution
2. A known problem with an unknown solution
3. An unknown problem with an unknown solution

It is essential to know that waterfall traditional methodology is most suitable to simple production like projects where the problem and the solution are both known. Yet in those projects, efficiency and improvements are achieved using agile practices like lean development, Kanban, and value stream mapping; just to list a few.

"Agile methodologies are applicable to small projects and do not pertain to large teams" is a myth and is still imposed by the limited understanding. PMI and earlier agile implementations still continue to reinforce this identifying that the Development Team size is generally 7 ± 2 (5 to 9 team members), though it very well scales to large projects. Today agile team sizes are even over 100 team members that successfully deliver large and complex products. Though such teams appear identical to traditional waterfall project teams, they essentially feel like agile project teams and have embraced agile principles and values via incorporating the practices and framework.

A Roadmap plan is long-range plan with high level capabilities as deliverables composing sets of minimum marketable features (MMFs). Roadmap plan normally pertains to a couple of year long duration with multiple releases, addresses product feasibility, and product release to the customer with significant value driven deliveries and capabilities.

A Release plan is long range plan, with many waves, with details and granularity achieved by iterative planning using a product backlog that is prioritized based on value associated with opportunity (cash inflow) and risk (cash outflow). A release plan is normally 3 to 6 months and at times even up to a yearlong, addresses product delivery at capability level with multiple features, addresses project feasibility and results in a final release to the customer.

A Wave plan spans multiple sprints and is typically 3 months long. Waves are more detailed planned at story level addresses feature aspects, and results in releasable product to customers. It is common to have three or four waves in a release.

A Sprint plan (aka iteration plan) is short-term plan expanding from 1 to 4 weeks duration where releasable product functionality is ensured and allows product and process reviews to inspect and adapt for value delivery. Sprints plans are at much detailed levels providing visibility at story and tasks level. Most common are two week sprints. For a wave of 3 months duration, it is common to have six two week sprints followed by a hardening sprint of a week.

An agile scaling model is expanded upon the product planning structure as shown:

Figure 24-1: Product Planning Structure

An agile scaling model is built on three layers: Business goals, Organization goal, and Agile core values and principles. The Organization is further segregated in different teams that define the product details in Product Backlog and the process. The product backlog is at three levels: capability, features and stories. The stories are further achieved by the identified tasks that lead to a developed deliverable functionality of value. Hence, collectively the five crucial elements to Agile scaling are: Business goals, Agile values, Organization, Product and process.

An agile scale model identifies how the layers are expanded to allow large teams to be agile and once you put this in perspective with the principles and core values expanded by the practices, it would be all clear. Thus, not much needs to be expanded further as you would have a clear picture by the end of this book! Details of the scaling model are out of current scope here and are briefly discussed for enthusiasts seeking awareness. This aspect is covered in detail in "Agile Enterprise Framework Evolution" and application aspects are covered in "Agile PMO."

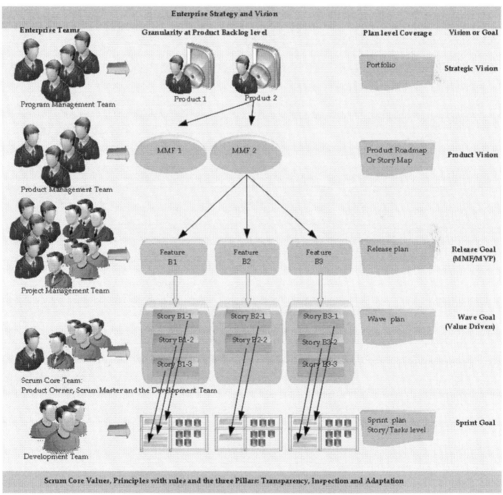

Figure 24-2 An Agile Scaling Model

In a large organization, a project could be a fit to a methodology based on three critical factors [HIGHSMITH, 2009]:

1. Project factors (complexity and uncertainty)
2. Cultural factors
3. Governance and compliance factors

Theme or capabilities

Theme is a high-level objective and is expected to apply across multiple releases and even projects.

In bottom-up approach, combining stories is done when stories are too small. Sometimes developers feel that fixing would be faster than documenting such stories. Common approach for such tiny stories is to combine these into a story from half-a-day to several days of work. This can be done by stapling or clipping the index cards with a cover card. This set is treated as a single story for estimation and planning. Such a set is known as a *theme*. An epic can also be referred as theme.

Features

Features here mean "product features." Features are mostly considered similar to themes due to their high level structure. These are essentially sub-themes that may span multiple releases in a project. A product may include multiple features in a given theme. An epic can also be used to designate a feature.

Epic

As the name suggest, epic is a set of multiple associated stories. Epics typically fall into two categories: *The complex story and compound story*. A *compound story* is one that can be split into multiple shorter stories. Unlike a compound story, a *complex story* is inherently large and cannot be disaggregated into a set of smaller stories. A story is identified complex due to uncertainty can be split into two smaller stories: an investigative story and another developing the new feature. For example, developers analyze a complex story: "A buyer can pay for the sale item with a credit card" and they have not done credit card processing ever; can break this into two stories:

1. Investigate payment processing using credit card - *a spike*
2. User can pay for the sale item with a credit card

In this case, the first story would be a spike. Adopted from XP, a *spike* is an investigative story identified for learning. Spike is timeboxed though they may be hard to estimate accurately. When complex stories are split in this way, always specify a timebox around a spike. Spike should be put in different sprint when possible and developing story in the following sprint. This allows easier estimation of developing story in case the spike is successful.

User stories

User story represent a complete function or feature the product provides. User stories originated from XP – an Agile methodology. User story is most widely used technique to represent requirements. User stories are light-weight as can be expressed in a sentence or two. User stories allow a platform for the customer and development team to collaborate easily through Card-Conversation-Confirmation technique. A good user story is Independent, Negotiable, Valuable, Estimable, Small and Testable; represented by acronym: INVEST. User stories are right sized to be at sprint level.

Agile Planning

Agile planning onion introduced new dimension to the planning aspect. While in the beginning, the Product Backlog could meet the needs, it was not sufficient with the introduction of intermediate levels between product planning and Sprint planning. The progressive elaboration over rolling wave planning with the introduction of release planning and wave planning resulted in more depth and visibility. This led to roadmap.

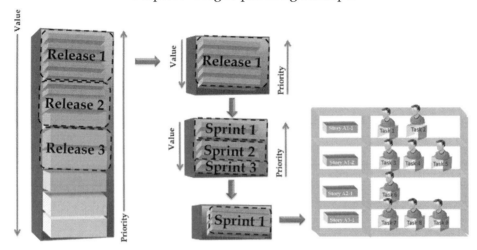

Figure 24-3: Product Backlog to Sprint planning

Here we shall keep the description with Release planning as understanding it will clarify how intermediate steps could be elaborated. The rolling wave planning as shown in Figure 24-3 applies to simple projects with short and clear release cycles. Yet it has drawbacks as it does not help identify progress related to releasable product.

Hence, the Product Backlog is expanded into two dimensions where the Backlog Item hierarchy is clearly visible with the identification leading to MMF. The Product Backlog could be displayed in two dimensions from the Product Backlog and is covered in Chapter 26: Product Planning.

Agile Release Planning

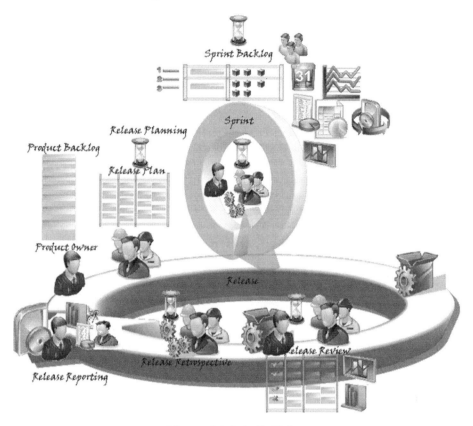

Figure 24-4 Agile Release

A release plan is essential for various reasons:

1   release plan helps to determine the effort and time it would take to build a releasable product

2   hence, a release plan identifies the features of the product for the release

3   provides a plan for the project to focus on instead of agile teams going from one sprint to the next without keeping the focus on minimum marketable feature (MMF)

4   release plan helps optimize return-on-investment (ROI), so the project can start realizing revenue and benefits from the product release

Agile Sprint planning

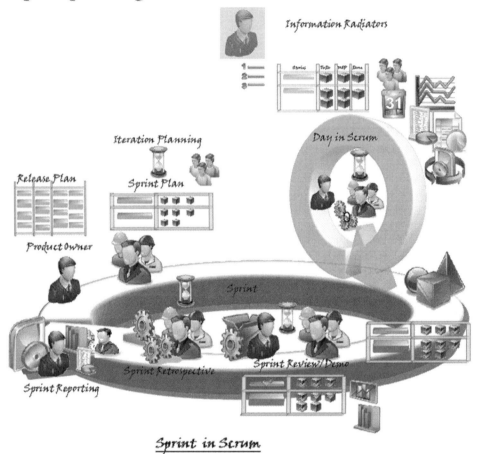

Sprint in Scrum

Figure 24-5 A Scrum Sprint (Agile Iteration)

Sprint planning allows the release plan to be further detailed into Sprint plan where the individual user story is expanded upon and tasks are listed against each user story. The Development Team members own the tasks and develop the functionality during the Sprint. Daily Scrum is where inspection and adaptation occurs where team tunes and plans its activities for the day. At the end of Sprint, Sprint review and retrospectives occur to tune the product and the development process.

A Day in Sprint on Scrum project

The Development Team focuses on development efforts to meet their commitments made during Daily Scrum, resolving any issues, collaborating with the customer.

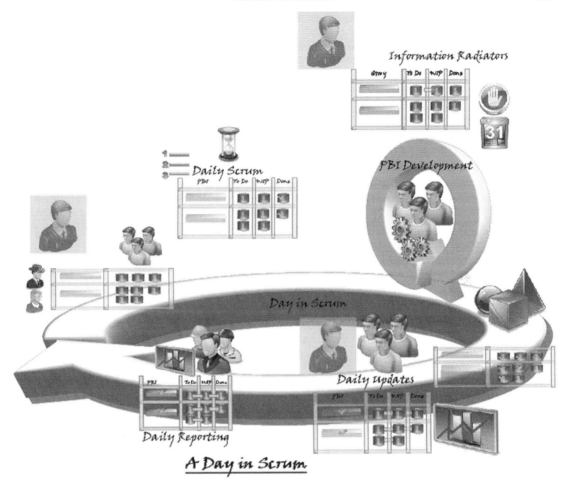

Figure 24-6 A Day in Scrum Sprint (Agile Iteration)

The planning is done early in the day where commitments are made in Daily Scrum sessions where the Development Team inspects-and-adapts to align itself with the common goal of Sprint. The commitments made in Daily Scrum are sought over the course of the day and reports are updated to reflect the progress and any issues.

The Scrum Master works on removing impediments, facilitating Scrum ceremonies, provide support, mentoring and coaching to the Product Owner and the Team. The Product Owner focuses on supporting team and collaborating with the stakeholders to ensure Product Backlog and roadmaps are kept DEEP.

Summary

In this chapter, we explored Agile Project Management model with insight on envisioning and exploration cycles.

In subsequent chapters, we shall explore Agile estimation and planning aspects. User stories and estimation techniques as some are borrowed from XP methodology since 2001 are also now considered part of Scrum Framework.

Chapter 25 Planning Layers

"All men can see these tactics whereby I conquer, but what none can see is the strategy out of which victory is evolved." - Sun Tzu

Introduction

Originally Scrum appeared to only appeal to small teams as the team size was identified to be 5 to nine members. The Product Owner role was not well defined and most of the responsibilities fell on the Scrum Master's shoulder. With the need to address complex projects that are also large, the journey has been long and tedious one. It took over a decade to really evolve strategies to scale Scrum for enterprises. Agile planning onion [COHN, 2006] was the first attempt which had mixed results. Later each layer was strategically segregated from the layers above and below which allowed the scalability to become evident and more visible. However, when enterprises approach this without clear segregation, they are bound to encounter challenges as the early adopters did.

Agile Planning Onion

Agile planning onion is illustrated with brief description in Figure 25-1.

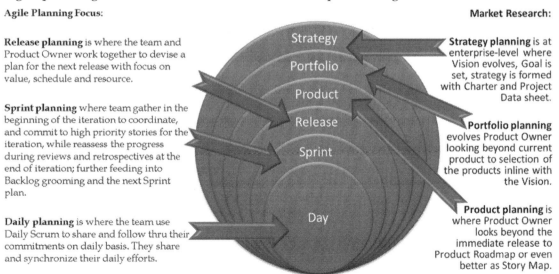

Agile Planning Focus:

Release planning is where the team and Product Owner work together to devise a plan for the next release with focus on value, schedule and resource.

Sprint planning where team gather in the beginning of the iteration to coordinate, and commit to high priority stories for the iteration, while reassess the progress during reviews and retrospectives at the end of iteration; further feeding into Backlog grooming and the next Sprint plan.

Daily planning is where the team use Daily Scrum to share and follow thru their commitments on daily basis. They share and synchronize their daily efforts.

Market Research:

Strategy planning is at enterprise-level where Vision evolves, Goal is set, strategy is formed with Charter and Project Data sheet.

Portfolio planning evolves Product Owner looking beyond current product to selection of the products inline with the Vision.

Product planning is where Product Owner looks beyond the immediate release to Product Roadmap or even better as Story Map.

Strategy
Portfolio
Product
Release
Sprint
Day

Figure 25-1: Agile Planning Onion

Each layer for a product is elaborated in the following sections and Chapters 16-29 in detail for enthusiasts seeking to learn to scale Scrum for large and complex enterprise projects.

Product Planning

Product planning is discussed in detail in next Chapter #26. Here an overview is provided to help provide an insight as how the layers work together. Progressively the backlog is refined at each layer with specific focus. All development is performed in Sprint while above layers help with product backlog grooming for estimation and planning. Product Development may be identified to consist of two or more releases. In each release, an incremental product is delivered to the customer. There are multiple sprints where development for releasable product occurs. All levels are timeboxes as shown in Figure 25-2.

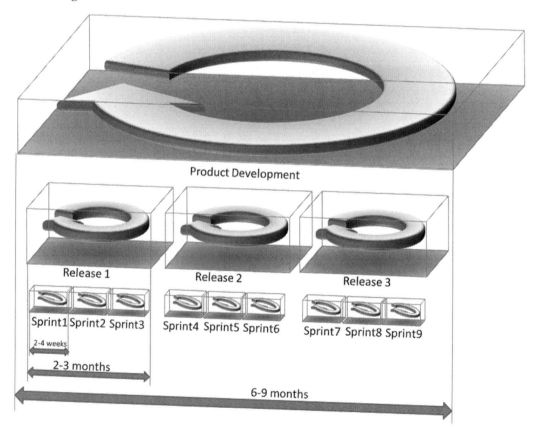

Figure 25-2: Product Planning layers in Timeboxes

Scrum allows scaling where the aspects allow providing additional layers of planning, reviews and retrospections at different layers. Figure 25-3 shows a scalable model where strategic vision at each level is expanded to allow rolling wave planning to refine, estimate, describe and prioritize Product Backlog. The details at different levels are discussed in next series of chapters 26 through 28.

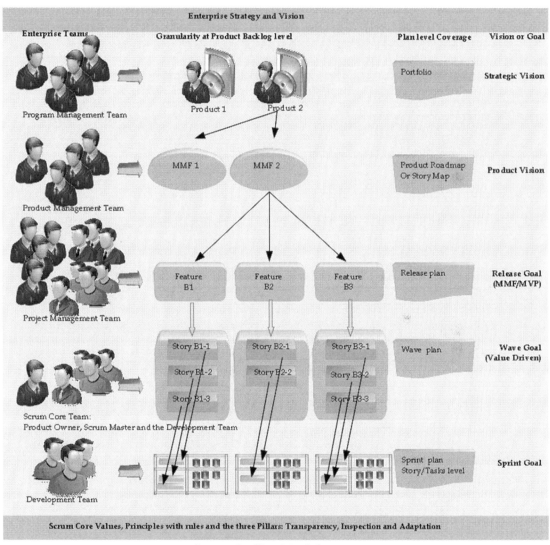

Scrum Scaling Model

Figure 25-3: Scrum Scaling Model

At each layer, the planning aspects gain importance, as illustrated in Figure 25-4. This expands on earlier discussion in Chapter 12: Agile management model.

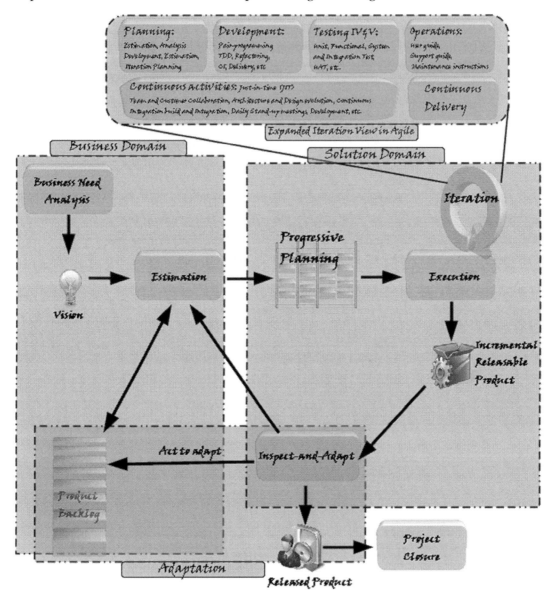

Figure 25-4: Scrum Framework with responsibility sharing at adaptation layers

Hence, the domains are displayed at release level. Adaptation level is highlighted where Business domain and Solution domain share. This used to be considered as owned by solution domain. However, in time, it became clear that this is actually an accountability of Business domain while the Development Team and the Scrum Master collaborate as responsible for planning, while they are accountable for development.

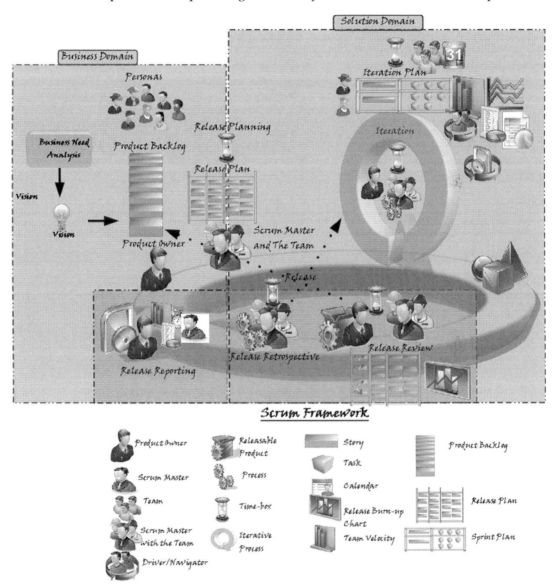

Figure 25-5: Adaptation layer is shared with Business in Scrum Framework

Continuous Improvement Model

Scum does not enforce development practices as XP. The Development team employs the best suitable development practice. Mostly the teams use many of XP practices like pair-programming, TDD, Continuous integration and others. All these allow further visibility to inspect and adapt at levels below a day.

Figure 25-6: Continuous improvement model

Summary

This chapter describes various layers of scaling with the corresponding artifacts and participants to allow effective scaling of Scrum. The next set of chapters take a deep dive in individual layers and provide further insights. Chapter 26 discusses product planning and how roadmap provides a new perspective of looking at customer needs as originally represented in Product Backlog.

Chapter 26 Product Planning

"A satisfied customer is the best business strategy of all." - Michael LeBoeuf

Introduction

The focus in Product Planning is to evolve MMFs from the Product Backlog. A Roadmap is created where MMFs are identified as an incremental releasable product.

Agile Planning

Agile planning onion introduced new dimension to the planning aspect. While in the beginning, the Product Backlog could meet the needs, it was not sufficient with the introduction of intermediate levels between product planning and Sprint planning. The progressive elaboration over rolling wave planning with the introduction of release planning and wave planning resulted in more depth and visibility. This led to roadmap. Here we shall keep the description with Release planning as understanding it will clarify how intermediate steps could be elaborated. The rolling wave planning as shown in Figure 24-3 applies to simple projects with short and clear release cycles. Yet it has drawbacks as it does not help identify progress related to releasable product.

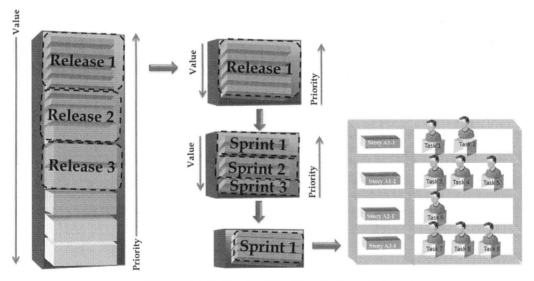

Figure 26-1: Product Backlog to Sprint planning

Hence, the Product Backlog is expanded into two dimensions where the Backlog Item hierarchy is clearly visible with the identification leading to MMF. The Product Backlog could be displayed in two dimensions from the Product Backlog as shown in Figure 24-4.

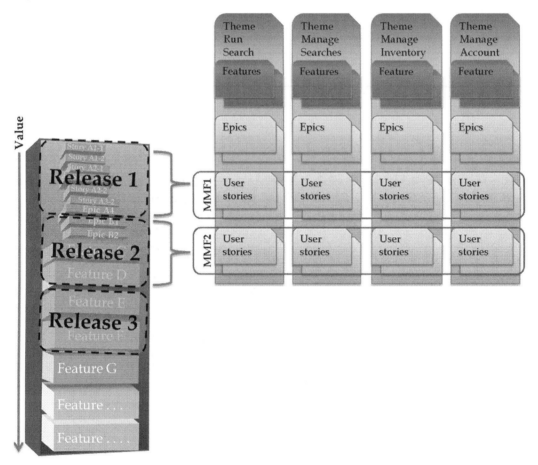

Figure 26-2: Roadmap from Product Backlog

This allows the Backlog hierarchy to be visible and layout for estimation and planning.

Agile Product Planning

For advancement in Agile project management, beyond basics of Scrum purpose, here we shall be discussing the first two evolutionary stages of Backlog grooming and how simple roadmap is derived with various stages. Advanced level of story mapping and detailing are advanced concepts and are covered in our book: *Coaching Agile Enterprises and Leadership Teams.*

Agile product planning focuses on MMFs/MVPs. The focus is on identifying the set of features to form a releasable product to the customer. The Product Owner works with leadership teams, customer, end-users, marketing and other essential stakeholders to identify the necessary features, epics and user stories. Then the Product Backlog is groomed to build a product roadmap and MMFs are identified. This further gets elaborated as part of grooming and rolling wave planning at lower levels. An initial product roadmap is illustrated in Figure 24-5.

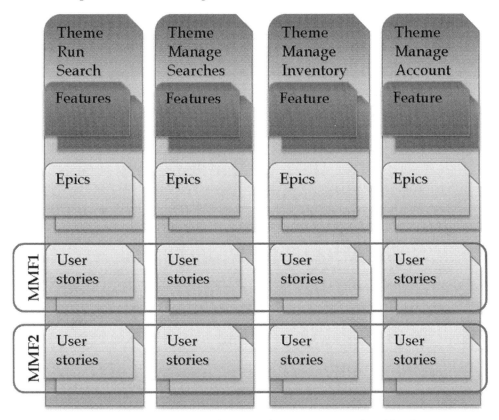

Figure 26-3: Sample Product Roadmap – MMFs identification

The MMFs are further expanded into specific user stories listing and rough releases are derived. In above roadmap, the features are split into various epics which are in turn split into many user stories. The user stories are groomed and elaborated upon as more information is available. Product Owner needs to collaborate with the stakeholders, the

Scrum Master and the Development Team to ensure this process is kept visible so any new information is immediately reflected to ensure that the Backlog is DEEP.

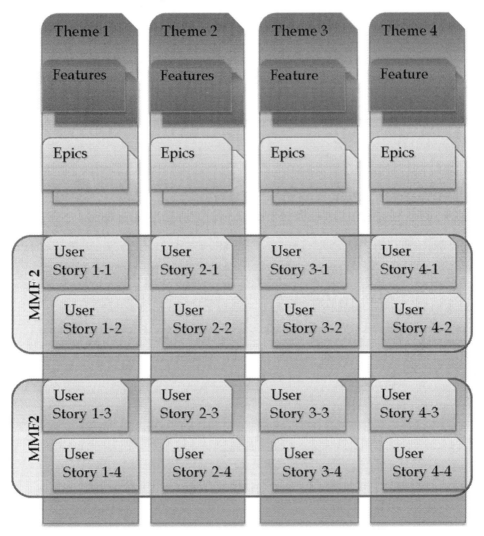

Figure 26-4: Roadmap - Step 2 - MMFs identification

These are then further expanded over releases with rough prioritization from market analysis as shown in Figure 26-5. The different legends based on MoSCoW value driven analysis are displayed.

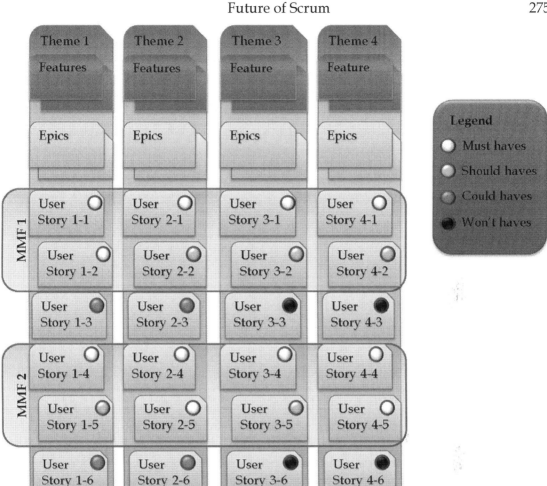

Figure 26-5: Product Roadmap with MMFs and Prioritization- shown MoSCoW based above

The roadmap is further groomed with the Development Team(s) to derive a clear map of anticipated deliverables once the releasable incremental product is identified as MMFs and the estimation is received. The estimates here are generally very high level and correspond to affinity sizing like T-shirt sizes: Extra Large (XL), Large (L), Medium (M), and Small (S). These with the prioritization of customer value helps derive rough release boundaries. These are taken to plan rough releases as shown in Figure 26-6.

With estimation done based on team velocity and knowing the number of Sprints in each Release, the team can split the stories to get further refinement so that the estimates can be derived with well-defined stories and the Product Roadmap starts to appear more groomed in release planning.

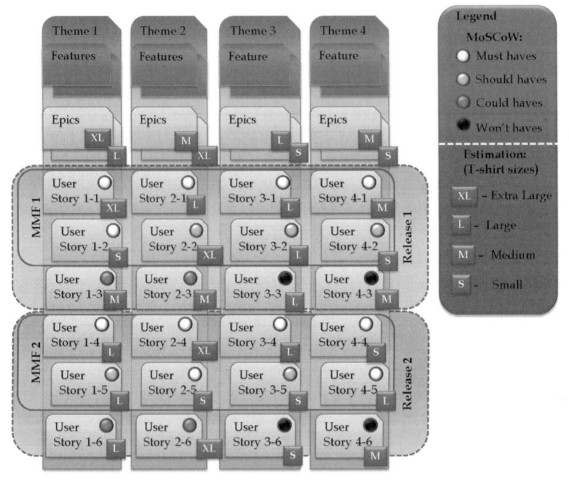

Figure 26-6: Product Roadmap with Estimated Releases

Summary

This chapter describes Product planning in Scrum Framework. As Scrum is being scaled, the aspects of planning are also expanding. The strategy and focus on product planning with differing commitments are addressed and planning is used to reflect the customer satisfaction as the highest priority.

Release planning is covered in next chapter.

Chapter 27 Release Planning

"By failing to prepare, you are preparing to fail." - Benjamin Franklin

Introduction

Release planning in Scrum delivers valuable software to the customer. The release planning is based on MMF's. Customer realizes collective value of features in an MMF.

Roadmap

Release planning creates a high level plan that spans over three to six months.

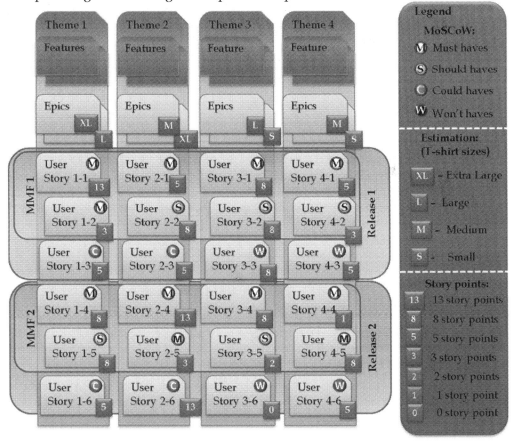

Figure 27-1: Sample Roadmap – Release level

Release planning enables a value delivery to customer. The value realization brings the conceptual analysis of ROI to actual returns. This fills in the gap of any analysis to realization of the real value. Actual value realized and current market trend allow further optimization. Business domain focuses on inspection and adaptation at release level. Product Roadmap reflects the strategy planned and is constantly reviewed as new information is available.

When schedule is estimated based on velocity, this can be reflected on the product roadmap. The completed sprints are shown in solid boundaries while the dashed-boundaries are displaying the estimated release. The roadmap continues to be groomed to ensure the stories are INVEST'ed.

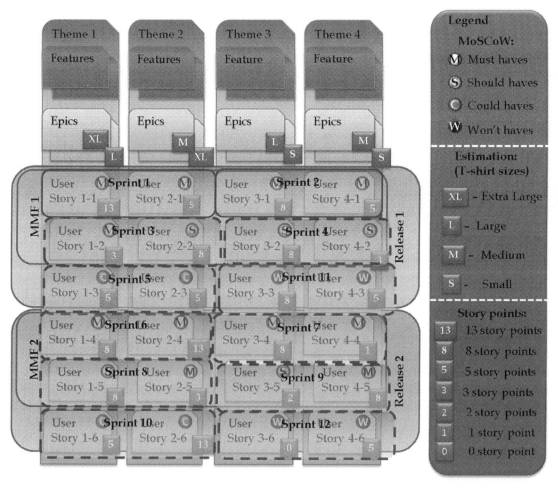

Figure 27-2: Product Roadmap with anticipated sprints

Release execution in Scrum is illustrated in Figure 27-3.

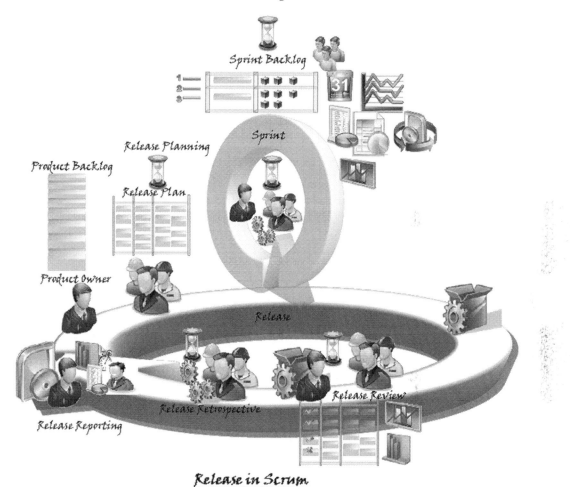

Figure 27-3: Release in Scrum

Constraints

Time and scope are identified as constraints in Agile Triangle. Most of the projects have either defined scope or definite time by which they must finish. The market is trending to always meet either or both of these constraints. These aspects get initially planned in product planning with MMFs analysis. Later, these get more detailed during release and sprint as part of rolling wave planning technique with more refinement occurring and details are captured at later stages.

Constraint based Release planning

In the following sections we shall address constraints based release planning. In essence, if a project provides value driven approach, it does not state that it is not going to meet either of the constraints. Constraints are important part of planning and become evident in release planning more than ever. The releases are delivered to the client. These releases may have time constraints like the product must be released before a trade show or upcoming market dependency. For instance, we see most software companies releasing their products during falls season. This is also the case with new car models. The driving force actually is the upcoming holidays as we see during Thanksgiving, Christmas, and New Year. Marketing and sales department drive these to optimize the opportunity to incite the customers with needs and excite them with the oncoming of spending season – umm... we mean – holiday season. Let's look at the essential aspects of release plan next.

Release plan

Release plan is created in Release planning ceremony where Product Owner and the team collaborate. Release plan helps bring a high level plan into perspective for the team. A release plan does not focus on assignment of stories and tasks for development efforts by the team. This is misleading. Rather individuals select the work as part of pull model which ensures better commitment and ownership. Release plan consists of users stories which describe the product features. The release plan focuses on prioritizing and estimating the user stories for maximum value and optimized ROI. Product Owner is responsible for prioritizing and maximizing ROI while the team is responsible for estimating the user stories.

As discussed earlier, a release plan could be feature-driven or date-driven.

Feature driven release plan identifies the stories implementing a set of features that need to be developed for the release. The stories are then estimated to derive the effort required. *Velocity is a measure of a team's progress rate.* Velocity is the number of story points the team can deliver in a sprint. Hence, the number of sprints can be derived by dividing the story points estimate for the release divided by the team velocity. Release date can be derived from the duration to complete the number of sprints and start date of release. For example, if release plan needs to deliver 200 points and team velocity is

40 story points per two week sprint; it'd take 5 two-week sprints. Given the start date of July 1st 2012, the release date could be as early as: Sept 10th.

Date driven release plan helps identify the duration for the release. The number of sprints that can be executed in this duration is identified by dividing the duration with sprint length. Total number of story points that can be delivered is identified by multiplying team velocity with the number of sprints. The release plan then includes stories whose total sum is equal to or less than this total number of derived story points. For example, if the product is to be released quarterly, there are approximately 13 weeks. This allows planning for 6 two weeks sprints in the release. If team velocity is 40 story points, then the release plan could include prioritized stories that have a cumulative sum equal to 240 story points (6 sprints * 40 story points). Team has the option to seek extra week for a shorter sprint at the end; if so desire. There are more general practices where this week is used by the team as it prefers - for refactoring, removing any technical debt, and other activities after six two-week sprints. For example, we have following stories for online retail website:

Rank	Prioritized User story	story points	Cumulative story points
1	As a buyer, I can search for an item, so that I can view items of interest to purchase	20	20
2	As a seller, I can post an item for sale, so as to make a sale	15	35
3	As a seller, I can limit the lowest acceptable price for my product for sale, so that I can manage it for acceptable profit	35	70
4	As a buyer, I can view the price for the item, so as to make a purchase decision	25	95
5	As a buyer, I can view the picture of the item, so that I can verify the product for sale	20	115
6	As a buyer, I can view the specifications of the item on sale, so that I can verify the product	20	135

7	As a buyer, I can save a search just ran with for later reuse	35	170
8	As a buyer, I can create a search for later reuse	25	195
9	As a buyer, I can update a saved-search that I had created or saved earlier	15	210
10	As a buyer, I can delete a saved-search	35	245
11	As a buyer, I can run search which should return result within 3 seconds	20	265
12	The search should return only premium results for free accounts	25	290
13	The search should return top 10 premium results and then maximum of 500 results for premium users	25	215
14	The search should identify recommended high quality item reviews to premium buyers	20	235
15	The search should allow option to compare products for premium buyers	40	275

Normally, the rank is not identified as it states that the backlog is prioritized. The rank column is added to guide you. Similarly, cumulative story points are also not required. However, they are provided here for easy reference and clarity. For release, the team can deliver first nine stories with total story points of 210. Since adding story 10 would increase the total to 245 story points which is five story points more than 240 story points to estimate for the release, story 10 is left out. However, if team gains five or more story points during execution, rank 10 story can be pulled in for development if there is time. Also, the extra week (week 13 in the quarter) could provide the opportunity where team could deliver additional 20 story points. Hence, with this new information, it could be planned, as release could have 260 story points instead of originally estimated 240 story points.

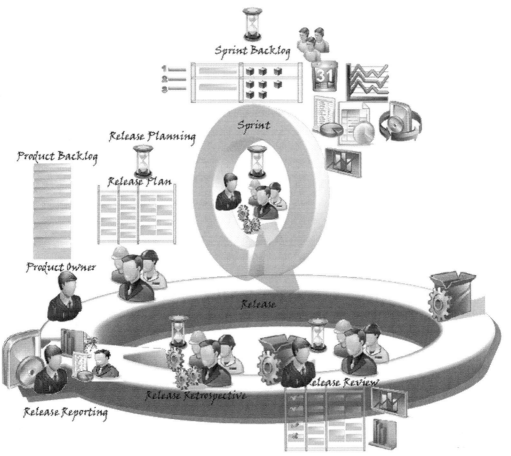

Release in Scrum

Figure 27-4: Release in Scrum (Overview)

The release plan is high level and hence, carries an inherent disadvantage of less knowledge as we gain more details and better estimation at the beginning of a sprint in Sprint planning ceremony. So, it is recommended to plan for first few sprints and leave others in a generic pool. As we approach sprint start, we can continue to assign with greater precision. Most software products for Agile project management provide this at release level where the stories could be assigned for first few releases (one to three normally) and rest stories are not assigned though sprints are planned. The stories could be assigned to later sprints as time comes close and precision increases on story details for better estimation and planning.

Release planning based on velocity

Initial Velocity

Initial velocity can be determined in any one of these three ways:

1   Use historical values
2   Run a sprint and use the velocity of that sprint
3   Take a guess

Best option is to use historical values if the current project is identical to the project whose historical value we are taking.

Running a sprint is good for start. However, as experienced, little is known in the beginning of the project, team may be new to the project and building on the tacit knowledge, the customer and users may seek many changes, may not be easily available, and other factors.

Guessing at velocity should be done so that we can explain it to others. However, this can be done based on the Estimating user stories exercise covered earlier. If we identify the ideal hours, then we need to identify how many actual hours would it take to do an ideal hour worth of work. Since the sprint duration is known, it can be used to derive the initial velocity. For example, if we estimate that an ideal hour of work can be done in 2 actual man-hours. Story points are defined as one point for four ideal hours. Then, for a sprint of two weeks (10 actual days), we can cover for a team of 5 developers, total of 80 * 5 = 400 actual hours which is equivalent to 200 ideal hours, which in-turn is equivalent to 50 story points. Hence, the initial velocity would be guessed as 50 story points.

Release estimation

Similar strategy of using velocity can be utilized to determine the number of sprints required for a release. During the planning session, the customer and development team discuss and estimate the stories for a release. The stories are provided an estimate in story points. This could enable in identifying the number of sprints it would take to complete a release.

For example, if we know the estimate velocity of 50 story points for a two week sprint. The stories selected for the release may come to 200 story points. Then, the release is expected to take 4 two weeks sprints.

Once the velocity is known, the customers provides the prioritized list of stories and collectively with the team select 50 story points worth of stories in each sprint in sequence.

- During the sprint, various strategies can be utilized:
- When users and teams are collocated, the development team will post the information through Information radiators, Kanban boards, etc. They will collectively review the progress at the end of each sprint and make updates.
- For distributed teams, these can be posted and updated on wiki sites or managed through tools like VersionOne, Rational Team Concert, SharePoint, etc.
- For global teams, again utilizing wiki, SharePoint sites, Rational Team Concert, VersionOne and similar products provide exposure to team's progress through information radiators.
- Yet there could be high level executives still asking to see a project plan, then mapping the tasks to different stories listed as deliverable and balancing them by mapping Stories and tasks on the MS Project has worked well.

Release plan is fluid and if in real life, we run into exact match, we need be cognizant to the fact that it is still a plan with coarse estimates for stories. Later discovery of new information during discussions could impact the estimates. Hence, it is safe to provide a range instead of exact sprints as we shall discover soon.

Another way of release planning is when the customer has a release date in mind. We can estimate from the estimate velocity, how many sprints we can run up to the date. Thus, allowing us to estimate the total story points for the release. The customer and team can then discuss to identify the set of stories that can be covered during the release. Then, those stories can be allocated to each release in sequence based on their prioritization. For example, on July 1st, we identify that we want to launch our retail website on Oct 1st, giving marketing department sufficient time for promotions efforts. This gives us a total of 13 weeks. We are running two week sprints. Thus, we can have total of 6 sprints and one week extra. Using our estimate velocity of 50 story points, we can deliver 300 story points (6 sprints * 50 story points). Now, customer and team discuss on what features they can have for the release. Further, MoSCoW as release estimation technique can help optimize it for the customer. Next step is to identify stories allocation for the sprints.

Planning with Stories

The Product Manager and the development team collaborate to select a sprint length for the project; usually between one and four weeks. Sprint length is constant for the project. *A release consists of one or more sprints.* A release could be from three to six months long duration. Hence, it could have three to twelve sprints.

A key feature of Agile planning is that the size is estimated but the duration is derived. For example, for a product, the cumulative sum of story points of all stories is 200. The team has velocity of 40 story points for two weeks sprint. Hence, the derived schedule would be ten weeks as 200 story points would take 5 sprints. Each sprint is two weeks, hence, 10 weeks.

Collaboratively, the team work cooperatively and delivers stories at the end of sprint. The pace of the team is identified as the cumulative sum of story points for stories completed for the sprint. It is not always possible to derive velocity and sometimes estimates have to be drawn; referred to as estimated velocity. There are three ways to estimate velocity:

1   Use historical values; for project identical to the current project w.r.t. technology, domain, team, product owner, tools, same work environment, etc.
2   Run a sprint; so as to use the velocity from the sprint
3   Make a forecast;

Velocity is the number of story points the development team delivers at the end of a sprint. For example, developers deliver four stories: A(5 story points), B(3 story points), C(7 story points), and D(8 story points) at the end of a sprint, the velocity for the sprint is: 5+3+7+8 = 23 story points.

To plan a release, prioritized stories into various piles are formed for each sprint of the release. Prioritization of a user story is based on following considerations:

1   The desirability of the feature to a broad base of users or customers

2   The desirability of the feature to a small number of important users or customers

3   The relationship of the story to the other stories. For example, an export to excel spreadsheet may not be high priority on its own; however, it could be considered as import feature story is high priority.

Basic rules on selecting a story in a sprint

- A story is skipped if it is too large to be included in a sprint
- If a story fits in a sprint through the next story may be closer to the estimated velocity, it should be considered for the sprint
- A story is not selected to meet the velocity, rather it's based on priority and size of story
- Selection Formula:
  a   Let's call bucket-size = expected velocity for the sprint
  b   Move the top story to sprint if story points of the story is less than or equal to bucket-size else skip the story

Each pile contains stories whose estimate for story points should not exceed the estimated velocity. For example, a release consisting of three sprints and an estimated velocity of 10 story points has the following prioritized story pile in descending order:

Story	Story points
Story A	3
Story B	7
Story C	3
Story D	3
Story E	4

Story F	4
Story G	6
Story H	3
Story I	4

The expected velocity is 10 would result in following stories distribution for the sprints:

Sprint	Story	Story points	Explanation
Sprint 1	A and B	3+7 = 10	Start Stack: ABCDEFGHI Selecting from top matches expected velocity of 10 story points
Sprint 2	C, D, and E	3+3+4 = 10	Start Stack: CDEFGHI Next 3 stories at top of stack match the expected velocity of 10 story points as well
Sprint 3	F and G	4+6 = 10	Start Stack: FGHI Sum of story points of the two top stories in the stack match the expected velocity of 10 story points

A complex scenario with three sprints with estimated velocity of 12 could be:

Story	Story points
Story A	3
Story B	2
Story C	7

Story D	3
Story E	3
Story F	7
Story G	5
Story H	2
Story I	2
Story J	3
Story K	5

The expected velocity is 12 would result in following stories distribution for the sprints:

Sprint	Story	Story points	Explanation
Sprint 1	A, B, and C	3+2+7 = 12	Start Stack: ABCDEFGH Selecting from top matches expected velocity of 12 story points
Sprint 2	D, E, and G	3+3+5 = 11	Start Stack: DEFGH F is too large to select here
Sprint 3	F, H, and I	7+2+2 = 11	Start Stack: FHIJK F is in priority though it is sized at 2 while J is sized at 3 but it is lower priority, hence, lower value to customer

Another complex scenario with three sprints with estimated velocity of 15 could be with prioritized stack of stories in descending order of priority:

Story	Story points
Story A	3
Story B	7
Story C	6
Story D	5
Story E	3
Story F	6
Story G	2
Story H	5
Story I	2
Story J	5
Story K	3

The expected velocity is 15 would result in following stories distribution for the sprints:

Sprint	Story	Story points	Explanation
Sprint 1	A, B, D	3+7+5 = 15	Start Stack: ABCDEFGHIJK Selecting from top matches skipping C for velocity of 15 story points
Sprint 2	C, E, G	6+3+2 = 11	Start Stack: CEFGHIJK C is in priority, F and H are too large
Sprint 3	F, H, I, K	6+5+2+3 = 15	Start Stack: FHIJK I is higher priority than J, J is too large to be included here.

Above scenario for sprint 3 planning is little more tricky and don't be fooled to think I and K are better choice as if J is preferred over I due to story size, it matches the velocity. Don't worry about sprint 2 with less story points than expected velocity. If development goes faster, developers may always ask for a small/suitable story and the Product Manager can update the stories in the stack at the start of new sprint. Alternatively, If a story does not fit in a sprint, it can be split into two or more small stories. Then one or more of the smaller stories can be included in the sprint.

Prior to start of a sprint, customer can make changes to the pile of stories by added new stories or shuffling the priority of various stories in the stack. However, customer cannot make changes in midway of a sprint, to the stack of tasks for allocated stories being developed in the sprint. These are owned by the development team. At the end of sprint, team delivers the code based on stories. Velocity of the sprint is measured by summing up the story points of all the stories accepted as done for the sprint. Releases and sprints are planned, thus, by assigning stories into sprints from the prioritized stack of stories with descending order of priority (based on relative value to the organization) from the top.

Release planning using velocity

Calculate the missing values:

Sprints >	Sprint 1	Sprint 2	Sprint 3	Sprint 4	Sprint 5
Story points at the start of sprint	100		100	67	
Completed story points during sprint	35	35		35	35
Story points due to new stories	6	8	0	16	8
Estimate changes by team during sprint planning	19		-4		
Sprint velocity	90			43	0

Release execution using roadmap

Once a roadmap is derived based on backlog grooming as discussed in earlier sessions, it is possible to align a roadmap for further estimation. A sample roadmap prior to estimation using velocity is shown below:

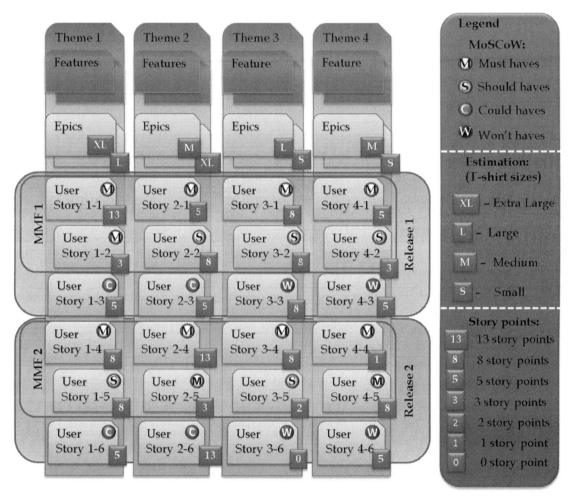

Figure 27-5: Roadmap - estimation using story points

A sample roadmap based on velocity can be used to show executed sprints as illustrated in Figure 27-6 where the stories are delivered in various Sprints. This updates are done in Sprint Review ceremony for 'done' stories. Any story that is not 'done' is reflected back on the roadmap. In this case Sprint 11 and Sprint 12 show the low priority items that were taken up later. In this case, the constraint could be 'scope' as all stories in the roadmap are completed.

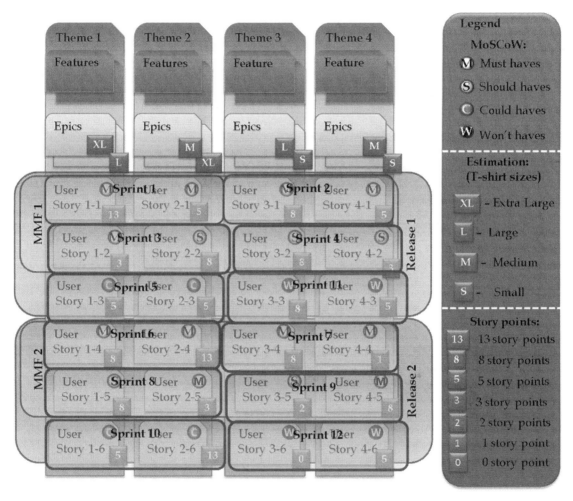

Figure 27-6: Roadmap - release execution using velocity

Summary

This chapter describes Release planning in Scrum Framework. As Scrum is being scaled, the aspects of planning are also expanding. The strategy and focus on release planning with differing commitments are addressed and planning is used to reflect the customer satisfaction as the highest priority.

Chapter 28 Sprint Planning

"Our greatest glory is not in never failing, but in rising up every time we fail."
- Ralph Waldo Emerson

Introduction

Sprint planning in Scrum focuses on development. During all other planning layers, planning is the major focus. Sprint is the execution phase. Team develops various valuable deliverables during Sprints. The other planning layers enable the backlog to be groomed so that it is ready for the Development Team to accept items for development. This chapter will elaborate on the concepts with supporting examples.

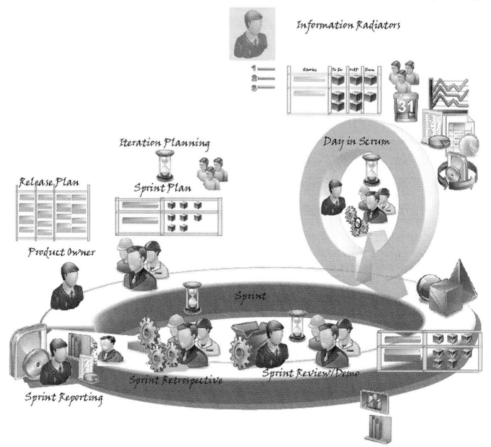

Figure 28-1 A Sprint in Scrum

Sprint Plan

Sprint plan is created in Sprint planning ceremony where Product Owner and the team collaborate. During the release plan, a rough plan for initial sprints with stories is identified. During the Sprint planning meeting, the Product Owner provides further details to the team on each story in the prioritized stories in the release plan. Team asks questions to understand the scope of each story and provides the estimate and tasks for the story. Team could utilize the index cards, white board or tools supporting APM to identify the required tasks with ideal hour estimates to complete the story. For example, a sprint plan for the first sprint for retail website could be as follows:

Rank	Prioritized User story	Ideal hours	SPs
1	As a buyer, I can search for an item, so that I can view items of interest to purchase 1 Determine the search engine logic..................... 2 Specify tests for search engine logic.................. 3 Setup database schema for items...................... 4 Design search engine.. 5 Code search engine... 6 Code UI.. 7 Run unit and integration tests............................ 8 Build configuration setup.................................... 9 Build and run automated acceptance tests........	30 40 20 30 40 10 20 10 20	20
2	As a seller, I can post an item for sale, so as to make a sale 1 Add database tables.. 2 Design UI for sellers to list an item..................... 3 Code retail engine... 4 Run unit and integration tests............................ 5 Add configuration setup for builds..................... 6 Build and run automated acceptance tests........	10 30 40 10 10 20	15

Sprint and release plan have following common aspects:

1   Product Owner brings a prioritized set of stories to both planning ceremonies
2   Product Owner describes the stories to the team and the Development Team inquires to identify scope
3   Acceptance criteria is reviewed and discussed and "done" criteria is defined for each story
4   The team estimates or re-estimates the stories at any time when something new is discovered
5   The Product Owner can also prioritize the stories during the planning meeting
6   Stories are relatively estimated based on size due to effort, risk, etc.
7   Large, compound, complex, and mixed stories are split to make them easy to estimate for a sprint

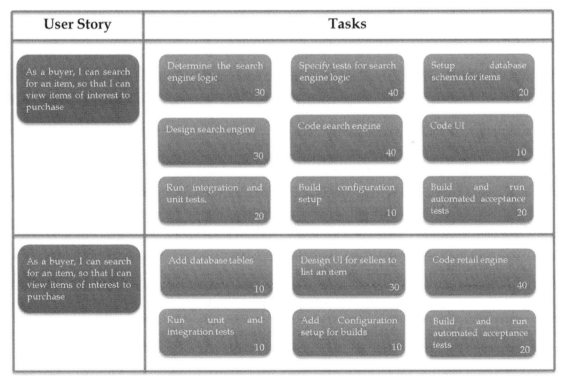

Figure 28-2: Sprint plan

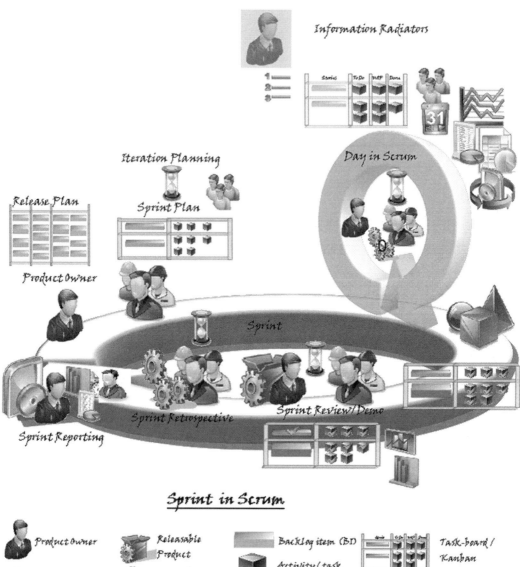

Figure 28-3 Overview of Sprint in Scrum

Sprint plan and release plan differ on the following:

	Release planning meeting	Sprint planning meeting
Duration of estimate	3-6 months	1 to 4 weeks
Input to plan	Product Backlog containing prioritized stories with acceptance criteria	Release Backlog containing prioritized stories with acceptance criteria
Output of planning ceremony	Release plan containing prioritized set of stories, release date, and estimated story points or ideal days	Sprint plan containing tasks identified with estimated ideal hours of effort

Sprint plan can be tracked with index cards in a taskboard or Kanban as shown:

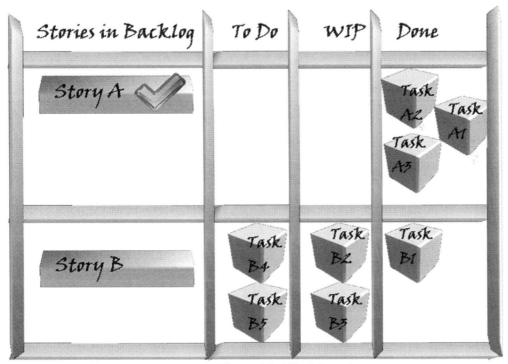

Figure 28-4 Task board

Sprint planning can be done by two factors: *Velocity or Commitment*. These two approaches are normally used and can be combined as well. Steps of velocity-driven Sprint planning are as follows:

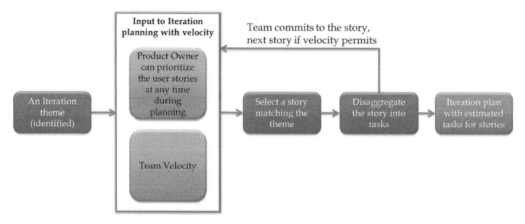

Figure 28-5: Velocity Driven Sprint Planning

An alternate approach with all stories as meeting the team velocity identified and then each story are disaggregated into tasks:

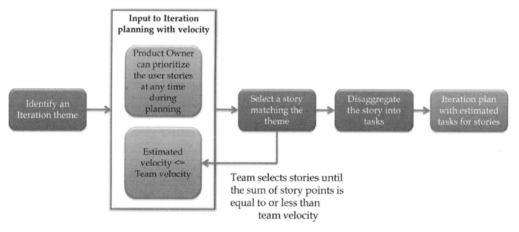

Figure 28-6: Alternate Velocity driven Sprint planning

Velocity Driven Sprint planning

Velocity-driven Sprint planning starts with two inputs: *a prioritized release backlog* containing stories and team velocity. Product Owner and team collaborate to identify the theme for the sprint. Then stories from the top of the stack are picked matching the theme. Product Owner describes the story and team inquires to identify the scope and related effort. Acceptance criteria for the story is discussed and "done" criteria are clearly defined for each story. Team disaggregates each story into tasks and associated effort to complete the tasks in ideal hours. Only relevant work to deliver value is included. As alternate shown above, some teams prefer to estimate tasks once all user stories are identified from the prioritized release backlog for the given team velocity. Tasks should be correct sized. If a task exceeds 8 hours, it is split into multiple tasks. Some teams maintain that a task cannot exceed 16 ideal hours.

Commitment driven Sprint planning

Commitment driven sprint planning is similar to velocity-driven planning approach except that stories are selected from the top of the release backlog containing prioritized stories until team cannot commit to any additional story. The sprint theme is identified as before. The inputs are the prioritized release backlog with team estimates for the stories. The sprint theme is identified as in velocity driven approach. Now a story is selected from the top of backlog and discussed. If team commits to the story, based on velocity, another story from release backlog could be selected for discussion. Once team has committed to stories, it could disaggregate stories into tasks and estimate the tasks. Some teams prefer to disaggregate stories one at a time into task and estimate before committing to the story for the sprint. If team does not commit to a story, it is put back on the release backlog and next story is selected for discussion; until the team can commit no more.

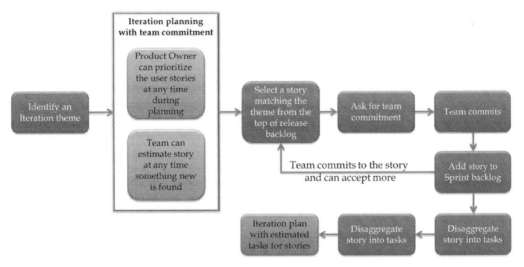

Figure 28-7: Commitment driven Sprint planning

an alternate approach where team prefers to disaggregate the story into tasks and estimate the task before committing to it for the sprint; as shown:

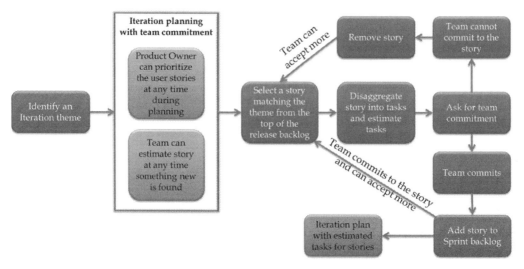

Figure 28-8: Alternate Commitment driven Sprint planning

The alternate approach is becoming more common as team can sum the estimates for the tasks and see if it is reasonable for inclusion to the sprint. Though the uncertainty exists, the task estimates in ideal hours give sufficient insight for the team to make the commitment. For example, if we have five developers working on resale website sprint 1. If the estimate of two stories as done earlier where Story 1 has 220 ideal hours of task estimates and Story 2 has 120 ideal hours of estimate for two-week sprints. The team has total hours as: 5 developers * 80 hours for two-week sprint/developer = 400 hours. Team can then estimate if it can complete total of 340 ideal hours for both the stories in 400 actual hours for the sprint. Team can then estimate and after a few sprint team will have a better feeling based on the value-stream analysis to know their ratio of actual vs. ideal hours. If team finds out that it's estimate is 5 hours of ideal hours in 8 hours day, then the ideal hours that can be achieved in 400 actual hours would be 5 developers * 10 days * 5 ideal hours = 250 hours. Thus, team would only commit to Story 1 for 220 ideal hours and leave out Story 2. After value-steam mapping and analyzing to optimize the process, say the team can achieve 7 ideal hours of work in a day, it'd be able to take up to 350 ideal hours of work in a sprint - an increase by 100 ideal hours!

Summary

This chapter describes Sprint planning in Scrum Framework. As Scrum is being scaled, the aspects of planning are also expanding. The strategy and focus on sprint planning with differing commitments are addressed and planning is used to reflect the customer satisfaction as the highest priority.

Chapter 29 A Day in Scrum

"Edison failed 10,000 times before he made the electric light. Do not be discouraged if you fail a few times." - Napoleon Hill

Introduction

A day in Scrum is where the core team works on tactics in sync with the strategic vision and goals. A Sprint starts with all members assessing their commitment from previous day. Then the team gathers for Daily Scrum where daily status is shared and team collaborates on strategy for the next day. As self-organizing team, the team collaborates to achieve the target set for the day.

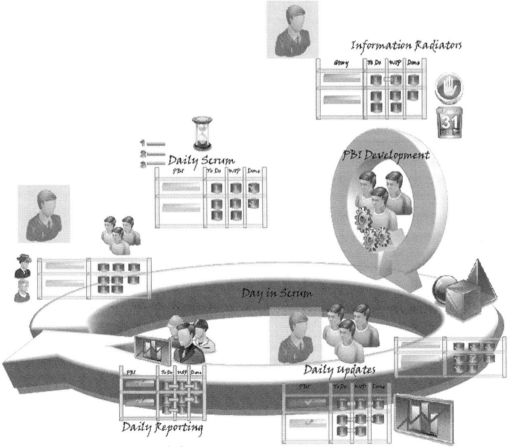

Figure 29-1: A day in Scrum

Daily Scrum

Daily Scrum ceremony occurs at the same location at the same time on every working day. This ceremony is timeboxed to 15 minutes and has been elaborated in Chapter 40 in detail. In essence, the core team gathers and looks at their commitments from the previous day, makes commitment to take on tasks for the next day and discusses any roadblocks. Scrum Master facilitates this session.

Team Development activities

Team members collaborate together to device the development process and practices. This is following the Agile principle #11: "The best architectures, requirements, and designs emerge from self-organizing teams."

The development team can utilize various practices as suitable. They may decide to pair-program, Test Driven Development (TDD), etc. There are many development practices promoted in eXtreme Programming which allow visibility to allow the team to inspect and adapt. Pair programming helps the team to share and able to inspect-and-adapt in seconds. Test Driven development promotes feedback in minutes. Continuous Integration (CI) can provide feedback multiple times during the day. Daily Scrum covers daily transparency and related feedback to enable inspection and adaptation.

Customer Collaboration

The development team and customer collaborate throughout the day with focus on development activities and Daily Scrum commitments. These are reflected in information radiators like Sprint Burndown or Burnup graphs, team calendar, task board, etc. Agile principle #4 supports the activities: "Business people and developers must work together daily throughout the project."

Raising issues

The roadblocks and any issues encountered during the day need not wait till the next day. The team realizes and discusses any new information, risks and issues as soon as they are evident and analyzed. The team seeks to find possible resolutions, tactics and ways to handle these and works together. The leadership team and other members of extended team seek to provide full support to ensure the development team has all the resources and support to carry out their work. This aligns with agile principle #5:

"Build projects around motivated individuals. Give them the environment and support they need, and trust them to get the job done."

Ideal hours reporting

Estimating for tasks is recommended to be in ideal hours instead of actual hours. While the actual hours are the hours worked, ideal hours provide the effective time spent in completing the tasks. The estimation is specific to project and could be in story points as well.

Task ideal hours vs. Story points

Remember the analogy of sieve when filtering right sized pebbles? This applies here and hence, story may have an average estimate relationship to ideal hours and not an exact value. This is represented by a bell-graph where a story of 1 point could take 8 ± 4 hours, story of 2 points could take 16 ± 4 hours, story of 3 points could take 24 ± 4 hours. This shows some distribution and hopefully balances out over the sprint period. Though there are many other factors that can influence this, an approximate relationship could be perceived. This is an important aspect to know for real world experience.

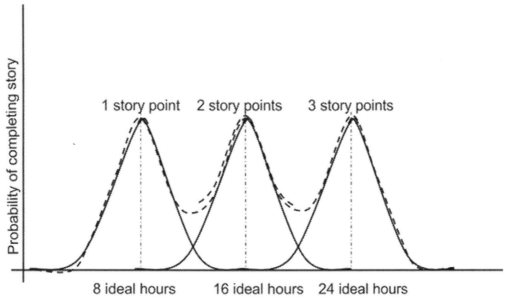

Figure 29-2: Task ideal hours vs. Story-points analysis

Summary

A day in Scrum is focused on the delivering value in optimal way. The core team collaborates to focus on delivering value to the customer on daily basis. There is transparency provided at daily level during Daily Scrum ceremony. The team continues to work on the set goals and organizes its approach while inspecting and adapting to any risks and changes it sees. The focus is on trees instead of the forest. Details and getting the team to self-organize is essential.

Section VII
Scrum Ceremonies

Chapter 30 Planning Ceremonies

"A good plan violently executed now is better than a perfect plan executed next week."
- George S. Patton

Introduction

Planning aspects were discussed in previous section. This chapter focuses on various activities that are carried out in each planning ceremony. The distinctions at different planning levels are profound and closely interrelated with backlog grooming as progressive elaboration results in refining, splitting and prioritizing the backlog items while new ones are added and existing ones are updated or deleted. The planning ceremony requires the backlog grooming to be done extensively to ensure further planning levels can elaborate effectively. Scrum Master facilitates planning ceremonies.

Figure 30-1: Scrum Planning Overview

Sprint Planning

Sprint planning participants are: The Product Owner, Scrum Master and the Development Team. For two week iterations, Sprint planning ceremony is 4 hours timebox. The input to Sprint planning ceremony varies with the type of project and its structure. At a minimum, it should be Product Backlog that is DEEP.

Sprint planning ceremony has two sessions: Commit to BI and Assign Tasks to BIs.

First session, Commit to BIs, is where the Product Owner discusses the backlog items top down with decreasing value. The team inquires to understand each backlog item to assess the various aspects and build a clear understanding of the effort it would take to get it done. The Development team identifies collectively the set of backlog items for the Sprint. These form the Development Team's commitment for the Sprint.

Second session, Assign tasks to BIs, is where the members of Development team collaborate to list all the tasks required for each backlog item. Once all the tasks have been listed, the team collectively discusses each task in some detail to ensure all options, alternatives and directions are shared to build a common perspective. The Scrum Master and the Product Owner are also welcome to share comments to ensure no gaps are left out, uncertainties and to realize known-unknowns are out in the open. These tasks are listed against each backlog items. Here the Sprint plan is an intermediate stage where the tasks still need to be owned. Team members take on ownership of various tasks. Team calendar is an essential input to ensure balanced ownership. Though an attempt is made to list and own tasks, it is still considered as an estimate. With more unknowns emerging later and clarification of known-unknowns could result in addition tasks or update to the current list of tasks. Tasks can be created, updated, and deleted during the Sprint Execution phase. The Development Team owns the Sprint plan though it should always keep the focus on priorities as the Product Owner identifies the priorities (aka Order or Rank - when a backlog item will be done) just as the Development Team provides the estimates to the backlog items.

Important rules of conducting the planning ceremony are:

- The Sprint planning ceremony is attended by the Scrum Master, the Product Owner and the Development Team
- Scrum Master facilitates the Sprint planning ceremony. In absence of Scrum Master, another Scrum Master, Scrum Coach or Agile Coach can facilitate the ceremony. Scrum Master must coordinate to ensure a facilitator is assigned.
- The Product Owner provides the prioritized Product Backlog and help the team understand the Product Backlog items
- The Development Team seeks to create a Sprint Backlog with Backlog items and required tasks to complete the Backlog items.

- No chickens (other stakeholders) are allowed unless provisioned by the Product Owner. Other team members acting as SMEs and required support personnel are allowed as observers.

- The Product Owner provides the updated and prioritized Product Backlog prior to the meeting

- In absence of the Product Owner, the Scrum Master prepares an adequate Product Backlog and stands in for the Product Owner

- The Team selects the Product Backlog items from the top (highest priority) to identify the items it can commit to. The Team determines what it will attempt to achieve during the Sprint.

- The Product Owner decides what items constitute the backlog for the Sprint.

- The team can offer suggestions and recommendations though for the Product Owner's consideration. Team calendar, velocity and other radiators are used for this analysis.

- Further analysis on Product Backlog items (PBIs) can be done during the Sprint.

- Product Owner is responsible to address any inquiries the Team has for understanding PBIs.

- During the second half, the Team breaks down each PBI into the various tasks needed to perform to achieve the PBI. The Product Owner must be present to provide answers to the Team. However, the discussion on analysis can continue during the Sprint, if both the parties agree as the ceremony is timeboxed.

- The Team manages the Sprint Backlog. The Team organizes Sprint plan to deliver the PBIs during the Sprint. Hence, the Team is responsible for deriving tasks needed to deliver each PBI. The Team collaborates with other stakeholders in case of inquiries or when it needs support.

- A set of rules apply to the Sprint and are thus, addressed in that section

- Every PBI in Sprint Backlog must have acceptance criteria defined (as to what 'done' means") to estimate effort and know when PBI is complete. The definition of 'done' should be defined and core team (the Product Owner, the Scrum Master, and the Development Team) agree as to what "done" means.

- During the Sprint, any changes to this definition must be agreed upon by the Product Owner and the Development Team.

Release Planning

Release planning seeks to distribute MMFs across various releases. The key participants in release planning are: The Product Owner or Product Owner Team(s), Scrum Master(s), key stakeholders, the Development Teams and Management and Leadership teams. Input to Release planning ceremony varies with the structure of the project and product planning strategy. The minimum input to release planning should be a DEEP Product Backlog with MMFs. Scrum Master or Agile Coach facilitates this session. We have seen many times Product Owner or Chief Product Owner trying to facilitate these sessions and also seen it fail badly on almost every occasions as there is inherent conflict of interest and it takes great character to stand through such conflicts. One perfect example of a Product Owner who repeatedly succeeded in being both: the Product Owner and the Scrum Master was Steve Jobs who didn't even need to use the term Scrum but ran every session as perfect Scrum ceremony at Ri-level (Transcending over to be the rule).

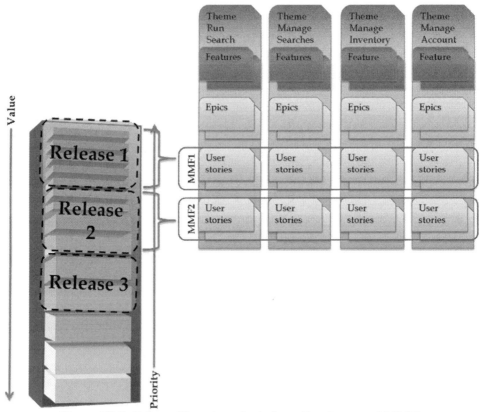

Figure 30-2: Release Planning starts from Roadmap and MMFs

Release planning session is split into two sessions: During the first half, the Product Owner or the Chief Product Owner discusses the MMFs in their respective order and addresses each backlog item contained in and how it all ties in. The participants inquire to build a common understanding of the MMFs and individual components in MMFs with interrelationships and dependencies. On some occasions, we have seen that MMFs get redefined during this session with prioritization occurring at times too. That occurs when new information has not made it to the backlog grooming. Once MMFs are defined, estimated and prioritized, any residual grooming is completed.

Release planning is done in Business domain. Scrum Master facilitates the Release planning and similar rules as that of Sprint planning apply except participants now include key stakeholders like marketing and sales team representatives, Operations, and Program Manager.

During the second half, the participants seek to identify the priority and build a release plan. Product prioritizing Techniques like MoSCoW or Kano analysis are employed to derive a value-driven approach. Participants play innovation games to build the set of backlog items. The focus is not to overload the release plan with value-driven items. It is essential to keep a balanced release plan with the understanding of empirical process at hand.

The release is balanced to cover MMF that delivers highest value with set of supporting user stories that could be technical, foundational and related to provide a mix. There is a

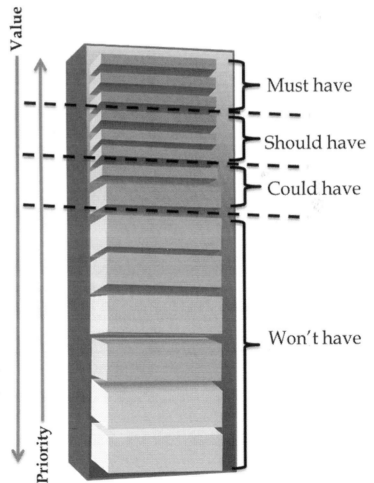

Figure 30-3: MoSCoW'ed Product Backlog

tendency of providing buffer stories in case the Development team feels that it'd finish the stories early. These are "won't haves" and may be substituted, as needed, with higher priority backlog items.

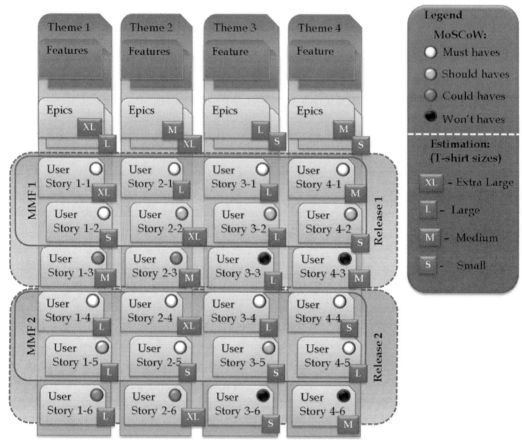

Figure 30-4: Release planning using value-driven approach (MoSCoW)

Product Planning

Product planning ceremony is held at stakeholders' level. The main participants of product planning ceremony are: the Management and Leadership teams, customer, end-users, marketing and sales teams, the Product Owner and the Scrum Master. If the Development Team is identified, they are welcome to attend as watchers or extended members. Product planning is focused on market analysis and identifies MMFs. This planning ceremony requires a Product Backlog item that is groomed at high level – Features and Epics. Other input includes one or more of the followings: the Product

Vision or elevator statement, Product Vision Box, Project Data sheet, planning constraints, and strategies.

Product planning ceremony is split in two sessions. In the first half, the Product Owner presents the Product Backlog items to the participants. The participants inquire about each item to build a common understanding. During the second half, the participants collaborate together and also employ agile games like innovation games for planning and Affinity sizing like T-shirt sizes for estimation (if any item was not estimated or new ones identified), to identify MMFs that could be attained in identified constraints.

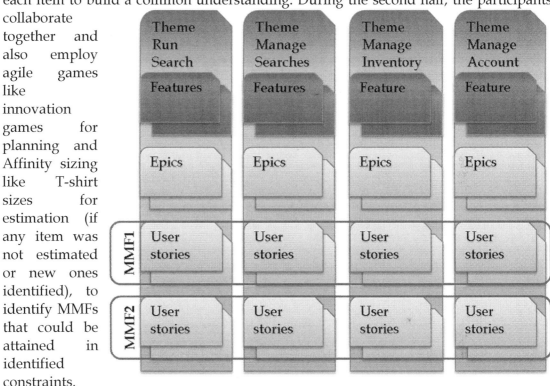

Figure 30-5: Product Planning - MMFs identification

Summary

This chapter describes the planning ceremonies and the essential ingredients of each of the planning ceremony. The portfolio and strategy planning are not covered here as they fall outside the scope. Those are addressed in detail in our book: *Coaching Agile Enterprises and leadership teams.*

The next chapter focuses on Daily Scrums where the Development team employs various tactics during the execution phase focusing on the development process.

Chapter 31 Daily Scrums

"Productivity is never an accident. It is always the result of a commitment to excellence, intelligent planning, and focused effort." - Paul J. Meyer

Introduction

Daily Scrum is the single most important empirical process control activity that has continued to provide visibility to the progress to be able to effectively inspect and adapt. Most Scrum teams start with holding Daily Scrums. Though easiest of all the ceremonies to get started with Scrum, Daily Scrum is also the most misunderstood. Scrum Master plays a key role in ensuring that the team is able to grasp and follow Scrum rules, values, and principles for an effective Daily Scrum sessions.

Figure 31-1: Daily Scrum

Ceremony

Daily Scrum is held daily at the same time at the same place where team gathers to inspect the progress and make further commitment for the day and address any impediment blocking progress. Scrum Master facilitates this ceremony. The participants include: The Development Team and the Product Owner. Other stakeholders can attend as watchers and are not allowed to speak.

Scrum Master starts the session with identifying the agenda for the ceremony. Scrum Master facilitates with suitable information radiators in focus. The participants normally gather around the information radiators or Team wall. Each participant takes turn to answer three questions:

1   What have you done since the Last Daily Scrum on this project?
2   What do you plan to do before the next Daily Scrum on this project?
3   Is there any impediment or roadblock in your way on this project?

The first questions focuses on assessing the progress based on previous meeting's commitment for the day. It is not a status reporting like – "I am working on so and so story or so and so task." It is to address specific task(s) the team member committed to finish. One essential ingredient is that the task should be sufficiently sized that it can be finished in the committed duration. This is based on best estimate. For new teams, it could take some time to get good estimates. However, mature teams, running for 3-4 sprints, should be getting good at it.

Second question focuses on the new commitment. Each participant focuses on various tasks they are taking on along with any unknowns and risks. The unknowns and risks are to be addressed proactively. Reactive approach ensures failure before even start. Before coming to the Daily Scrum, each member should think about what it would take to finish a task. When there are unknowns, they should be identified here so that other members have an opportunity to provide insight or at least brainstorm various options later.

The last question is related to a roadblock in development process. This should be a task for Scrum Master if it pertains to solution domain or a task for the Product Owner if it pertains to the Business domain. However, though the accountability is owned individually, everyone in the ceremony is equally responsible and committed.

Utilizing SharePoint or Wiki site to post Daily Scrum updates is found very effective for Release, project and product retrospectives.

Rules of Daily Scrum

As per the rules of Scrum, following aspects are important and the Scrum Master is responsible to enforce these rules:

- The Daily Scrum is conducted at the same time and same place every day
- Everyone needs to be punctual to Daily Scrum Ceremony
- Daily Scrum ceremonies are timeboxed to 15 minutes duration
- Participants are the Core Team members: the Scrum Master, the Product Owner, and The Team. Extended Team members may attend as observers and are not allowed to speak during the ceremony.
- Scrum Master facilitates the ceremony. In absence of Scrum Master, another Scrum Master, Scrum Coach or Agile Coach can facilitate the ceremony. Scrum Master must coordinate to ensure a facilitator is present with the agenda.
- Only the three questions [as stated above] are answered by the team members
- Only one conversation continues where a team member answers the three questions
- No one other than the team members can speak in these ceremonies. Only one team member talks at a time and answers the three questions.
- Anyone can request specifics on any item of interest for parking lot and plan for a follow-up ceremony to discuss them with the Team or team member.
- No lengthy solutions to any identified impediments are discussed during the ceremony. These are recorded as parking lot item. Parking lot items are tackled in a follow-up session by the Team, Scrum Master and the Product Owner.
- Participation is normally decided by the team for extended team members which includes stakeholders
- If a team member cannot attend, he or she must provide the status beforehand or provide a proxy with the status
- The Scrum Master can limit the attendance of participants other than the team and the Product Owner.
- For team members not following the rules, the Scrum Master can remove them from the Team if unable to get compliance

Though these rules are followed, a mature Scrum Master uses soft-skills and leadership skills to make these ceremonies interesting. Outcome of Daily Scrum ceremony is current status and list of any impediments the Team has. Thus, any follow-up session can be held to address those and achieve the short-term deliverables. As evident, extended team members are not allowed to speak and are only observers.

So they cannot provide instructions and direction to the team on how to complete the work.

Summary

This chapter describes some essential key aspects of Daily Scrum ceremony. Scrum of Scrums is discussed in the next chapter. It is effective when more than one team is involved in product development and has inter-dependencies. Sometimes programs use Scrum of Scrums to ensure the visibility across multiple products.

Chapter 32 Scrum of Scrums

"I count him braver who overcomes his desires than him who conquers his enemies; for the hardest victory is over self." - Aristotle

Introduction

Scrum of Scrums ceremony is performed when there is more than one Development Team working on a product. Currently, Scrum of Scrums is performed at product development level. However, it can be equally utilized at Product or Portfolio level when there are multiple project teams developing product components. Scrum of Scrum provides multiple teams to collaborate and synchronize their activities toward the common goal – delivering incremental product to customers.

Currently, Scrum of Scrums ceremonies were introduced for large team sizes or multiple teams working at project or program level. These apply to larger teams where development representatives from each Scrum team meet regularly to collaborate with other teams. These ceremonies occur once or twice a week to focus on project progress. This is a short ceremony; similar to Daily Scrum as focus is on providing transparency.

Figure 32-1: Scrum of Scrums Overview

Scrum of Scrums is held regularly at the same day at the same time. It is 15 minute timebox. Each Scrum core team representative answers the following four questions:

1. What has your team done since we last met?
2. What will your team do before we meet again?
3. Is there anything slowing your team down or any roadblock is in its way?
4. Are you about to put anything in other team's/teams' way?

Rules of Scrum of Scrums

As per the rules of Scrum, following aspects are important and the Scrum Master is responsible to enforce these rules:

- The Scrum of Scrums is conducted at the same time and same place every day
- Everyone needs to be on time as this ceremony is kept short and quick
- Scrum of Scrums ceremonies are 15 minute timeboxes
- Attendees are the Core Team members: Scrum Master(s), and individual Development Team leads or representatives.
- Scrum Coach or one of the Scrum Masters facilitates the Scrum of Scrums ceremony. In absence of Scrum Master, another Scrum Master, Scrum Coach or Agile Coach can facilitate the ceremony. Scrum Master must coordinate to ensure a facilitator is present with the agenda.
- Only the four questions [as stated above] are answered by the team members
- Only one conversation continues where a team member answers the four questions
- No one other than the team members can speak in these ceremonies. Only one team member talks at a time and answers the questions.
- Anyone can note specifics on any item of interest and plan for a follow-up ceremony to discuss them with the Team or team member. However, extended team members are not allowed to provide instructions and direction to the team on how to complete the work.
- No lengthy solutions to any identified impediments are discussed during the ceremony. These are recorded as parking lot item. Parking lot items are tackled in a follow-up session by the Team, Scrum Master and the Product Owner.
- Participation is normally decided by the team for extended team members which includes stakeholders

- If a team member cannot attend, he or she must provide the status beforehand or provide a proxy with the status
- The Scrum master can limit the attendance of participants other than the team. For team members not following the rules, the Scrum Master can remove them from the Team

It is essential that the objectives, perspectives, and goals of all the teams represented in Scrum of Scrums are aligned. In absence of the driving factors and shared vision, the ceremony encounters ambiguities, challenges and could fail to be effective.

Summary

This chapter described various aspects of Scrum of Scrums ceremony. This ceremony is effective in empirical process control for large project teams working on same project, program or portfolio. Effectiveness of this

Chapter 33 Review Ceremonies

"The price of success is hard work, dedication to the job at hand, and the determination that whether we win or lose, we have applied the best of ourselves to the task at hand."
- Vince Lombardi

Introduction

Review ceremony is held on the last day of the development timebox. Review is a timebox ceremony. For two week Sprint, Review is normally four hour timebox. The Product Owner or the Chief Product Owner facilitates this ceremony. The Development Team members demo the product to the stakeholders and at the end feedback are taken and praises are shared for the efforts undertaken.

Figure 33-1: Review Ceremony Overview

Sprint Review

Review ceremony is held on the last day of the Sprint. Review is a timebox ceremony. For two week Sprint, Review is normally four hour timebox. The Product Owner or the Chief Product Owner facilitates this session. In the past, Scrum Masters were facilitators. However, it soon became evident that in such cases, the Product Owner may not have the level of commitment; needed in this ceremony. Product Owner prepares for this ceremony early on with the Development Team. This allows them to collaborate and accept the completed stories; prior to the ceremony. An essential aspect of this acceptance is the review of acceptance criteria and ensuring that all the acceptance criteria for a completed story are met. Then the story is moved to 'done' state. During the ceremony, the Product Owner identifies the acceptance criteria for the story and the Development Team displays the compliance to that criteria. This makes the explicit statement to the stakeholders on the scope.

The hind-sight is normally 20-20. We have seen that in Sprint Retrospectives there are bulbs flashing all over the place. The stakeholders and sometimes even the Product Owner and the Development Team discover new findings during the Review. These are an essential output as the Scrum Master can help capture these new discoveries. These discoveries are actually owned by the Product Owner and Scrum Master just functions in support role to keep the session focused. These new findings are then considered for the Product Backlog; not the Release Backlog. A greater view is desired as Release backlog may not provide full insight to all the themes and related Backlog items. The new items are analyzed and result in creation, updated, review and removal of the Backlog items in the Product Backlog.

The Product Owner takes the Product Backlog after the Review session for grooming. This is to ensure a DEEP Product backlog for the next planning ceremony.

Release Review

The Product Owner or the Chief Product Owner facilitates Release Reviews. The Scrum Master helps in capturing the session details as a support role. The Development Team demonstrates the integrated Minimally Marketable Feature (MMF) as a Minimum Viable Product (MVP) of value to the customer. Inputs from Sprint Reviews feed into Release Review where the inspection of the product is done at MMF level which spans across many themes. The inputs from stakeholders are taken and leads to Product Backlog grooming to ensure it stays DEEP. Further any impact to oncoming releases is also actively undertaken during this review. Agile is all about the ability to inspect-and-adapt and this is an important juncture in the process.

Releases mainly focus on MMF/MVP aspect. The deliverable from the release ends up in the hands of end-users. This requires that the product features provided in the product meet the marketable aspect and provide an integrated solution to the customer needs. Release reviews focus on these aspects where the focus is on the integrated whole instead of individual story, as was the case in Sprint Reviews.

The rules pertaining to Sprint Review ceremony are:

- Sprint review ceremony is attended by the Core Team viz. the Scrum Master, the Team and the Product Owner, and essential stakeholders.
- Only PBI(s) that are "done" based on the acceptance criteria established during the Planning ceremony are addressed. Any PBI not done is not addressed during the ceremony.
- Any work item not part of Sprint Backlog can be presented. This is to discourage gold plating
- PBI completed during the Sprint is presented (demoed) on a production or production like workstations closest to the production configuration
- Completed PBIs are presented by the team though it is a growing practice for the Product Owner to present the completed functionality to the stakeholders
- During the second half, the Product Backlog is updated with "done" PBIs noted, additional PBIs identified for consideration based on stakeholders' feedback and input
- The Product Backlog updates and prioritization is the responsibility of the Product Owner
- Product Owner facilitates Sprint Review ceremony and in the absence of Product Owner, it can be covered by the Scrum Master. Product Owner is responsible for ensuring the coordination to ensure a facilitator is available with agenda for the ceremony.
- In first half of the ceremony, the Team demos the product deliverables
- In second half, backlog items are accepted and reviews received

Product Review

Product Review is differs from lessons learned as carried out at the end of the project. Hence, the focus is on success of the product. The Product Owner is accountable for the product success. This success is built on various levels. Ultimately, the success is tracked and analyzed with a common goal to learn and grow. The Product Owner or the Chief Product Owner facilitates Product Review ceremony. The Development Team(s) participates and conducts demo of various features and shares many outstanding aspect of the product. The project timeline is shared with various aspects where successes and failures were encountered and how opportunities were explored and threats were reduced. Market analysis, vision to concept, proving market analysis to the results and feedback

The main criteria of successful project retrospectives highlight the following factors:

1. The Core Team would continue to work in similar fashion in future
2. The Management and Leadership team remains intact after the project
3. The Development Team members continue to work together as an entity
4. The Product Owner continues to perform on their role and may take on additional projects
5. The Review provide an essential insight to enterprise vision and portfolio

Summary

This chapter describes the various levels of Scrum Reviews at Sprint, Release, and Product levels. These reviews allow the Core Team to share the product deliverables with the stakeholders in their effort to ensure they are aligned with the initial commitments while also seeking important feedbacks from this session to re-align themselves for the arising needs and external factors.

The Product Owner plays a key role in ensuring that this ceremony generates sufficient upsurge of ideas and feedback for ensuring that the Product Backlog is optimized to ensure maximum ROI and customer satisfaction.

Chapter 34 Retrospectives

"Excellence is an art won by training and habituation. We do not act rightly because we have virtue or excellence, but we rather have those because we have acted rightly. We are what we repeatedly do. Excellence, then, is not an act but a habit." - Aristotle

Introduction

Retrospective is the last activity of the development timebox; be it Sprint, Release or Product development cycle. In Retrospectives, the team inspects the development process to optimize it and adapt it for efficiency and effectiveness. The development process includes three key factors: The methods or processes used, the resources used for development, and people involved in development. It is misleading to only focus on processes and leave out other two.

Figure 34-1: Retrospective Overview

Retrospectives Model

Retrospective model as proposed by Esther Derby and Diana Larsen [DERBY and LARSEN, 2006] is the minimal set for agile retrospective ceremonies:

1. Set the Stage
2. Gather Data
3. Generate Insights
4. Decide what to do
5. Close the Retrospective

All Retrospectives irrespective of their types follow these. However, the higher the level, more strategic focus and aligned it is to the vision. Sprint retrospectives are more tactical in approach where the Core Team gathers to identify ways to optimize the development process.

Sprint Retrospectives

We have been using a Retrospective template based technique for Sprint Retrospectives for normal sprints. This template allows easy flow through the session and seeks to keep the session effective while focusing on tuning the development process which is composed of three elements: People, processes and resources. It is evident that for this template to be effective, a collaborative and supportive environment is provided for the teams to grow. The layout of the sections visited is as follows:

1. Express your feelings about the problem – This is carried out in free-for-all manner. For new teams, it is better to carry in round-robin fashion to help the team express. It is normal for participants to go overboard with expressing more than just a few words. Asking them to keep it for the next session works. In early sessions, providing an agenda early on helps the team to be ready appropriately. Scrum values are exercised and reinforced when members are able to share their feelings openly.

2. What went well: It is effective to get the members to focus on the good aspects of the development effort during the Sprint. Now that everyone feels that they have been heard about their feelings in earlier section, this starts to instill positive feelings about the project. The resource crunch, individuals and interactions, and processes and procedures are the focus here.

3.   What didn't work well: This is an important area to capture where the strategies and tactics may not be effective. The resource crunch, individuals and interactions, and processes and procedures are the focus here as well.

4.   New ideas: For each item in "what didn't work well," the participants brainstorm various solutions, decide on the solution to implement, discuss detail activities for the solution and own activities to implement the solution are address.

5.   Assess confidence level and build buy-in: Each decision is recorded here with ownership. SMART goals activity: Specific, Measurable, Attainable, Relevant and Timely [Derby and Larsen, 2006]. This activity takes longer (30-60 minutes) on first few Sprint retrospectives and then gets completed quickly (10 to 20 minutes) on the following ones for the project team.

6.   Appreciations: It is important to help team members recognize each other's effort. This is a reflection of supportive and collaborative environment.

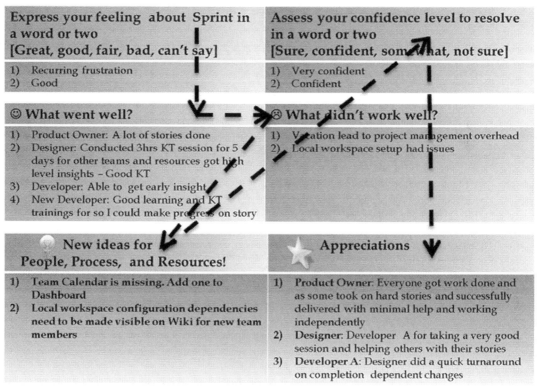

Figure 34-2: Sample Retrospective Template

Rules of Sprint Retrospective

The rules pertaining to Sprint Retrospective ceremony are:

- Sprint Retrospective ceremony is attended by the Scrum Master, the Product Owner and the Development Team.
- Scrum Master facilitates the Sprint planning ceremony. In absence of Scrum Master, another Scrum Master, Scrum Coach or Agile Coach can facilitate the ceremony. Scrum Master must coordinate to ensure a facilitator is present with the agenda.
- Attendees are the Core Team members: the Scrum Master, the Product Owner, and The Team.
- The Product Owner's participation is optional. No other stakeholders are allowed.
- Sprint retrospective ceremonies do not have a specific format of questions. However, it must address the following two questions, at the minimum:
  - What went well during the Sprint?
  - What could be improved in the upcoming Sprint?

Additional questions that should be addressed are:

  - What did not go well during the Sprint?
  - What process improvements from past Sprint(s) are still applicable?
  - Any new ideas that can be tried to improve current process?
  - Any appreciations for the team and others for the last Sprint?

These additional questions provide further retrospection as part of continuous improvement goals. When team records data in information sharing tools like SharePoint or Wiki site, it helps to refer and analyze the data from Daily Scrums, Product Council sessions, and other Team collaboration sessions.

Sample agenda for a normal Sprint Retrospective:

9AM-9:15AM   Set the Stage: Welcome, Discuss Goal, and activities: Focus on/Focus off, discuss ground rules

09:15AM-10AM	Gather Data – #1: Overall feeling, #2: What went well, and #3: what did not go well
10AM -10:15 AM	Generate insights – #4: New ideas
10:15AM -11:45 AM	Decide what to do – #4: Select one or two new ideas to implement and detail tasks – SMART goals
4PM- 5:15PM	Closing: #5: Assess confidence level on the decisions from the session, #6: Appreciations, followed by ROTI on Retrospective. Thank the participants

When there are exceptions like a cancelled or failed Sprint, it helps to dig deeper and retrospective agenda and exercises would have to be modified to get appropriate details.

Release Retrospectives

Release retrospectives are normally full day ceremony for 2 to 3 months long release timebox. Release expands over a longer time span. This requires better visibility over the long period. The strategic planning and execution are inspected here for further tuning and addressing greater aspects. Release retrospectives also include more stakeholders to join as fly-on-the-wall and the support teams or their representatives.

For a 2-3 month release, Product retrospective ceremony could be 6 hour timebox. There need to be sufficient breaks for 15 minutes. 4 breaks and 1 hour for lunch consumes a whole day in Product Retrospective.

The participants to Release retrospective extend beyond the Core Team. This requires identifying the stakeholders to invite; inviting identified stakeholders; and educating them on the importance, agenda and retrospective process. These include support teams like network, MIS, Operations, Key customers, and Marketing and Sales team representatives.

Release retrospection is more effective using timeline techniques. The events are tracked and recorded and also the retrospectives from sprints in the release are used to quickly grasp the tuning of development process during the release.

Rules of Release Retrospectives

The rules pertaining to Release Retrospective ceremony are:

- The Core Team identifies key Business and Solution stakeholders and extend invitation to the release retrospective
- Scrum Master ensures that the key stakeholders are educated on the purpose, activities and scope of release retrospectives
- Participants to Release Retrospective ceremony are: the Scrum Master, the Product Owner, the Development Team and key Business and Solution domain stakeholders.
- Scrum Coach, Scrum Master or Team lead can facilitate the Release retrospective ceremony. In absence of Scrum Master, another Scrum Master, Scrum Coach, or Team Lead can facilitate the ceremony. Scrum Master must coordinate to ensure a facilitator is present with a prepared agenda.
- Release retrospective ceremonies need to focus on higher level of streamlining the development process. Hence, uses timeline to gather data effectively:
  - What went well during the Release development?
  - What could be improved in the upcoming Release development?

Additional questions that should be addressed are:

- What did not go well during the Release?
- What process improvements from past Release(s) are still applicable?
- Any new ideas that can be tried to improve current process?
- Any appreciations due for the Release development process?

These additional questions provide further retrospection as part of continuous improvement goals. Communication tools like SharePoint and Wiki help capture sprint data that can be referred and utilized for release retrospectives.

Sample agenda for Release Retrospective:

9AM-10:15AM   Set the Stage: Welcome, Discuss Goal, and activity: Focus on/Focus off, ground rules

10:15-10:30AM   Break

10:30AM-11:45AM	Gather Data – Timeline analysis and review major project events
11:45AM-12:45PM	*Lunch*
12:45PM-2PM	Generate insights – Timeline analysis
2:15PM-2:30PM	*Break*
2:30PM-3:45PM	Decide what to do: Retrospective planning game
3:45PM-4:00PM	*Break*
4PM- 5:15PM	Closing: ROTI, Appreciations, Thank the participants

Product Retrospectives

Product Retrospectives are similar to lessons learned as carried out at the end of the project. Hence, these are also sometimes referred to as project retrospectives. The success of a project is also reflected in the outcome of this retrospective. The main criteria of successful project retrospectives highlight the following factors:

1. The Core Team and Stakeholders would continue to work in similar fashion in future
2. The Core Team would utilize the established processes to further tune and tailor to the needs
3. The Management and Leadership team remains intact after the project
4. The Development Team members continue to work together as an entity; though on new project
5. The Product Owner and the Scrum Master continue to perform on their role and may take on additional projects
6. The Retrospectives provide an essential improvement enterprise-wide
7. Process tailor continues based on the outcome of project retrospectives

Rules of Product Retrospective

Product retrospective is an important ceremony to learn what worked and what could have been used to enhance the product development process. The participants to this ceremony include all the participants from release retrospectives and key management and leadership stakeholders like program management, PMO representatives, and

C/D level management. For a 12-24 month project, Product retrospective ceremony could be 6-12 hours timebox. There need to be sufficient breaks for 15 minutes every 75 minutes. 4 breaks and 1 hour for lunch consumes a whole day in Product Retrospective.

The rules pertaining to Product Retrospective ceremony are:

- The Core Team identifies key Business and Solution stakeholders and extend invitation to the Product Retrospective
- Scrum Master ensures that the key stakeholders are educated on the purpose, activities and scope of Product Retrospective
- Participants to Product Retrospective ceremony are: all participants from Release Retrospectives and key Business and Solution domain stakeholders like Program managers, PMO representatives and upper management.
- Scrum Master facilitates the Product Retrospective ceremony. In absence of Scrum Master, another Scrum Master, Scrum Coach or Agile Coach can facilitate the ceremony. Scrum Master must coordinate to ensure a facilitator is present with the agenda.
- Participants are the Core Team members: the Scrum Master, the Product Owner, and The Team.
- Sprint retrospective ceremonies do not have a specific format of questions. However, it must address the following two at the minimum:
  - What went well during the Product Development?
  - What could have been improved in the product development?

Additional questions that should be addressed are:

- What did not go well during the product development?
- What process improvements from past Sprint(s) are still applicable?
- Any new ideas that could have improved the development process?
- Any appreciations for the team and others for the product development process improvement?

These additional questions provide further retrospection as part of continuous improvement goals. Communication tools like SharePoint and Wiki help capture release data and longer timelines that can be referred and utilized for release retrospectives.

Sample agenda for Product Retrospective:

9AM-10:15AM	Set the Stage: Welcome, Discuss Goal, and activity: Focus on/Focus off, ground rules
10:15AM-10:30AM	*Break*
10:30AM-11:45AM	Gather Data – Timeline analysis and review major project events
11:45AM-12:45PM	*Lunch*
12:45PM-2PM	Generate insights – Timeline analysis
2:15PM-2:30PM	*Break*
2:30PM-3:45PM	Decide what to do: Retrospective planning game
3:45PM-4:00PM	*Break*
4pPM- 5:15PM	Closing: ROTI, Appreciations, Thank the participants

Summary

This chapter describes Retrospectives ceremonies and how these have evolved with the scaling of Scrum. The ceremony is an essential aspect and also identified as Principle #12 of Agile Manifesto - #12. *At regular intervals, the team reflects on how to become more effective, then tunes and adjusts its behavior accordingly.*

The next chapter describes various types of reports needed after each scale layer and the essential aspects of inspection-and-adaptation using these reports.

Chapter 35 Reports

"Quality is not an act, it is a habit." - Aristotle

Introduction

Reports are essential to allow inspection at higher level layer. Daily Scrum reporting is used to provide transparency and inspection at Sprint Review and Sprint Retrospectives. In turn, Sprint reports allow inspection at Release level and so forth. This is essential to enable empirical process control to be effective. When reports are left out or ignored, the effect replicates at higher level of planning. With little or no transparency, it is harder to be able to adapt to changing needs. Most agile planning and project management tools support reporting. Thus, reports are essential to success.

Reports are collection of information radiators with actual execution values. These when analyzed with estimation and planning allow adaptation.

Sprint Reports

At the end of the Sprint, the Product Owner and the Scrum Master are responsible for four reports:

1. The Product Backlog at the start of the previous Sprint
2. The Product Backlog at the start of the new Sprint
3. The Changes report that details all of the differences between the Product Backlogs in the first two reports
4. The Product Backlog Burndown chart: A Burndown chart that shows the amount of work remaining across time.

Release Reports

1. The Product Backlog at the start of the previous Release
2. The Product Backlog at the start of the new Release
3. The Changes report that details all of the differences between the Product Backlogs in the first two reports

4   The Release BurnUp or Burndown chart: A Burndown chart that shows the amount of work remaining across time. A BurnUp chart shows the amount of work completed across time.

5   Release notes – accompany the delivered product with features included and supporting documents

6   User guide is normally inherent in the software as help files and are provided to guide the users on software usage

7   Maintenance guide is to help support and maintenance personnel

Product Reports

1   The Product Backlog at the start of the project
2   The Product Backlog at the end of the project
3   The Change report that details all the differences between the Product Backlog in the first two reports
4   Market analysis with ROI and Product revenue chart
5   Release progression report with realized ROI versus planned ROI

Summary

This chapter describes the various types of reports generated at Sprint, Release and Product levels. These reports allow transparency to the process and help allow inspection and tuning to get refined at Portfolio and program levels. These are essential, for successive execution as well as for higher levels of planning, to adapt.

Next section, we discuss various aspects that follow in Scrum. Story mapping, an advanced concept than roadmap, is discussed. Common myths about agile methodologies are identified. Various agility aspects of Scrum are also addressed. The limitations of Scrum are more imaginary than actual. Creativity and innovative approaches can provide solution. These can ensure Scrum Framework adaptation to achieve success.

Section VIII
What's next!

Chapter 36 Story Mapping

"Sometimes when you innovate, you make mistakes. It is best to admit them quickly, and get on with improving your other innovations." – Steve Jobs

Introduction

User Story mapping technique is adopted from Feature Driven Development (FDD); an agile methodology. Jeff Patton showed the Story mapping concept borrowing terms like activity and tasks from UX Development. Story map was commonly referred to as the new backlog [http://agileproductdesign.com/blog/the_new_backlog.html].

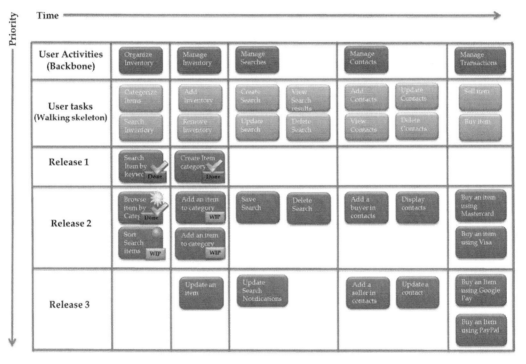

Figure 36-1: Story map as information radiator

Story map is also referred to as User story map; as it lays down the user stories in two dimensions in relationship using time and value-driven priority. Story map is navigated left-to-right and then top-to-bottom for each segregated (lined) row or section in row.

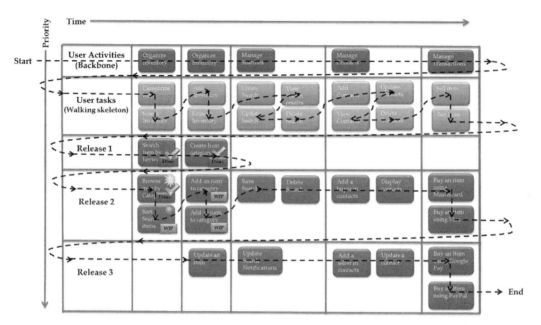

Figure 36-2 User story map - as information radiator with default flow

While looking at the backlog, Kanban, task board, it is very hard to predict what business process the team is working on in the current sprint. There are user stories that are transitioning from ready state to WIP to finally getting done and accepted. Yet with INVEST qualities to focus on keeping the stories, the business process is not visible. Also, another aspect missing is the ability to predict the coverage of business flow. What is needed to complete the business flow? When we look at a process map, it helps in understanding the various user activities and the sequence they are performed. For instance, a web user can log onto the website and search for an item of interest, organizes inventory in various categories, manages inventory like adding, removing, updating quantity, identifying new category, and updating profile for an item in inventory, then they might manage searches to analyze other products, then manage contact list, and perform different transactions. When the core team works with customers, it helps to gain insight to business process to be able to reflect the various transactions. These transactions help in understanding the various user activities performed frequently, repeated paths navigated, common user stories that are visited frequently, the sequence and details. When the user stories are captured in backlogs, a lot of this information is lost. Roadmap helped initially dissipate some of the concerns. However, it was still not enough when it came to tying together themes and MMF.

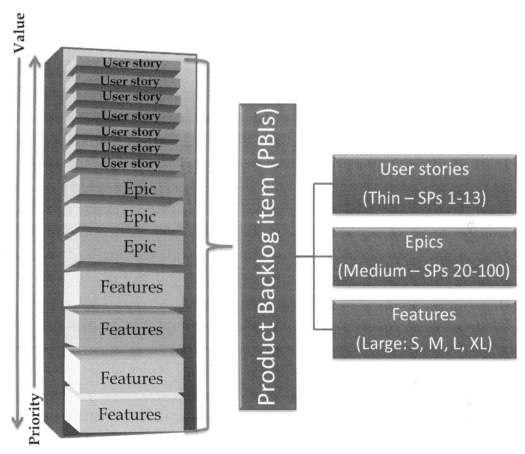

Figure 36-3: Groomed Product Backlog

Before we explore the concept, let's visit some of the reasons that evolved as the need for this concept. When the core team works with Backlog items transitioning through the various backlogs viz. Product Backlog, Release Backlog, and Sprint backlogs, the team uses various information radiators to provide visibility to the process and progress which further feeds into inspection and adaptability. During release planning, it becomes hard to look at the single dimension Product Backlog to derive an effective release. Even though MoSCoW and other techniques are available, the gap on inter-relationship is not apparent. Sometimes when we create a release backlog and deliver the incremental product at the end of release, the customers come back with feedback on differing preference and at times the value prioritization is built in relationship with other stories. Product Backlog fails to address these concerns as it is prioritized based on value and effort estimates determine the optimal value. However, value is not always determined bases on single backlog item and is a relationship of many when working in combination. The quote: "*The whole is more than the sum of its parts. –* *Aristotle* is directly applicable in this case.

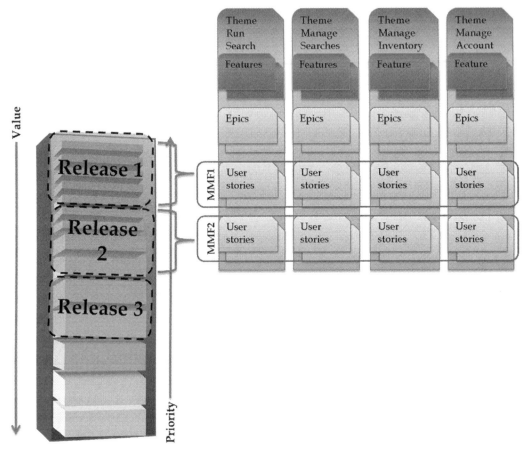

Figure 36-4: Roadmap with releases

Planning releases with Product Backlog is easier for small scale application development where the team is able to develop and deliver an incremental product of value in 30 days Sprint as was originally addressed. For large scale application, it does not meet the need of release planning and hence, roadmap came into practice. The concept of roadmap was to enable Product Backlog and vision be utilized to provide the two dimension view. This is addressed further in next section.

Roadmap

Roadmap provides a second dimension to align product marketability and vision. Roadmap takes the groomed backlog i.e. **D**etailed appropriately, **E**mergent, **E**stimated, and **P**rioritized (**DEEP**) [Roman Pichler and Mike Cohn, 2010] product backlog for product and release planning. This product backlog is then estimated using various value-driven approaches like MoSCoW, Kano Analysis, etc. While DEEP aspects only identify the single dimension based on value as priority to arrange in single dimension, release plan also encompasses a marketable aspect. Released product must make sense to the customer as a unit. Thus, the release must include various user tasks in a set of combination to be useful in meeting the needs. The features that constitute to a release are, thus, also referred to as **M**inimally **R**eleasable **F**eatures or **M**inimum **R**eleasable **F**eatures (**MRF**). These are also referred to as **M**inimum **V**iable **P**roduct (**MVP**) as it corresponds to a minimum set of features to recognize the product as viable and meeting the customer needs. Another common term is: **M**inimally **M**arketable **F**eatures or **M**inimum **M**arketable **F**eatures (**MMF**). These are the set of features that are marketable and are considered a viable product.

Agile methodologies are still evolving to come to a common syntax and semantics. ITIL standards have provided some help in this aspect. It is recommended that project identifies common glossary and semantics to follow to enable efficient communication. As teams work on various releases, the release backlog is used to derive the next level, say Sprint backlog. The Sprint backlog is then elaborated to include tasks that need to be performed for each user story. This flow is covered in Figure 36-5.

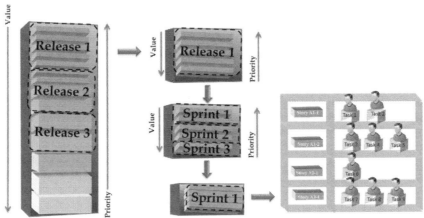

Figure 36-5 Roadmap for release to Sprint and task planning

As is evident, it is not possible to know the status of progress based on business flow, marketable features, and status as a viable product during development using a roadmap.

Metaphors

Product Backlog

Using product backlog is like a walking blind man and trying to reach the goal. With no eyes, the blind man cannot see if he is on the right path or not. There is no clues except taking chances on stepping forward blindly on the leap of faith. If there happens to be a pit, the blind man would fall and try to get up as quickly as possible and try to inspect-and-adapt by evaluating various options. While at each step, there are landmarks achieved when the blind man reaches the landmark. These are like cheers he can hear as he continues to pace.

Vision

A vision is akin to a visionary with no legs to walk to the goal. Visionary can see the goal in sight, knows how to go there, can watch for pitfalls and hurdles on the path, only if he had legs to walk. Even though a person with vision cannot see all the way, he can surely see where the end goal is, has a good sense of direction, can avoid pitfalls and trenches in the way. Yet without any mode of travel, he finds it hard to progress from his current position.

Road Map

Roadmap is akin to a blind man taking the visionary man on his shoulders to travel to the goal. The blind man just needs to follow the direction of the blind man and walk on the path. The visionary needs to watch the path and prompt the blind man to avoid any pitfalls while en route to the destination. In midst of grooming and detailing user stories, it is easy to lose the forest for the trees with limited vision and ability to navigate.

Story Map

Story map tries to achieve more than roadmap as it ties the steps to the route to the goal. It is like the visionary can see the path and also has a map which shows the trail leading to the end goal. As there are trenches, instead of just being able to seek possible options in sight, the visionary can use the map to find the optimal path to reach the goal. Story maps provide ability to see the forest and the trees while still prioritizing the stories and knowing the business flow, relationships, sequence in time and user activities and tasks. Focus is attained on prioritization with greater visibility of the big picture. Story map exposes multiple parameters like MMF, themes, business flow, and value to optimize approach for value-driven delivery. These are discussed further next.

Transition to Story Map

Product Backlog and vision are used together to form a Roadmap. Further integrating roadmap with business flow concept helps to derive a Story map. Story map provides a unique view to the optimal value with delivery strategy for planning. During product planning, using Story map would allow the depth needed. It allows the set of product feature set to be identified that a customer is ready to pay for. This improves marketability and acceptance of the product by end user. If some of the features are missing, the product would have a serious setback and is unable to optimize ROI.

While Scrum started with Product Backlog to manage the requirements, Story maps extends it by addition another dimension and tying together the time and priority in relationship to the capabilities, features, minimally marketable feature (MMF) and user stories. Thus, the single dimension of Product backlog extended with the additional dimension across time allows planning to optimize on marketable releases of the product. Below is a simple Story map with backbone, skeleton, and various releases, themes and MMF's identified for a product.

Step 1: Define backbone and walking skeleton

Story map concept is to groom Product Backlog so that you have the theme identified with their corresponding features, epics and user stories in a column. These themes are listed in the sequence as identified in the business flow. Thus, they provide the sequence in time. The top level backlog items are listed at the top which are termed as "**user activities**." These user activities are listed at the top of the map and are referred to as "**backbone**." For instance, a user activity like "Manage Searches" could be further split into various user tasks like Create search, save search, update search, delete search, view search results, etc. These are the individual tasks an end-user would perform when using the product. The "**user tasks**" are then listed below the "**user activities**." These are referred to as **Walking skeleton**. Conceptually, a "walking skeleton" is a simple "proof-of-concept" based implementation of the user tasks that the user can perform as an end-to-end function. This does not pertain to be on final architecture. It should be able to, however, tie all the components together for end-to-end functionality. It helps tie the concepts and work through various spikes to allow getting the navigation through various transactions completed; as in a business flow. It need not be extensive or detailed. As the name suggests, it should be just enough to get the transaction work. For instance, for a search, it should be able to send the request and get a valid response from various application layers successfully. The display, data details and other aspects would evolve as the architecture and functionality evolves over time.

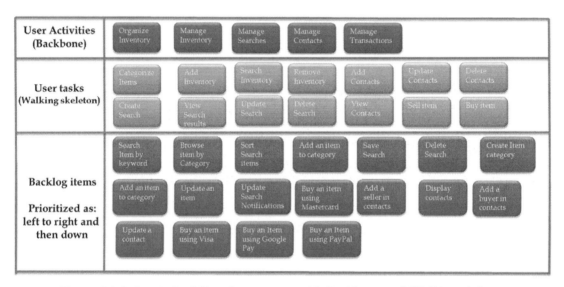

Figure 36-6: Step1: Building Story map - with Backbone and Walking skeleton

Once the backbone and walking skeleton are identified, then user stories with detailed functionality on various aspects are listed in the priority under various themes. Since the themes have already been organized in the sequence, it allows tying in various user stories to derive a minimally marketable feature (MMF). This is an important aspect to keep the Themes in sequence help identify the sequence and is designated with time of evolution as the individual user story is developed. In each flow from left to right, it helps tie in the sequence in which the user stories could be executed. Then the user stories under each theme based on their priorities further help segregate and build MMFs which are then aligned with various releases.

Step 2: Identify themes

Below is a conceptual layout of a Story map. Here the themes are listed in the sequence from left to right in time. User activities are listed in the first row as backbone. Backbone includes: Organize Inventory, Manage inventory, Manage searches, Manage contacts, Manage transactions. Conceptually, these are the big items of interest under each theme. User tasks are listed in "Walking Skeleton" as individual tasks that the end-user of the product would perform. Again these are listed with simple transactions under each theme and mostly spikes are performed here to identify any fast fail scenario. After the user tasks, user stories are listed in each theme and are set in priority with descending value.

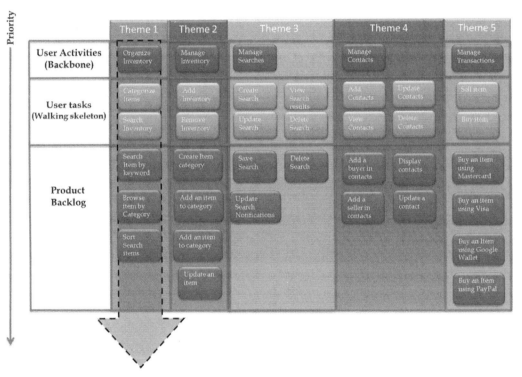

Figure 36-7: Story Map - step 2: Align backlog items to themes

Step 3: Align story map items to themes

The business process is essential aspect to align various backlog items to derive a marketable combination. Customers are willing to pay and value a combination of functions to be able to address their needs effectively. Hence, Scrum team collaborates with the customer to understand the process flow. These help align the sequence in which the tasks are performed and helps identify any dependency, relationship and repeated pattern of usage of the product. Hence, the themes are aligned to match the sequence in which the user would perform various tasks. There are various ways to achieve this. The customer could either show the team their current system, if they have. Value stream mapping also helps identify the value driven delivery with user tasks of interest and value in meeting the need. A process map provides valuable insight in this process as well. Using any of these, the team can align the sequence of the themes in horizontal order – left to right. This is done initially for the backbone at high level; as shown below.

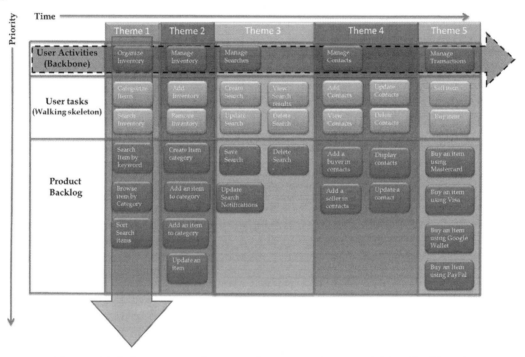

Figure 36-8: Story map - Step 3a - Sequence of user activities (backbone)

Once backbone is aligned, the themes under each item in backbone can be aligned for the user tasks (Walking skeleton) and the backlog items. This allows the story map structure to appear where the sequence provides dual purpose:

1. Business flow sequence is maintained with end-to-end transactions and usage
2. The value is tied closely to the process mapping with development effort

This keeps the value prioritization aligned for easier alignment of various backlog items for further analysis into marketable feature set.

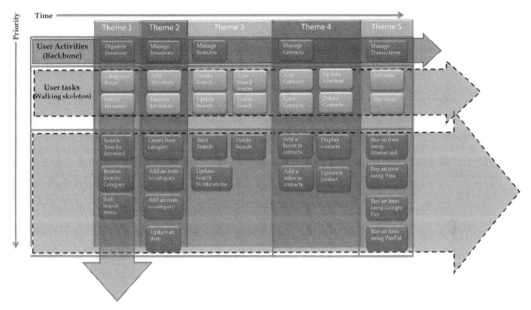

Figure 36-9: Story map - Step 3b - Skeleton and Backlog items aligned in sequence

Step 4: Plan releases in Story map

In this example, First release consists of: *User activities (backbone), user tasks (walking skeleton), and two user stories: Search item by keyword and Create item by category.* These backlog items are selected based on team velocity, team calendar and committed to as per release planning strategy.

Second release consists of *Browse item by category, Sort search items, Add an item to category, Delete an item, Save search, Delete search, Add a buyer in contacts, Display contacts, Buy an item using MasterCard, and Buy an item using Visa.* Third release consists of *Update an item, Update search notifications, Add a seller in contacts, Update contacts, Buy an item using Google pay, and Buy an item using PayPal.*

Third release consists of *Update an item, Update search notifications, Add a seller in contacts, Update a contact, Buy an item using Google pay, and Buy an item using PayPal.*

These releases are easily visible in a layout as shown in Figure 38-10. These releases form individual MMFs that can be delivered to end-users as an incremental product.

Figure 36-10: Story map – Step 4 - Release planning using Story map

Above layout of releases in simplified for clarity into different sections. MMFs are easily identified for each release with various stories; as shown in Figure 36-11.

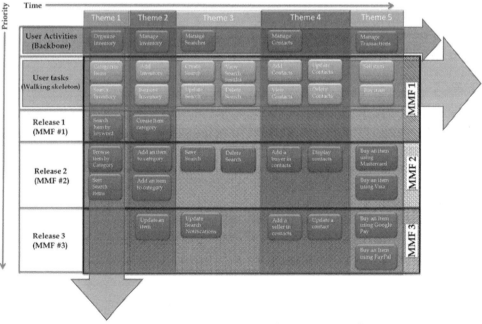

Figure 36-11: Story map with Releases in rows layout

When the various detailed labeling is removed, we get a Story map suitable as radiator. A story map serves an important purpose as it allows easier release planning, tracking and quick updates.

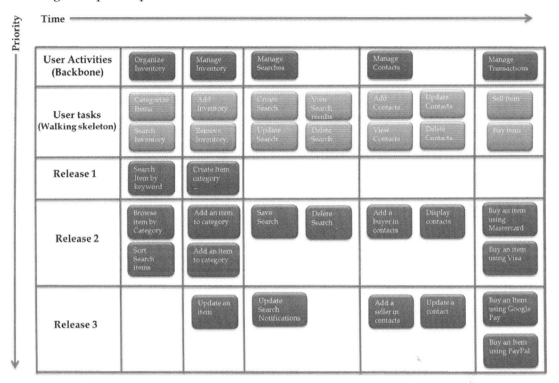

Figure 36-12: Story map with releases planned

As the story map is used in a release, it allows working on themes in different Sprints as focus; if so desired. There is another advantage on keeping this as simple structure. As customer identifies, the priority of a user story in the map can be updated quickly. In order to identify preference, the Product Owner can identify various indicators to show priority, roadblocks, done, work-in-progress and other statuses. Some easy to grasp and simple ways story map functions as information radiator is displayed below:

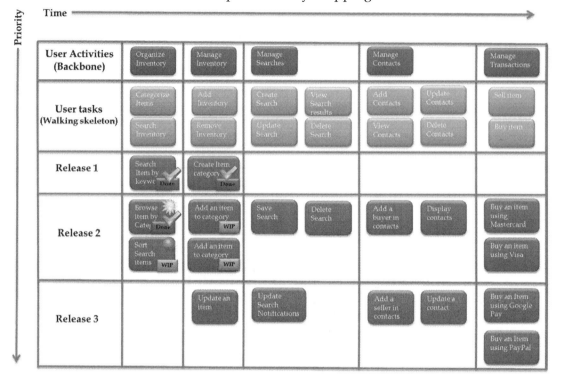

Figure 36-13: Story map showing progress as information radiator

Product planning

Story map based planning reflects reality. Before any development effort can begin, it is essential to have the infrastructure in place. Sprint 0 as initiation sprint to setup the environment is hardly sufficient for a large organization adapting to Scrum methodology. It normally is a parallel activity set after an initial setup of environment. Though story mapping concept has provided ease on product planning for software development, it still stays a challenge to address large projects that include infrastructure, COTS, deployment components of architecture layers and continuous deployment. There have been various strategies being utilized; which are mostly a stepped adoption of existing traditional practices. Continuous integration has enabled once the infrastructure and components have been deployed to speed up integration and providing quick feedback to inspect-and-adapt.

An important aspect to planning based on story map requires MMF analysis. Innovation games are a great way to identify the minimum set of features for MMF.

While customer would pay for a feature over another, it is known that there are a set of features that could demand together a higher value than the sum of each feature. The whole is better than the sum. This enables the Product Owner to optimize on ROI.

Groom a Story Map

Story Map grooming follows Product Backlog grooming. Story map is groomed based on similar strategy where features, epics and stories are presented on same story map. New information and any change in product vision triggers a need to groom the story map. Both of these changes would reflect on the product. Story map helps formulate a strategy of product feature delivery. Hence, updating Story map to reflect and be in sync with the two is essential.

Story map is groomed in similar fashion as the Product Backlog. The user stories can be split in similar manner as it was in the product backlog. While agile planning tools are still far behind, hopefully they would catch up to the concept of Story mapping.

Summary

In this chapter, the shortcomings of Product Backlog and Roadmap were discussed. These have been effective tool to help prioritize and identify MMFs to deliver a minimum viable product (MVP). However, there are many shortcomings as it pertains to business process flow. Process chart are utilized along with roadmap to build user story map. Story mapping technique is expected to gain more popularity as it enhances the success of product development with enhanced planning insights. It removes the blurs currently not addressed using product backlog or roadmap. Application of story map using the sample application is discussed in the next chapter.

Chapter 37 Application of Story Map

"Being busy does not always mean real work. The object of all work is production or accomplishment and to either of these ends there must be forethought, system, planning, intelligence, and honest purpose, as well as perspiration. Seeming to do is not doing."
- Thomas A. Edison

Introduction

A common challenge is evident as Product Owners work with Product Backlog. Though the grooming session allows value prioritization, trying to devise a release has always been a challenge. Product Backlog on its own is not sufficient for planning at release level.

Release plans are depicted using story maps which allows grouping of stories based on dependency and functionality. Story maps provide additional benefits in viewing the Product Backlog as:

1. Knowing dependencies between stories in the Product Backlog
2. A great view to be able to manage the stories in Product Backlog with categories based on functionality
3. Differentiating associated values for assigning stories to a release
4. Planning phases of functionality to manage MMFs (Minimally Marketable Features) that can be provided to customers to generate early revenue and delivering value
5. Managing releases with stories and thus providing Roadmap for the product
6. Help the team look beyond release planning and provide visual alternate to project plans
7. allows assessing the options for project/product and adapt strategies as

Developed by Jeff Patton et al. User Story map also known as "Story map" adds another dimension to the Product Backlog. The steps in creating a story map are:

- 3-5 stakeholders gather who understand the product from customers' perspective as has been discussed using role modeling techniques:
- The project needs a customer to help identify and write stories. So, the first step is to identify the Customer.

- Identify Initial user roles and write the user role cards.
- Consolidating and Narrowing phase: Once the user role names are written on index cards, remove duplicates or near duplicates, consider whether any user roles should be merged, and come up with a refined list of user roles that the project will start with.
- Next, we consider each user role and add details to the role cards known as "Role Modeling"
- Adding Personas is the final step after analyzing Individual personas derived from the user roles
- They take about 5-10 minutes individually to write down "user tasks" on index cards. These story cards with dependencies and   functionality result in the "walking skeleton" of the story map
  a. Identify functions performed by the personas
  b. then breaking these functions down into implementable chunk stories
  1   When   done, the high level scope is gathered, the team groups the index cards in silence by moving related stories together. These stories   are then arranged based on dependencies and related categories based on functionality.
  2   Arrange the story groups from left to right in the order the personas would typically perform the activities
  3   Initial base stories form the backbone and can be referred to as "User Activities"
  4   Next is the rows of stories identifying the tasks user performs and is referred to as "skeleton and timeline"
  5   Next is set of stories based on functionality can then be aligned based on MMF(s) to optimize ROI – these can be assigned to individual releases based on value and grouping for MMF(s)

For example, in online retail website the following user activities are identified as shown below as "backbone":

- Organize inventory
- Manage inventory
- Manage searches
- Manage seller and buyer contacts

- Manage invoices and sales

The "walking skeleton and timeline" could consist of the following stories as user tasks:

- Search inventory
- Categorize items in inventory
- Add inventory items
- Browse inventory items
- Remove inventory items
- View Searches
- Create Searches
- Update Searches
- Delete Searches
- Add new contact
- Update existing contact
- Delete contact
- View   Contacts
- Sell an invoice item
- Buy an item

Now that backbone and walking skeleton are defined across time in which these are executed, based on value and then group user stories in MMF to optimize ROI

Release 1: MMF could consist of user stories of value in the series desired:

- Search item by keyword
- Create categories of inventory items
- Add inventory items to the category
- Delete inventory items in a category
- Buy an item
  - Using MasterCard
  - Using Visa

Release 2: MMF could then consist of next set of valued stories in the sequence desired:

- Browse items by categories
- Update item

- Save Search
- Delete Search
- Add a buyer in contacts
- Display Contacts
- Buy an item using MasterCard

Release 3: MMF could then consist of next set of valued stories in the sequence desired:

- Sort search items
- Update search
- Add a seller in contacts
- Update a contact
- Buy an item using PayPal

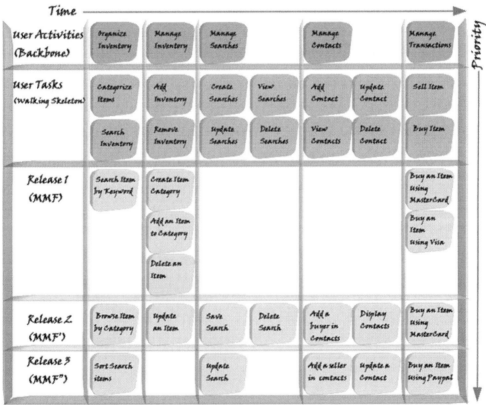

Figure 37-1: Story Map

Grooming Story Map for theme

Themes help align various functional streams in a story map. These themes also align the functional areas where large teams can be organized to work on individual or collection of themes. Collaboration is required to align Sprint and Release goals.

Figure 37-2: Story Map with Themes identified

Grooming Story Map for MMF

Minimally marketable feature (MMF) is essential to determine a releasable product. The customer recognizes value when a minimal set of features are provide to attain a realized value. While individual features help in individual task, a complete user task is attained through performing various tasks in a sequence. Story map depicts this flow as shown in time. The tasks are carried out in a sequence from left to right to meet a specific user need.

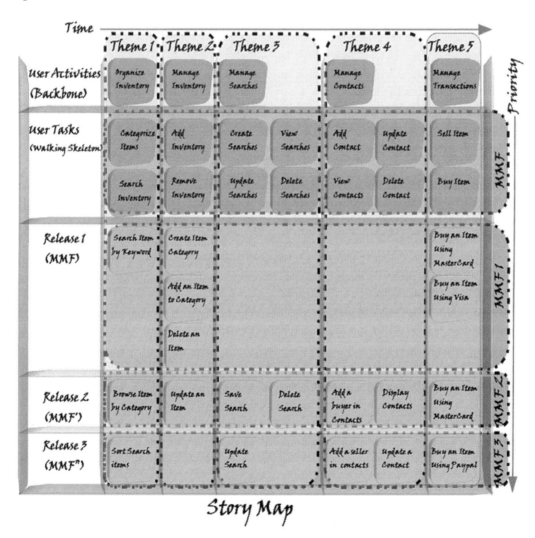

Figure 37-3: Story Map with MMF's identified

Story Map during Execution

Story map reflects the status during product development. Below

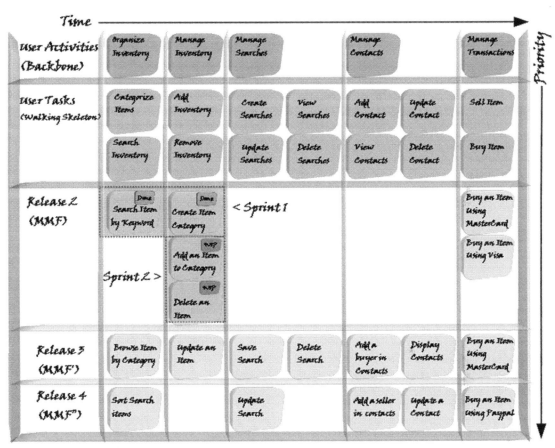

Figure 37-4: Story map showing: Release 1 – 2nd Sprint In-progress

Summary

This chapter describes application of Story map with a variation to the initial navigation strategy defined in the previous chapter. Story map is explained in details in our books: 'Coaching Agile Enterprises and Leadership Teams' and 'Agile PMO.'

Chapter 38 Why is Scrum so hard?

"The difference between stupidity and genius is that genius has its limits." - Albert Einstein

Introduction

Scrum is easy to understand but hard to do. Why is that? This is the most common question asked when projects try to adapt to Scrum and find it challenging. You could attend a session on Scrum overview in an hour and feel comfortable that you understand the framework and its workings. Watch out! It may appear too simple. That is the good part. It is too powerful, that's the hard part. Let's take an instance of travelling from point A to point B. In order to keep it simple, we can walk from point A to point B. No problem. Then comes a point where we have to travel the distance in half the pace. Now if we have to travel a distance of 20 miles in an hour, running would be hard and exhausting. We might seek alternatives. We could decide to ride a bicycle. From the face of it, cycling appears simple. You get on, keep your balance and pedal while using handle to change direction. It is simple, right? Not so fast. It may appear simple but it is much different from walking. Walking requires balancing and shifting of body weight from one leg to another; as you lift the feet to take a step. Cycling, on the other hand, is balancing in the center and also engages hands. There is a change of mindset, techniques and skills. This is like change of values and principles. While there may still be similarities like the front foot presses to move forward, it still has a different motion. Same is the case when we tend to adapt to Scrum from traditional or iterative development methods.

Focus on values and principles

Scrum has five core values: Focus, Commitment, Openness, Courage and Respect. It is essential to understand these. The three pillars of Scrum: Transparency, Inspection and adaptation are built into the framework. Further agile manifesto and its twelve principles provide the fundamental criteria to maintain agility. It is essential to focus on these core values and principles while adapting Scrum. This has been addressed at length in each aspect of Scrum.

Adaption challenges

There are many challenges that come when adapting to Scrum. These are also discussed in the series of myths that prevail and many practices that have come as a matter of past habits. These have been discussed at length in our book: *Get Fragile out of Agile.*

Agile manifesto is misunderstood in the industry. Common myths like there is no planning in agile, no contract negotiations in agile, no need to document or no need of processes and tools; are common ones. All these are myths. Agile manifesto compares two values and weighs the items on the left more than on the right. Not that it ignores the item on the right altogether.

Summary

Mostly, it is not the failure of Scrum Framework itself; it is the failure to adapt to Scrum. Little creativity goes a long way to building innovative products.

Chapter 39 Scrum is not ---

"Make everything as simple as possible, but not simpler." - Albert Einstein

Introduction

Scrum is easy to understand but hard to do. Why is that? This is the most common question asked when projects try to adapt to Scrum and find it challenging. You could attend a session on Scrum overview in an hour and feel comfortable that you understand the framework and its workings. Watch out! It may appear too simple. That is the good part. It is too powerful, that's the hard part. Let's take an instance of travelling from point A to point B. We can simply walk from point A to point B. No problem. Then comes a point where we have to travel the distance in half the pace. Now if we have to travel a distance of 20 miles in an hour, running would be hard and exhausting. We might look for alternatives. We could decide to ride a bicycle. From the face of it, cycling appears simple. You get on it, keep your balance and pedal while using handle and shift weight to change direction. It is simple, right? Not so fast. It may appear simple but it is much different from walking. You know from experience that cycling is much different than walking. Walking requires balancing and shifting of weight from one leg to another as you lift the feet to take a step. Cycling on the other hand is balancing in the center. There is a change of mindset. Change of values and principles. While there may still be similarities like the front foot presses to move forward, it still has a different motion. Same is the case when we tend to adapt to Scrum from traditional or iterative development methods.

What Scrum is not

Scrum is not:

- ❖ A silver bullet
- ❖ A cure all
- ❖ New and upcoming
- ❖ Fix for resource issues
- ❖ A way to skip planning
- ❖ A way to skip documentation
- ❖ A way to skip analysis

- ❖ A way to skip architecture
- ❖ A way to skip design
- ❖ Hacking license
- ❖ Way to excuse from poor quality
- ❖ Renegade development
- ❖ To promote undisciplined approaches
- ❖ Enforce cross-functional team expectations
- ❖ A way to ignore specialization
- ❖ Used only on small projects
- ❖ Used only on independent projects

A silver bullet

Scrum is not to be taken as a solution to any development effort. As discussed earlier, agile methodology is most applicable in complex environment. For simple environment, waterfall methodology or iterative development methods still offer the benefits. When coupled with lean principles, the value delivery can be achieved efficiently. In the case of chaotic environment, Scrum cannot fix the chaos and get the product delivery as well.

A cure all

When a project is faced with many problems, transition to Scrum is not a cure all to fix issues. Scrum still requires the values and principles to be upheld.

New and upcoming

Scrum has been here for over two decades and has been constantly evolving. Scrum has been proven to work on many complex projects successfully. Thinking of Scrum as not something that has been proven and well established is undesirable. Do not give up on Scrum just because you have not used it or it sounds unfamiliar. Rather for complex projects, seek out to understand and start small yet strong with good foundation on the three pillars and core values. Teams normally start Scrum with adapting to Daily Scrums and then expanding on to the Product Backlog grooming followed by including the Sprint planning with all its ceremonies. There are varying approaches based on specific situations. These situations are based on enterprise culture, work environments, team structures, customer interactions, etc. Seek out what are the specifics and ways to embrace Scrum for your individual environment accordingly. An agile coach can surely help you assess and take an efficient approach to embracing Scrum in an effective manner.

Fix for resource issues

Scrum does not help with managing resource turnover. Scrum cannot fix the resource issues if there is lack of skilled personnel. Also, if there is specialization required, Scrum should not be used to piggy back new resources on seasoned ones to replace highly paid resources with low paid resources. Too direct but this is not what Scrum help accomplish. Scrum Framework promotes cross-functional team. It expects the team to stay for the duration of the project. Scrum team members have a broad domain understanding while could still hold specialization in a specific domain. Scrum adaptation is not a key to resource retention either. Hence, Scrum teams should experience no or minimal turnover during the project lifecycle.

A way to skip planning

Scrum is not a way to skip planning. It is not to not have plan. Rather Scrum includes planning to inspect-and-adapt to fix the plans as part of its planning. This requires continuous planning while elaborating and enhancing the plans Just-in-time in rolling waves.

A way to skip documentation

When there are project requirements to deliver documentation, Scrum is not an escape goat. Scrum encourages minimum documentation to keep the development effective. The focus is to have minimum documentation and encourage more individual interaction and collaborative sessions. Scrum fosters open team environment, brainstorming and collaboration with the delivery team and customers. Constant visibility to the delivery process also points towards reducing the documentation and not eliminating the need altogether.

A way to skip analysis

Scrum is not to give up on requirements analysis. Backlog grooming and planning at various stages encourages analysis as the details are known. These allow the customer and the delivery team to work hand-in-hand collaborating to analyze as part of development process.

A way to skip architecture

Scrum encourages the architecture to evolve as the development effort is undertaken. Spikes further help in getting early insights to this. Scrum does not expect complete upfront architecture and design to be completed. Agile principle: Simplicity – the amount of work not done – is essential; encourages that aspect. Architecture evolves as the planning, execution and delivery cycles progress.

A way to skip design

Design is essential for the focused scope. Scrum does not skip design or for that matter any of the development phase. Rather all the phases are done in parallel to ensure they stay in sync and not get outdated.

Hacking license

Scrum is not a license to renegade development. Hacking the code in whatever manner is not encouraged. Shu-Ha-Ri path of progression should be followed. It is not that at Ri-level, the delivery team members can break away and do not have to follow the rules of Scrum. Rather they are so experienced in Scrum, they transcend over to new ideas, improvements and ways of developing while keeping the rules intact yet not have to follow the specific order. A seasoned practitioner at this level is seeking mastery on development and management aspects while continuing to improve Scrum practices. Continuous improvement is an ongoing goal. Once a Scrum Master approached and asked me, "I have been using Scrum for over a year effectively. Do not you think I have mastered it?" My response was that even though I had been using it for many years, I have not yet mastered it. He further asked, "How long do you think it takes to master Scrum?" My response, "How long do you plan to live?" Mastering is a lifelong pursuit. It is not something achieved over a few Sprints. Scrum practices can be learned at an accelerated rate by following the rules, core values and principles.

Way to excuse from poor quality

Scrum provides transparency to inspect-and-adapt. Ignoring the feedback loop and moving forward with technical debt and resulting poor quality is undesirable. Poor quality is not a by-product of Scrum. Rather it is a by-product of failing to upheld Scrum values and principles. Seek to inspect-and-adapt when something new and different is encountered. Constantly changing the plan to adapt to new understanding helps with staying on target.

Renegade development

Scrum encourages disciplined approach. Renegade development is not encouraged when adapting to Scrum. At higher level of experience and Scrum usage, the individuals grow to use development practices in an informal and open environment. This may give the wrong impression. However, it is not renegade development.

To promote undisciplined approaches

Scrum approaches and fosters more disciplined approaches. Further it encourages these in an open and transparent environment. This makes any undisciplined approach to quickly become visible. Such practices are avoided and team stays focused on the delivery of incremental deployable valuable product as its highest priority.

Enforce cross-functional team expectations

Scrum is not an excuse to make individuals learn the depth of each other's skill set. The team members are cross-functional as they get more insight to the broader perspective of each other's skills as they continue to work together. Collaboration, osmotic communication, tacit knowledge sharing, transparency and team workspace are important factors to broaden the horizon where team members get to understand various aspects of product development. Yet it should not be taken as a scapegoat approach to have backup resources or have such expectations.

A way to ignore specialization

Cross functional team has broader level of understanding of different development phases to foster collaboration. It is not a solution to have jack-of-all and master of none. Skill is an essential aspect and a skilled professional can surely help the project delivery faster than having a team of unskilled or low skilled professionals. With skills come the experience, domain knowledge and understanding are important factors when building a Scrum team.

Used only on small projects

Scrum surely started small. It was initially used on small-scaled projects where the Sprints were 30 days long. At the end of each Sprint, an incremental product delivery was made to the customer. The delivered product was directly put in the hands of the end-users to get quick feedback. However, over the last two decades, Scrum has scaled to support enterprise-wide development to large and complex projects. Scrum of Scrums help with collaboration and getting multiple Scrum teams to collaborate for successful product development and delivery. Self-organizing aspect of the team also fosters growth and expansion of Scrum methodology at higher complexity and sophisticated team structures.

Used only on independent projects

Scrum fosters individual and interactions. Scaling Scrum for complex domain includes working on programs, inter-dependent projects and large projects. It is not that Scrum cannot scale, it is the failure of adapting to Scrum rules and principles at larger scale that fails.

We have a slogan posted in our offices which states: "Yes, you are right when you say that it cannot be done. It just means that you cannot do it." This reminds us that creativity and can-do attitude matters. Yet the effort should be focused on product delivery and exciting our customers and not replacing skilled professionals, hiring renegade developers, building cross-functional teams or controlling resource turnover. Those are easily managed when we foster Scrum values and bring forth the idea of worth-and-purpose to override carrot-and-stick approach.

Focus on values and principles

Scrum has five core values: Focus, Commitment, Openness, Courage and Respect. It is essential to understand these. The three pillars of Scrum: Transparency, Inspection and adaptation are built into the framework. Further agile manifesto and its twelve principles provide the fundamental criteria to maintain agility. It is essential to focus on these core values and principles while adapting Scrum. This has been addressed at length in each aspect of Scrum.

Adaption challenges

There are many challenges that come when adapting to Scrum. These are also discussed in the series of myths that prevail and many practices that have come as a matter of past habits. These have been discussed at length in our book: *Get Fragile out of Agile.*

Agile manifesto is misunderstood in the industry. Common myths like there is no planning in agile, no contract negotiations in agile, no need to document or no need of processes and tools; are common ones. All these are myths. Agile manifesto compares two values and weighs the items on the left more than on the right. Not that it ignores the item on the right altogether.

Summary

This chapter describes the common misconceptions about Scrum. Some of the challenges are encountered due to limited understanding of Scrum values and principles. Start with prescriptive approach while focusing on supporting and enhancing the values provide an easier path. Take to the initial Scrum Framework and make it your own. Scrum framework may take on many flavors as it allows the team to learn and grow.

In the next chapter, we discuss how Scrum supports agility. The framework is extremely effective for empirical process.

Chapter 40 Scrum promotes agility

"Thinking well to be wise: planning well, wiser: doing well wisest and best of all."
- Malcolm Forbes

Introduction

Scrum is not a silver bullet. Though there are some myths in the industry and sometimes even agile practitioners seem to put their emotions and beliefs behind proving that Scrum is THE solution. Yet it is not so. There are many factors to this:

1. Scrum Framework applies to empirical process where there are uncertainties in software development. These uncertainties could be related to technical domain, business domain, technology, skills, etc.
2. Waterfall and iterative methods are more effective in simple domain where there are no uncertainties in the development process, skills are easily available, business and technical domains are well known and complete cycles run as well-oiled engine.
3. Scrum addresses the methodology aspect and not product domain. While Scrum could be used to develop a product, it does not mean that the product would be a hit. Just as having MS-Word does not guarantee a best seller, Scrum does not guarantee a great product. It does make it easier to derive optimal value driven approach to optimize resources.
4. Scrum fosters individuals and interactions for collaboration. The ability helps with effective planning and focusing on stay on target. Agile principles bring forth many of these aspects and are fully supported in Scrum. Scrum is about providing an environment where teams can deliver great products and innovations flourish.

Scrum does not guarantee success

Scrum does not guarantee success. However, it makes it easier to manage complex projects. Scrum Framework removes the hassle and troublesome aspects from project planning and software development approaches to make it easier for the enterprise to deliver value to the customer. Scrum seeks to enable collaboration and brings forth best practices while breaking the practices that have known to cause bottleneck in the system.

Scrum is common sense. Just as common sense does not give you success but can help you in much profound manner, similarly Scrum can enable project planning and software development in simple and effective manner.

Agile values and principles must be upheld

Scrum fully supports Agile manifesto and the twelve principles. While Scrum has its own set of values and foundational pillars, it does not mean that it overwrites the need to upheld Agile manifesto. Rather the two work hand in hand.

Summary

This chapter focuses on aspects that make Scrum so agile. Agile manifesto and its twelve principles further enhance the ability to stay agile. The agility comes easy when the enterprise culture and teams embrace Scrum core values and principles. The adaptation is effective when rules are followed while keeping transparency to the customer collaboration and development efforts. Staying true to the values is essential for the framework to stay effective.

Glossary of terms

Acceptance criteria are a set of conditions identified from business perspective. Acceptance criteria help identify the criteria to be met to know when the backlog item is complete. A deliverable is done when acceptance criteria are met.

Adaptation: It is necessary to adapt to changes and especially when things are not going as planned. Scrum focuses on adapting to changing conditions to be able to say effective. Adapting to any aspect not covered in planning allows the planning to be changed to quickly adapt to new direction to reach the goal.

Burndown graph is a graph that shows the effort estimate completed over time and could also be traced against expected values for comparison to achieve the timebox goal. Y- axis represents the effort estimates (normally in story points) and X-axis represents time of the lower timebox planning layer like days, Sprints, Waves or Releases. X-axis for Product Burndown graph is Release; that of Release Burndown graph is Sprint, and that of Sprint Burndown graph is days. A metaphor of a burning candle applies here. Just as a candle burns down over time, similarly the team completes the backlog items and the backlog gets smaller and smaller and finally finishes when all backlog items are considered done and accepted.

BurnUp graph is a graph shows the effort estimate building over time and can be traced against expected values for comparison. It is similar to Burndown graph but grows upward over time, instead of showing Burndown effect; as that of a burning candle.

Caves and Commons refer to work area setup for Agile Teams. Caves provide isolated work area for privacy like meeting room or individual office. Commons refers to an open large area where team members can openly discuss, work, brainstorm and have dashboards for discussions. Commons are easily accessible areas.

Ceremony is an activity performed with a well-defined agenda and focus. Scrum Framework has various ceremonies like Daily Scrums, Planning, Review, and Retrospectives. Additional ones used on large teams are: Backlog grooming and Scrum of Scrums.

Chickens are involved members who are responsible but not accountable to project success. They provide or receive services from the Core Team who are also called pigs as they are committed.

Collaboration is a negotiation style that promotes mutual interest of all parties involved where they working together for mutual interests.

Collocation is residing at the same location – same floor and building are implied. Collocation promotes osmotic communication and enables effective modes of communication. The ability to just be at same location allows expedites a group to build ties and become an entity with aligned objectives.

Cross-functional refers to an entity that contains wide knowledge. The Development Team is cross-functional where each team member has knowledge at some level about other phases while could be specializing in specific domain(s).

Customer is any entity willing to pay for the product or product features.

End-user is an entity that has a need that the product fulfils. The end-user utilizes the product to achieve a specific goal though various user activities and tasks.

Information Radiators are big visible graphs and charts posted in a common area to make the progress easy to convey with ease.

Information refrigerators are opposite in concept where the information is kept hidden in secured sites, restricted locations or emails.

Inspection: At each step in Scrum framework, inspection allows looking at the progress and seeks out any feedback to ensure the progress and related deviations. This allows the progress to be tracked and feedback to be viewed in proper perspectives. Inspection allows looking at variances to adapt.

Just-in-Time (JIT) is a time management technique where work is undertaken just when they are needed. This optimizes time utilization and avoids wastes like waiting. This is further extended and applied to progressive elaboration and rolling wave planning.

Kanban is a Japanese word which means sign, signboard, doorplate, poster, or billboards. Kanban is also commonly referred to as "signal card" or task board.

Osmotic communication occurs by just being in the vicinity. This occurs where other folks are discussing as if in unconscious eavesdropping. Osmotic communication is promoted heavily in agile software development. The Product Owner, the Scrum Master and the Development Team – all are encouraged to be collocated in same area to promote osmotic communication.

Pigs are committed members on the project. They are accountable to project success. Pigs normally refer to Scrum Core Team which includes the Product Owner, Scrum Master and the Development Team.

Progressive elaboration is a technique of looking at refinement in different stages as progression. In Agile, it is the inspect-and-adapt aspect where each item in the development and planning are visited when more information is available. As each item is visited, it is elaborated to the desired level of details for the progressive stage. Agile methodologies support different progressive levels in product development. These levels are identified in agile onion and are closely related to rolling wave planning.

Release is a planning layer where the delivered product increment is released to the customer to realize value.

Rolling wave planning is a technique to approach planning in different levels to allow distinct levels for easier planning and segregation. In agile, it allows the backlog items to be prioritized and move from Product Backlog to Release Backlog to Sprint Backlog with each level progressively adding more details and granularity. Some teams add Wave Backlog between Release backlogs and Sprint backlogs to identify another timebox. Rolling wave planning allows initial estimates to be high level and then progressively, in successive sessions, the requirements are detailed with sufficient insight for the team to be able to commit to the work. Agile planning onion utilizes rolling wave planning, progressive elaboration and Just-in-time concepts collectively.

Sashimi is a Japanese dish made from thin slices of raw fish. Each slice is complete in itself. Other conceptual metaphors are Sieving, slicing a cake or pizza. Each of them contains complete value pertaining to the product.

Scrum Master is a Scrum role and acts as Process Champion. Scrum Master is responsible for the Scrum Framework adaptation. Scrum Master manages the principles and principles manage the Scrum Team.

Scrum values: There are five core Scrum values: Focus, openness, commitment, courage and respect.

Self-organizing pertains to the aspect where the team organizes itself and the development work though adaptation to changing environment. This does not mean that the team organizes its structure and can have work area or organization hierarchy organized. The focus is on the development process which includes people, processes and resources.

Self-managing concept pertains to the aspect that management does not interfere in managing the Team. Rather principles guide and thus, manage the team. Self-managing does not imply that the team members hire new team members and fire existing team members. Human Resources department provides that aspect and related support. Ken Schwaber identified the Team to be utterly self-managing. (SCHWABER, Pg. 136)

Sieving pertains to splitting product into backlog items with layers that are individual unit that assemble to create a whole. Slicing a cake or pizza is similar metaphor. Sashimi and Sieving are used interchangeably to identify same concept.

Tacit knowledge is the implied business domain knowledge that occurs when working closely with customers and end-user. Tacit knowledge is easier to build when members are collocated and work together on daily basis.

Teamwork is the process where a group of motivated individuals working closely on a common goal with aligned visions. Everyone brings their abilities to best achieve the goal.

Transparency: Scrum provides complete visibility to the process and progress during development. This allows breaking the silos mindset, individual ownership, communication gaps, conflicts arising due to limited or twisted perspectives, and many other bottlenecks. This exposes complexities early.

Three pillars of Scrum: The Scrum framework for software development is an empirical process where the implementation is held by three pillars of Scrum viz. *Transparency, Inspection, and Adaptation.*

User story addresses production functionality of value to the customer. A Customer could be a user, purchaser, or a stakeholder: someone with interest in the product. A user story has three aspects known as 3C's [JEFFRIES, 2001]:

Velocity is a measure of a team's progress rate. At the end of sprint, team reviews and calculates the velocity as the sum of story points of completed stories. There are no partial story points to claim for incomplete stories at the end of the Sprint. It is either 100 percent or zero percent!

Bibliography

[ADKINS, 2010] Adkins, Lyssa: *Coaching Agile Teams: A Companion for Scrum Masters, Agile Coaches, and Project Managers in Transition.* (2010)

[MANIFESTO, 2001] Kent Beck, Mike Beedle, Arie van Bennekum, Alistair Cockburn, Ward Cunningham, Martin Fowler, James Grenning, Jim Highsmith, Andrew Hunt, Ron Jeffries, Jon Kern, Brian Marick, Robert C. Martin, Steve Mellor, Ken Schwaber, Jeff Sutherland, and Dave Thomas. 2001. *Manifesto for Agile Software Development.* http://www.agilemanifesto.org

[Arnold, 1993] Arnold, John D: *When The Sparks Fly: Resolving Conflicts In Your Organization.* New York: Mcgraw-Hill, 1993.

[Arrow, 1995] Arrow, K, Et. Al. (Eds.): *Barriers To Conflict Resolution.* New York: W. W. Norton & Company, 1995

[Bill Wake, 2003] Bill Wake: *Extreme Programming explored and Refactoring workbook.* 2003

[Bush, 1994] Bush, R.A.B. & Folger, J.P: *The Promise Of Mediation: Responding To Conflict Through Empowerment And Recognition.* San Francisco: Jossey-Bass, 1994

[COCKBURN] COCKBURN, ALISTAIR: *Agile Software Development: The Cooperative Game.* 2007

[COHN, 2009] Cohn, Mike: *Succeeding with Agile.* 2009.

[COHN, 2006] Cohn, Mike: *Agile Estimating and Planning.* 2006.

[COHN, 2004] Cohn, Mike: *User Stories Applied: For Agile Software Development.* 2004.

[DERBY and LARSEN, 2006] Esther Derby and Diana Larsen: *Agile Retrospectives: Making Good Teams Great.* 2006

[DOI, 2005] David Anderson, Sanjiv Augustine, Christopher Avery, Alistair Cockburn, Mike Cohn, Doug DeCarlo, Donna Fitzgerald, Jim Highsmith, Ole Jepsen, Lowell Lindstrom, Todd Little, Kent McDonald, Pollyanna Pixton, Preston Smith and Robert Wysocki. 2005. *Declaration of interdependence (DOI).* http://pmdoi.org/

[FOWLER, 1999] Martin Fowler, Kent Beck, John Brant, William Opdyke and Don Roberts: *Refactoring; improving the Design of Existing Code.* 1999.

[GRENNINGS, 2002] Grenning, James: *Planning Poker.* 2002.

[Garry, 2005] Furlong, Garry: *Conflict Resolution Toolbox: Models And Maps For Analysing, Diagnosing, And Resolving Conflict.* New York: John Wiley & Sons, Ltd., 2005.

[Goldratt, 1997] Goldratt, Eliyahu M. 1997. *Critical Chain.* North River Press.

[Grimshaw, 1990] Grimshaw, A. (Ed.): *Conflict Talk.* Cambridge, LJK- Cambridge University Press, 1990 Groups. San Francisco: Jossey-Bass Publishers, 1994.

[HBR-NACR, 2000] *Harvard Business Review On Negotiation And Conflict Resolution.* Boston: Harvard Business School Press, 2000.

[HIGHSMITH, 2009] Jim Highsmith: *Agile Project Management: Creating Innovative Products.* 2009.

[Isaacs, 1999] Isaacs, W: Dialogue: *The Art Of Thinking Together.* New York: Doubleday, 1999

[JEFFRIES, 2001] Jeffries, Ron: *Essential XP*: Card, Conversation, Confirmation. 2001.

[Kanban] Language work translation used to find specific meanings of the Japanese term: Kanban. http://www.eudict.com/?lang=japeng&word=kanban

[KERTH, 2001] Kerth, Norm: *Project Retrospectives: A Handbook for Team Reviews.* 2001.

[KANO] Dr. Noriaki Kano and his colleagues developed *Kano Model* in 1980s. Sources: http://en.wikipedia.org/wiki/Kano_model. International Journal of Quality & Reliability Management. 1984.

[LAUFER, 1996] Laufer, Alexander: *Simultaneous Management: Managing projects in a Dynamic Environment.* 1996.

[LEFFINGWELL, 2011] Dean Leffingwell: *Agile Project Requirements: Lean Requirement Practices for Teams, Programs, and the Enterprise.* 2011.

[Mitchell, 1989] Mitchell, C.R.: *The Structure of International Conflict* (Apr 15, 1989)

[MOORE, 1991] Moore, Geoffrey: Elevator statement is defined in his book: *Crossing the Chasm.* 1991.

[Patterson, CC-TFRBP] Patterson, Kerry. *Crucial Confrontations: Tools For Resolving Broken Promises, Violated Expectations, And Bad Behavior*. New York: Mcgraw-Hill, 2004.

[PATTON] Jeff Patton: describes story map, in an interesting way, at website: http://www.agileproductdesign.com/blog/the_new_backlog.html_keeping it simple and fun!

[PICHLER, 2010] Pichler, Roman: *Agile Product Management with Scrum: Creating Products that Customers Love*. 2010.

[PMI, 2013] PMI: PMBOK® Guide. 2013.

[Poppendieck, 2003] Mary Poppendieck and Tom Poppendieck: *Lean Software Development: An Agile Toolkit*. 2003.

[Pyzdeck, 2003] Pyzdeck, Thomas: *Quality Engineering Handbook*. 2003

[Rothman, 1997] Rothman, J.: Resolving Identity-Based *Conflict In Nations, Organizations And Communities*. San Francisco: Jossey-Bass, 1997

[SCHWABER, 2001] Ken Schwaber and Mike Beedle: *Agile Software Development with Scrum*. 2001.

[SCRUM GODFATHERS] Hirotaka Takeuchi and Ikujiro Nonaka: *The New New Product Development Game*. January 1986.

[SHALLOWAY et al, 2009] Alan Shalloway, Guy Beaver, James R. Trott: *Lean-Agile Software Development: Achieving Enterprise Agility*. 2009.

[SHORE, 2007] James Shore: *The Art of Agile Development*. Available at website: http://www.jamesshore.com/Agile-Book/. 2007.

[SINGHAL, SP, 2013] Singhal, Jai and Singhal, Anju: *Solving Problems – The Agile Way*. Agiliants, 2013

[SINGHAL, CAEALT, 2013] Singhal, Jai and Singhal, Anju: *Coaching Agile Enterprises and Leadership Teams*. Agiliants, 2013

[SINGHAL, PoG, 2013] Singhal, Jai and Singhal, Anju: *The Pursuit of Greatness*. Agiliants, 2013

[SINGHAL, PoH, 2013] Singhal, Anju and Singhal, Jai: *The Pursuit of Happiness*. Agiliants, 2013

[SINGHAL, TFOOA, 2013] Singhal, Anju and Singhal, Jai: *Get Fragile out of Agile*. 2013

[SLIGER,] Michele Sliger and Stacia Broderick: *The Software Manager's Bridge to Agility*. 2008.

[SMITH, 2009] Greg Smith and Ahmed Sidky: *Becoming Agile: ...in an imperfect world*. 2009.

[Stone et al. 1999]Stone, D, Patton, B & Heen S: *Difficult Conversations: How To Discuss What Matters Most*. New York: Viking/Penguin, 1999

[SUTHERLAND] Jeff Sutherland: White papers and interesting readings on Scrum Framework at website: http://info.scruminc.com/learn-how-to-get-started-with-scrum

[SUTHERLAND, 2011] Jeff Sutherland and Ken Schwaber: *Scrum Guide*™. Scrum Inc. Oct 2011. Downloadable at ScrumInc.com website: http://info.scruminc.com/Portals/191341/docs/Scrum%20Guide%20Scrum%20Inc.%20Oct%202011.pdf Ken Schwaber had tried to register this title as trademark in 2009 and 2010 but was unsuccessful. Later a new application for trademark for this was filed on Novermber 5th, 2013. A registration number has not been assigned as of this writing. However, to honor their dedication to the field and avoid any conflict, we changed the prior title of our book published on August 13th, 2013. Further info for enthusiast is at: (http://tmsearch.uspto.gov/bin/showfield?f=doc&state=4810:pgqyaq.2.2) (http://tmsearch.uspto.gov/bin/showfield?f=doc&state=4810:pgqyaq.2.1).

[SUTHERLAND, SCRUM GODFATHERS, 2011] Jeff Sutherland: http://scrum.jeffsutherland.com/2005/03/scrum-godfathers-takeuchi-and-nonaka.html Scrum Godfathers: Takeuchi and Nonaka: The seminal paper, *The New New Product Development Game*. Harvard Business Review. 1986.

[Schwaber, 2009] ScrumGuide 2009, ScrumAlliance

[Schwaber, 2010] Ken Schwaber: *Scrum* Feb 2010 http://evolvebeyond.com/resources/scrumguide/Scrum-Guide-1.pdf

[Schwaber, 2011] Jeff Sutherland and Ken Schwaber: *The Scrum Guide*. Oct 2011: https://www.scrum.org/Portals/0/Documents/Scrum%20Guides/Scrum_Guide.pdf

[Sutherland, 2011] Jeff Sutherland: The Scrum Papers. Jan 2011 in Paris http://scruminc.com/tl_files/scrum_inc/documents/ScrumPapers.pdf

[Ury et al, 2011] Roger Fisher, William L. Ury and Bruce Patton: *Getting to Yes: Negotiating Agreement without Giving In.* May 3, 2011.

[VersionOne, 2011] VersionOne.com: *The State of Agile Development: Sixth Annual Survey.* Available as downloadable PDF.

[WAKE, 2003] William C. Wake: INVEST in Good Stories and SMART Tasks/goals. 2003.

[XP123] www.xp123.com

Index

396 Index

Additional titles in Agile Project Management series are:

➢ Solving Problems: The Agile Way

➢ Get Fragile out of Agile

➢ Agile Games™

➢ Coaching Agile Enterprises and Leadership Teams

➢ Coaching Agile PMO

➢ XP Guide

➢ ScrumBan Guide

➢ Kanban Guide

➢ Lean-Agile Guide

➢ Future of Scrum: Your guide to the most popular agile methodology

➢ Agile Enterprise Framework Evolution

➢ PMI-ACP Exam Guide

➢ Scale Agile Enterprise-wide

➢ Agile Enterprise Transformation Guide

➢ Pursuit of Excellence for Enterprises

➢ Pursuit of Excellence for Projects

➢ Pursuit of Excellence for Agile Practitioners

Learn more information at:

www.Agiliants.com
Phone: +1 - (240) 654-5496
Fax: +1 - (301) 769-6253
Email: Info@Agiliants.com
Website: www.Agiliants.com

Agiliants™
Act Smart. Be Agile.

28116864R00250

Made in the USA
Charleston, SC
02 April 2014